VIOLENT ACTS AND VIOLENTIZATION:
ASSESSING, APPLYING, AND DEVELOPING LONNIE ATHENS' THEORIES

SOCIOLOGY OF CRIME, LAW AND DEVIANCE

Series Editor: Jeffery T. Ulmer

Recent Volumes:

SOCIOLOGY OF CRIME, LAW AND DEVIANCE   VOLUME 4

VIOLENT ACTS AND VIOLENTIZATION:
ASSESSING, APPLYING, AND DEVELOPING LONNIE ATHENS' THEORIES

EDITED BY

LONNIE ATHENS
Seton Hall University, USA

JEFFERY T. ULMER
Penn State University, USA

2003

JAI
An Imprint of Elsevier Science

Amsterdam – Boston – London – New York – Oxford – Paris
San Diego – San Francisco – Singapore – Sydney – Tokyo

ELSEVIER SCIENCE Ltd
The Boulevard, Langford Lane
Kidlington, Oxford OX5 1GB, UK

First edition 2003

Library of Congress Cataloging in Publication Data
A catalog record from the Library of Congress has been applied for.

British Library Cataloguing in Publication Data
A catalogue record from the British Library has been applied for.

ISBN: 0-7623-0905-9
ISSN: 1521-6136 (Series)

∞ The paper used in this publication meets the requirements of ANSI/NISO Z39.48-1992 (Permanence of Paper).
Printed in The Netherlands.

CONTENTS

LIST OF CONTRIBUTORS

George J. Allen

Psychology Department, University of Connecticut, Storrs, CT, USA

Lonnie Athens

Department of Criminal Justice, Seton Hall University, USA

Antonius H. N. Cillessen

Psychology Department, University of Connecticut, Storrs, CT, USA

Matthew P. Dumont

Belmont, USA

G. Roger Jarjoura

School of Public and Environmental Affairs, Indiana-Purdue University, USA

Joseph Nowinski

Tolland, CT, USA

Richard Restak

Department of Neurology, George Washington University, USA

Ginger Rhodes

San Fransisco, USA

Richard Rhodes

San Fransisco, USA

Joshua Sanborn

Department of History, Lafayette College, USA

Randy Starr

Illinois, USA

Ruth Triplett

Department of Sociology, Old Dominion University, USA

Jeffery T. Ulmer

Department of Sociology, Pennsylvania State University, USA

PREFACE

And Cain talked with Abel his brother; and it came to pass, when they were in the field, that Cain rose up against Abel his brother and slew him (Genesis 4:8).

Violence has beset human group life since the beginnings of history. Violence is both feared and used in interpersonal, intergroup, and international relations. Some violence meets the official disapproval of groups and societies (e.g. criminal violence), while other forms of violence are performed at the behest of groups or societies, and even honored (e.g. feuds, war). Therefore, any understanding of violence must be thoroughly social, because violence is so situationally contingent, culturally and subculturally patterned, and historically variable. For all of violence's ubiquity, we do not fully understood its causes and contextual variations very well, and its causes and risks are the subject of much misinformation.

Perhaps the first work I ever read on violence per se was Lonnie Athens' *The Creation of Dangerous Violent Criminals* (1989). I was a graduate student working as the editorial assistant for the journal *Symbolic Interaction*, and the journal received a review copy of Athens' new (at the time) book. I borrowed it and read it with interest. I was drawn to the fine empirical detail of Athens' ethnographic data, the thoroughly social nature of his theory, as well its emphasis on process, contingency, agency, and context. I was also drawn to its symbolic interactionist basis (the perspective that has always animated my own work), and to the compatibilities between violentization and the theoretical tradition of differential association in criminology (Sutherland, 1947; Glaser, 1956; Warr, 1992; Akers, 1998), which perhaps enjoys the most empirical support in criminology. I later learned that Athens does not place his work on violence within the differential association tradition (though he sees important and interesting overlaps). Rather, it is but a part of his own more general theory of the self, the social act, social interaction, and community, which extends the work of G. H. Mead and Athens' mentor, Herbert Blumer (e.g. Athens, 1994, 1995, 1998, 2002).

Later, when I began teaching criminology classes, I worked Athens' theory into my coverage of socialization favorable to crime. Students reacted well to it, and I also noticed that the students to whom the theory spoke to the most tended to be ones who had some sort of personal experience with serious violence. My familiarity with Athens' work deepened later in my career, when I was asked to review his paper "Dominance, Ghettoes, and Violent Crime" for *The Sociological Quarterly* (published in 1998), and to write a review of his *Violent Criminal Acts and Actors Revisited* (1997) for *Symbolic Interaction*. Both of these works incorporate a valuable extension of the theory of violentization and violent acts to the community and cultural level. In my view, this is one of the most potentially exciting and fruitful future directions for Athens' perspective – connecting violentization processes to larger and institutional and cultural contexts. In the beginning piece in this volume, Athens takes this line of work even further by developing a previously unpublished theory of institutions, communities and how they change, as related to violence.

Shortly after this, Pulitzer Prize winning journalist and author Richard Rhodes' bestseller *Why They Kill: Discoveries of a Maverick Criminologist* (1999) appeared in bookstores throughout the world, followed by a wave of both positive and negative media attention. Lonnie and I discussed the idea of putting together a volume of *Sociology of Crime, Law, and Deviance* centered on testing and further developing the theory of violentization and violent acts, and agreed that it was especially timely to do so.

My hope is that this volume will stimulate more interest and new dialogue concerning violence in general and the theory of violentization and violent acts in particular. For a variety of reasons well-described by Athens (1997) and Rhodes (1999), prior to the publication of Rhodes' book, Athens' work received disappointingly little attention in criminology (though it is cited sporadically in criminology textbooks and journal articles). I think the lack of serious engagement with Athen's work was a real shame, because it prevented more widespread empirical application, testing, and development of his concepts and propositions. It has also often kept many scholar from seriously engaging his concepts and propositions, which they might otherwise find very useful in fleshing out and improving upon their own ideas or existing theoretical frameworks (a point I will return to in the Afterword).

Though this volume centers around Lonnie Athens' work, the contributors and their contributions are extremely varied. The volume begins with Athens' own further extension of violentization into the larger realm of social structure and culture. In it, Athens not only further develops his ideas of dominance communities and their varying norms for dominance disputes (see also Athens, 2002), but also pays particular attention to the role of gender in the nature and probabilities of violentization. This piece actually goes considerably beyond anything Athens has published previously. First, it revises the theory of violentization and violent acts. It then presents a new theory, influenced by the work of Robert Park, of the embeddedness of violence in communities and how communities change. The new theory develops a typology of communities (civil, malignant, and turbulent communities, which can be minor or major), emphasizes the dominance orders of communities and the institutions within these communities for settling disputes. Athens squarely locates the revised theory of violentization and the dynamics of violent acts inside this new theory.

Psychiatrist Matthew Dumont then grounds Athens' unique perspective on violence in his childhood and adult biography, and explores the broader social and cultural implications of Athen's ideas for human nature, mental illness, and authority. Next, Athens and Randy Starr, an ex-offender with a history of substantial violence, tell Starr's narrative of his life experience and interprets it through the lenses of violentization. Medical Doctor and neuroscientist Richard Restak then presents a provocative, disturbing, and humorous satire of the scientific and ethical presumptuousness involved in the predictive and selective identification, incapacitation, or even treatment of would-be offenders based on their neurology. Richard Rhodes, author of *Why They Kill*, describes how violentization was a key ingredient in the transforming ordinary German citizens into mass murderers in the service of the Nazi SS and police. Joshua Sanborn, an historian at Lafayette College, discusses parallels between the socialization toward violent behavior of criminals and soldiers. Ginger Rhodes and her colleagues (all psychologists) develop and produce initial predictive validation for the first quantitative scale for measuring violentization. G. Roger Jarjoura and Ruth Triplett, sociological criminologists from Indiana University-Purdue University, Indianapolis and Old Dominion University, test and find support for aspects of the theory of violentization using interviews with 18 year-olds from a high-security juvenile detention facility. Finally, I conclude the volume with my own observation of the place of Athens' work in criminology, and the necessity of both further empirical testing and of dialogue with other sociological treatments of violence.

REFERENCES

Akers, R. (1998). *Social Learning and Social Structure: A General Theory of Crime and Deviance.* Boston: Northeastern University Press.

Athens, L. (1989). *The Creation of Dangerous Violent Criminals.* New York: Routledge.

Athens, L. (1994). The Self as a Soliloquy. *The Sociological Quarterly, 35,* 521–532.

Athens, L. (1995). Dramatic Self Change. *The Sociological Quarterly, 36,* 571–586.

Athens, L. (1997). *Violent Criminal Acts and Actors Revisited.* Urbana: University of Illinois Press.

Athens, L. (1998). Dominance, Ghettos, and Violent Crime. *The Sociological Quarterly, 39,* 673–691.

Athens, L. (2002). Domination: The Blind Spot in Mead's Analysis of the Social Act. *Journal of Classical Sociology, 2,* 25–42.

Glaser, D. (1956). Criminality Theories and Behavioral Images. *American Journal of Sociology*, *61*, 440–441.

Rhodes, R. (1999). *Why They Kill: Discoveries of a Maverick Criminologist*. New York: Knopf.

Sutherland, E. (1947). *Principles of Criminology*. Philadelphia: Lippincott.

Warr, M. (2002). *Companions in Crime: The Social Aspects of Criminal Conduct*. New York: Cambridge University Press.

Jeffery T. Ulmer

VIOLENTIZATION IN LARGER SOCIAL CONTEXT

Lonnie Athens

I. INTRODUCTION

addressing gender [handwritten]

Problem

Why do only some males and much fewer females become seriously violent while most of their peers do not? Why do more violence-prone people live in some communities rather than others? The answers to all these questions ultimately hinge on the answer to the more general question of why human beings become violent, which has baffled many for ages. Before this more *definitional* [handwritten] general question can be answered, however, it must be worded more precisely.

The question of why human beings become violent is based on a critical, hidden assumption that needs to be uncovered. Because we take for granted ? [handwritten] that people will resort to violence for purposes of self-preservation, we presume, at least implicitly, that they are "marginally violent." What we do not take for granted, however, is their resorting to violence for purposes other than self-preservation. Thus, when we ask why do people become violent, the question that we really want answered is not why people become "marginally violent" individuals, but instead, why they become "violent" or "ultra-violent" ones.

Theories about the origin of violence can be classified on the basis of whether their authors locate the causes of violence in the organism itself, its environment, or in both places. The biological purist spots the cause of violence in the

UR [handwritten]

**Violent Acts and Violentization: Assessing, Applying, and Developing Lonnie Athens'
Theories, Volume 4, pages 1–41.**

sensitive & dull as static!

Bio. gene-based LONNIE ATHENS

organism itself. Sarnoff Mednick (1977, 1982) has provided us with the best explanation of this type. According to him, punishment is both the most practical and efficient means at our disposal for teaching children to behave as we wish. He believes that children who become violent have a dull central system that prevents them from learning from punishment. His entire theory can be broken down to three simple propositions: (1) children's genes determine the sensitivity of their central nervous systems; (2) the sensitivity of children's central nervous systems determine their level of fearfulness; and (3) children's fearfulness determines whether they can learn from punishment.

w/o consid. of develop. post-birth?

If the reactions of children with sensitive and dull central nervous systems are compared, then the underlying causal dynamics of his theory can be clarified. First, let's take the case a child who inherited a dull central nervous system. When provoked, this child feels the urge to react violently. Because past punishment has failed to make him fearful of taking violent action, he acts on rather than inhibits this urge. No matter how repeatedly or severely these children are punished, they are incapable of learning to inhibit their violent urges. Now let's compare this child with one who inherited a sensitive central nervous system. When provoked, the child with a sensitive central nervous system, like the one with a dull central nervous system, feels the urge to react violently. Because of past punishment, however, the former child, unlike the latter one, becomes fearful, which makes him inhibit instead of act on his violent urge. The inhibition of this urge reduces greatly this child's fearfulness, which rewards him for his non-violent reaction. According to this theory, it is more common for boys than girls to become violent because the genes that wire the central nervous systems are sex-linked.

inability to adapt - learn

Purists Bio polar < social

Unlike the biological purists, the environmental purist spots the cause of violence in people's living habitats rather than in their bodies. Wolfgang and Ferracuti (1967, p. 143) still provide us with the best environmental theory of violence, stating, "We are led back to the external social environment as the area where the causative key to aggression must at present be found." They equate the environment with a culture, the principal components of which are norms and values. The cultural environment, however, is not homogeneous, but heterogeneous. The norms and values that prevail in one environmental niche may not prevail in another. Their basic underlying assumption is that people absorb the prevailing norms and values of their environmental niche like a dry sponge dropped into a large pool of water (Sutherland, 1973a, p. 43). According to Wolfgang and Ferracuti, people become violent from living in a "subculture of violence," an environmental niche in which "pro-" rather than "anti-violent" norms and values prevail. The subculture of violence explanation can be also broken down to three simple propositions: (1) people are exposed to different

*L.L.
L.R.*

environmental niches or subcultures; (2) people with more exposure to violent rather than non-violent subcultures absorb "pro-" rather than "anti-violent" norms and values; and (3) the absorption of pro-violent norms and values creates a violence-prone personality. *— Social*

Thus, it is the relative amount of exposure that people have had to violent and non-violent subcultures that accounts for their acting violently. This can be vividly illustrated by comparing different people's reactions to some perceived provocation. Let's first take the case of the person who has had greater exposure to a violent than a non-violent subculture. When someone provokes this person, his norms would prescribe that he act violently and proscribe his acting non-violently. His values would cast his taking violent action in a positive light and taking non-violent action in a negative one. Now let's compare this with the case of the person who has had greater exposure to a non-violent subculture. When someone provokes this person, her norms would prescribe that she act non-violently and would proscribe her acting violently. Her values would cast a favorable light on her taking non-violent action and an unfavorable light on her taking violent action. According this theory, males more often than females become violent, not because their central nervous systems are wired differently, but because males have more contact with violent subcultures.

Unlike the biological and environmental purists, eclectics spot the causes of violence in multiple factors located in the organism and the environment rather than located in just one or the other. We are indebted to Dorothy Lewis (1992, 1998) for the best eclectic theory. According to her, at least five factors located in one or the other of these two places must come together for children to become violent.

The first factor is the "XY syndrome," from which Lewis (1998, pp. 287–288) believes that all males suffer. Lewis locates this syndrome exclusively in the body because, according to her, it is a genetically determined condition that has two defining characteristics, high androgen production and a "masculinized brain." Like the XY syndrome, brain damage, the second factor, is also located in the body and is thereby an organic factor. If people suffer injuries that disrupt the pathways between their frontal lobes and the brain's reptilian base buried beneath them, then they cannot control their primitive urges. Lewis (1998, p. 288) describes this condition as analogous to driving a truck with worn-out brakes. *fearfulness regulation*

The third organic factor is an overly sensitive amygdala, the portion of brain "hidden within each temporal lobe," which is primarily responsible for "our sense of fear." Regarding this brain disorder, Lewis (1998, p. 288) observes: "We cannot do without the amygdala. But fear is often the nidus for paranoia. A certain amount of fear is necessary for survival. On the other hand, too much *units are dynamic?*

can make us dangerous." The concentration level of neurotransmitters in the brain is the fourth organic factor. Lowered levels of neurotransmitters, such as serotonin, cause children to be irritable and prone to anger (1998, p. 289). Unlike the first four factors, the fifth and final factor, "violent abuse," is the only environmental factor. It can result from people being either the actual victim of physical attacks or an eyewitness to them. In either case, the violent abuser becomes a role model for their own future violent behavior.

Social learning

In short, the coalescence of two or three of these factors in a child's life is not enough to make him or her become violent. Instead, all five of these factors must coalesce for this to happen (1992, pp. 387–389). Brain damage (factor two), amygdala disorder (factor three), and neurotransmitter depression (factor four) only make children susceptible to becoming violent. In order for them to succumb to this susceptibility, however, they must also be violently abused (factor five). More males than females become violent, not because females suffer significantly less often from brain damage, amygdala disorders, depressed neurotransmitter levels, or violent abuse, but because of their immunity to the XY syndrome (factor one).

independent factors

Unlike in the multiple-factor approach (where some of the factors that cause *one!* violence are found in the organism and others are found in the environment, but these factors are not explicitly linked together), in the integrated approach, they are expressly connected. This is where the lines are drawn between all the dots. James Gilligan (1996) has done us the favor of supplying the best example of the integrated approach of which I am aware. He connects together factors lodged in the organism with those lodged in the environment.

hormonal transmission (neurne)

He divides the factors lodged in the organism into those that reside in the body and those that dwell in the psyche. According to him (1996, pp. 221–223), the two most important factors residing in the body as far as violence is concerned are androgen and serotonin. Too much androgen together with too little serotonin, a combination from which males suffer more than females, predisposes people to violent reactions. Far more important than these biological factors, however, is an *unconscious* psychic factor – the deep-seated need for love and respect and to avoid shame, which according to him (pp. 45–80, 110–146, 261) is every bit as strong as the desire for self-preservation among human beings.

Gilligan splits the factors lodged in the environment into those that reside in our society and those that reside in our culture. By far the most important social factor is that our society is stratified. We are forced to live under a ridged class system (p. 187). The cultural factor of greatest importance is the sex role stereotyping that demands males and females to fulfill widely different societal expectations (pp. 196–208).

"Simplist" - violence occurs bec. of a choice

Unfortunately, males from the lower class, especially those from minority groups, are at a distinct disadvantage when it comes to fulfilling the cultural expectation that they become independent, respected members of society. Their failure to live up to this cultural expectation aggravates their unconscious need to avoid shame. When their self-esteem becomes threatened, their innate disposition to become violent, which is created from the high androgen and depressed serotonin levels that exists among all males, is easily ignited. Males become violent more often than females from a combination of their biological predisposition toward violence, sex role stereotyping, lower class status, but most importantly because of their absence of self-esteem, for which the latter two factors mentioned are primarily responsible (pp. 222, 237).

Anomie

Unfortunately, biological purists, environmental purists, eclectics, and integrationists cannot adequately explain how males or females become violent because they all disrespect the very essence of "human experience." A human experience refers to the overt physical actions together with the *conscious* thoughts and feelings that occur when human beings interact with their environment, including other human beings, at a particular point in time (Dewey, 1929). Conscious thoughts and feelings are not optional, but instead essential components of all human experience (Cooley, 1926). In fact, it is only because we think and can become aware of our feelings that we are able to play an active instead of a passive part in the creation of our experiences (Blumer, 1969a, pp. 12–15, 72–73; Denzin, 1989, pp. 19–34; Schutz, 1973, pp. 3–47).

YES !

physio bio processes i.e. - stress responses - unconscio. - sympathic CNS

Just as there are no environmental-less experiences, there are no higher organism-less ones. Both a higher organism – one with a mind – and an environment are needed for a human experience to occur. However, a human experience results from the interaction of the human organism *as a whole* and not some special organ of it, such as the brain alone, with its environmental niche or immediate operating environment. The biological purist, environmental purist, eclectic, and integrated approaches are based on a false dualism between the body and the environment because they all trace the alleged causes of violence back to factors that spring from either the body *or* environment instead of back to the experiences that spring from the *interaction* between them. Thus, a *holistic* approach that unites the body and environment rather than arbitrarily splits them apart must be taken in the study of violence. ✱ (*harmfulness*)

not just Brain!

✱

✱

Moreover, human organisms, their environmental niche, and their ongoing experiences exist in an *interdependent* relationship to one another (Lewontin, 1991, pp. 105–128; Mead, 1922, 1932, pp. 32–46, 84–85; 1934, p. 129, 245–252). The experience produced from the interaction between a human being and his environment changes, however slightly, not only the human organism, but also his environmental niche, which extends from his family, school, and

structures

ALAQ Attributes of any/all experience

non-dual, holistic theory building

interactionally developed

growing
adapted

neighborhood to the larger community that surrounds them (Mead, 1934, pp. 214–216). The newly changed organism and environmental niche, in turn, change all the human organism's subsequent experiences, which still in turn, change both the human organism and its environmental niche even further. Thus, the relationship between human organisms and their environmental niches are not only interdependent, but also *developmental* (Lewontin et al., 1984, pp. 265–290; Lewontin, 1991, pp. 119–123; 2000; Montagu, 1985). Because of the *conscious, interdependent,* and *developmental* nature of this relationship, children, like adults, always play a *proactive* rather than merely a passive role in their own violent transformations and in the transformations of the larger communities in which they live (Athens, 1997, pp. 22–27, 115–120; 1998, p. 676; Blumer, 1997, pp. iii–vi). Consequently, to gain a proper understanding of violence, not only must a holistic approach be taken, but one that respects the interdependent and developmental nature of human experiences.

invite in
unconscious
automatic

Purpose

I believe that the theory that provides the best answer to the questions posed at the beginning of this paper is "violentization" (Athens, 1992) because it honors rather than disrespects the essential nature of the human experience. I coined the term "violentization" by combining the words "violent" and "socialization." Although first published more than a decade ago (Athens, 1989), my theory remained relatively unknown until the renown author Richard Rhodes (1999) popularized it in *Why They Kill: The Discoveries of a Maverick Criminologist* (see also Rhodes, 2002, pp. 19–37).

In this essay, I will do two things. First, I will take this opportunity to integrate the scattered, piecemeal statements of my theory that I (1974, 1977, 1986, 1989, 1997, 1998, 2001) have progressively developed over the last quarter century (Rhodes, 1999, pp. 1–140, 267–285). I plan to accomplish this badly needed integration of my theory by re-stating it in more generic sociological terms. The newly integrated theory is based on my (1992, pp. 22–25; 1997, pp. 30–31) study of the life histories of 110 subjects,[1] which includes both adults and juveniles, males and females. My restatement of the theory will be based on four key assumptions.

The first assumption is that domination and subordination are the common denominators in all human conflict and violence (Athens, 1998, p. 686). The second assumption is that people always strive to make their lives more predictable by "institutionalizing," which I will define in part III, the critical social experiences that they undergo, although not necessarily in the same way. The third assumption is that violent and ultra-violent people undergo a special form of socialization, which I now dub the "violentization process," where they learn that violence is the basis for deciding who performs the super ordinate and subordinate roles in social activities. The final assumption is that whenever people undergo dramatic personal change (Athens, 1995), as in the case of the violentization process, or else live or work in a community in which they are "social misfits" for too long, they will suffer from at least some personal disorganization (see Thomas & Znaniecki, [1917]1958, pp. 1647–1653; Blumer, 1979, pp. 67–69). I want to underscore that I do not view personal disorganization as a "mental disease," but as only one of the trials and tribulations of life that sooner or later we all go through to one degree or another if we live long enough (see Athens & Starr, 2002; Clinard, 1949; Szasz, 1960).

adaptein again

Thus, in re-stating my theory, I will have to make more explicit the operation of domination and subjugation, as well as institutions. In making more explicit the operation of institutions, I will need to bridge the divide between "collective" and "institutional" behavior (Blumer, 1969b, pp. 67–69, 121). It will also be necessary for me to introduce the notion of "personal disorganization" and to more precisely define a "community." These changes will be reflected, among other ways, by changing the names of two of the violentization process' four stages (Athens, 2001), distinguishing different types of institutions and "major" from "minor" communities, as well as making "dominance engagements" the pivotal notion in the entire theory.

The second thing that I will do in this paper is to explain, according to my restated theory, why more males than females become violent, and why more people, both males and females, become violent in certain communities rather than others. In extending my theory to cover both of these admittedly critical matters, I hope to silence once and for all the criticism that my theory does not explain the widely different rates of participation in violent crimes displayed across the different sexes and communities in our society (Bailey, 2000, p. 548; Kruttschnitt, 1994, p. 334; Milovanovic, 1991, p. 112; Zahn, 1992, p. 336; but also see Ulmer, 2000).

II. VIOLENTIZATION IN GENERIC TERMS

Violentization is composed of both unitary and composite experiences. A unitary experience is a distinct, elementary experience that cannot blend with other elemental experiences any more than oil can mix with water. On the other hand, a composite experience is a compound of distinct, elemental experiences that coalesce. Whether unitary or composite, the experiences comprising violentization do not occur all at once, but over a process that has four separate stages that build on each other like the layers of a cake. The four stages that comprise the violentization process are: (1) brutalization; (2) defiance; (3) violent dominance engagements; and (4) virulency.

Brutalization

The first stage is "brutalization," a composite experience made up of three distinct elemental experiences: (1) violent subjugation; (2) personal horrification; and (3) violent coaching. During "violent subjugation," authentic or would-be subjugators, such as fathers, stepmothers, older siblings, neighbors, or school-mates, use or threaten to use physical force to make a perceived subordinate accept their domination. Violent subjugation can be practiced in one of two ways. On the one hand, it is practiced coercively when a subjugator seeks to make a perceived subordinate comply with a specific command; he uses only enough force to achieve this limited goal. On the other hand, when a super ordinate seeks to teach perceived subordinates a lasting lesson about his dominance over them and uses more than enough force to achieve their promise of future submission, he is practicing retaliative subjugation. Although both forms are brutal, coercive subjugation is relatively merciful. During coercive subjugation, subordinates can immediately stop getting battered by complying with their subjugator's present command; during retaliatory subjugation, however, a subordinate is not afforded this precious luxury.

The second elemental experience that comprises brutalization is "personal horrification." During this experience, perceived subordinates do not undergo violent subjugation themselves, but they witness someone close to them, such as a mother, brother, close friend, neighbor, or schoolmate, undergo it. Although not as physically traumatic as violent subjugation, it can be even more psychologically damaging. Moreover, after undergoing personal horrification, perceived subordinates can be effectively subjugated for a while, at least by physical intimidation alone. Thus, it is possible for a person who has never been physically attacked to complete the brutalization stage.

"Violent coaching" is the final elemental experience that comprises brutal-ization. During this experience, a super ordinate places himself in the role of coach and assigns a perceived subordinate to the role of novice. The coach instructs novices that they should not try to avoid, appease, ignore, or run from their would-be violent subjugators, but instead physically attack them. Thus, the coach's goal is to prompt violent conduct on the part of the novice, which ironically, the novice could later direct against his coach. In a west Baltimore neighborhood, violent coaching is known as "crimping'em up," which the locals define as "the process by which older kids toughen up younger ones, steeling them for the reality of Fayette Street with a thousand petty insults and savageries" (Simon & Burns, 1997, pp. 205–206).

Coaches have a variety of techniques at their disposal, each with its own teaching principle, for prompting novices to take violent action against would-be violent subjugators. One technique is "vain glorification." Here, the coach regales the novices with personal anecdotes about his own or his cronies' violent actions. Not surprisingly, the coach portrays himself or his intimates as heroes, or at least anti-heroes, and their would-be violent subjugators as villains. The teaching principle upon which this technique works is "vicarious enjoyment." The pleasure that novices derive from hearing their coaches' stories make them long for the day when they can finally have their own violent feats to brag about.

"Ridicule" is a second technique that coaches use to provoke violence on the part of novices. The coach belittles the novice for his reluctance or refusal to physically attack people who try to subjugate him violently. This techniques operates on the teaching principle of "torment." The coach continuously mocks the novice until the realization sinks in that it is better to physically attack a potential violent subjugator than to suffer any more derision from the coach.

If a coach prefers a less subtle technique than either vain glorification or ridicule, he can always use "coercion," a special case of violent subjugation (described earlier) where super ordinates either threaten or actually harm a novice for refusing to obey their instructions to physically attack some would-be violent subjugator. The teaching principle upon which coercion operates is pure and simple fear. Novices quickly get the message that it would be smarter for them to physically attack some other violent subjugator than to get physically harmed by their coaches.

"Haranguing" is still another technique. Here, the coach relentlessly rants and raves about hurting would-be violent subjugators without ever belittling, physically threatening, or appealing to novices' vanity, as the other techniques do. The teaching principle upon which haranguing operates is the "incessant melodrama" – if novices are repeatedly told the same thing with enough force and conviction, then it must eventually sink into their heads. Coaches who suffer from drug and alcohol abuse often display a fondness for this technique.

A final technique that a coach can use for prompting novices to take violent action is "besiegement," which combines all the techniques described previously, except for haranguing. Coaches who use this technique are usually in search of a quick fix for a "slow learner." Because haranguing takes time to work, there would be little point in including it among the other techniques. During besiegement, a coach can make novices endure the pain and anxiety of ridicule and coercion if they refuse to physically attack a would-be violent subjugator, while assuring them certain relief from this pain and anxiety, as well as the added enjoyment of vain glorification, if they do succeed in harming him physically. The teaching principle on which besiegement operates is "overkill" – if a single technique will not prompt a novice to take violent action against potential violent subjugators, then resort to a combination of techniques.

It should come as no surprise that males' and females' passages through the brutalization stage may differ. Although females may undergo violent subjugation and personal horrification as often as males, males undergo violent coaching more often than females. Because violent coaches suffer from the same gender bias as many other members of society, they usually find it more acceptable for females than males to play subordinate rather than super ordinate roles and that it is more acceptable for females to rely on reasoning, charm, and guile rather than brute force to settle dominance disputes. Thus, females may just as often as males enter the brutalization stage, but males much more often complete this stage.

Case 104 illustrates the case of a middle-aged, married woman who had repeatedly undergone violent subjugation at the hands of her second husband, but who had not completed the brutalization stage for, among other reasons, her failure to undergo personal horrification and her previous anti- rather than pro-violent coaching:

> *Case 104:* Besides for my second husband's attacks on me, I had never seen any violence except in the movies.
>
> My father and mother did not get into physical fights with each other. I had never seen any physical fights at home, school, or anywhere else before my second marriage. I did not like to see that type of behavior even in the movies. It was very unpleasant for me.
>
> While growing up, I lived a very sheltered life. My mother and father taught me that it was okay to talk things out or even argue, but you do not swear at people, or physically threaten or hit them. I think that it is wrong to do those things to people. It repulsed me. Bulldozing your way through life is stupid. There is no rhyme or reason to it. It is self-defeating and childish.

Defiance

The second stage in the violentization process is "defiance" (formerly labeled "belligerency"). Unlike brutalization, defiance is a unitary, yet nuanced experience. During defiance, subordinates want to find a nostrum for the personal disorganization from which they are suffering. More specifically, they seek to resolve the crisis into which their brutalization has thrown them. While agonizing over their brutalization, they repeatedly ask themselves why they are being brutalized and what, if anything, they can do about it. In a desperate search for answers, they revisit episodes of their past violent subjugation, personal horrification, and violent coaching. The reliving of these experiences, which consumes them with hostility toward themselves and other people, produces an epiphany: they realize belatedly that their violent coaches may have had a point after all. The only real way that you can put a stop to your brutalization is to become violent yourself. If, in the wake of this epiphany, the subordinates finally decide to heed their violent coaches' instructions, then they make a "mitigated violent resolution" – they resolve from this moment on to kill or gravely harm anyone who attempts to violently subjugate or degrade them. The making of this resolution not only marks the graduation from this stage, but also the birth of a potential violent individual whose motto is "don't tread on me." It is on the basis of this new principle that they start their personal re-organization (for examples, see Athens & Starr, 2002; Rhodes, 1999, pp. 143–155).

In contrast to males' and females' pointedly different passages through the brutalization stage, they pass through the defiance stage in much the same way. Females who enter this stage are no less apt than males to complete it. It must be remembered that both these males and females have undergone violent coaching during the earlier brutalization stage. Thus, the seed needed for them to have an epiphany during this stage about the necessity for taking grievous violent action against future subjugators and debasers has already been deeply planted in *both* their minds. Cases 74, 66, and 69 from my second major study (1992, pp. 60–61) provide examples of adolescent and young adult males who had attained this plateau in their violence development:

Case 74: I still get upset when I think about all the things that happened. I can never forget the beatings that my father gave me, the beatings that I saw my mother and older sister take from him and all his loud bragging about what he had done to people. The things my father did to us made me feel ashamed and mad. It built my anger up and up until I got mean and crazy. It got so that I wanted to stay away from everybody and wanted everybody to stay away from me. I didn't want to be fooled around with by people. I told myself that if anybody fools around with me bad anymore, I am going to go off on them. I was ready to kill people who fooled and fooled around with me and wouldn't stop.

Case 66: The beatings my stepfather laid on me, the terrible beatings he laid on my mother, and all the violent rhetoric took their toll on my mind. It inflamed me and made me want to go for bad. I was tired of always being messed with by people. I was ashamed of being weak and lame and letting people mess with me all the time. I didn't want to be messed with by people anymore. People had messed with me long enough. If anybody ever messed with me again, I was going to go up against them. I was going to stop them from messing bad with me. If I had to, I would use a gun, knife, or anything. I didn't mess with other people, and I wasn't letting them mess with me anymore. My days of being a chump who was too frightened and scared to hurt people for messing with him were over.

Case 69: I was tired of people putting their punk trips on me, calling me a "punk" and shoving me around. I didn't like people treading on me, and I wanted to scream at them, "Don't tread on me, don't tread on me." I was scared that people would be treating me like a punk all my life. I hated myself for letting people make me a punk. I was ashamed that I was a helpless cry baby who couldn't protect himself or his mother. I was being stomped into the ground both mentally and physically. I knew that I had to somehow dig myself out. I finally came to the conclusion one day that I was going to have to kick people's asses, like I had been hearing from my stepfather. I was down and determined not to let my stepfather or anyone else make me out as a punk. I was going to make sure that no one treated me like a punk anyway that I could. I was not out to make people punks, but nobody better try to make me out as one either. I had had it. This was it, the end of being a sissy punk for me. I wouldn't have ever wanted to hurt people bad if it wasn't for this punk stuff. It was what made me turn mean.

Violent Dominance Engagements

"Violent dominance engagement" (formerly labeled "violent performance") is the third stage in the violentization process. Unlike brutalization, but like defiance, a violent dominance engagement is also a unitary yet nuanced experience. Dominance engagements arise when disputes break out over dominance, but despite appearances to the contrary, such disputes do not occur instantaneously. Instead, they arise over a process that has a minimum of three basic steps.

First, a would-be super ordinate must cast himself into the role of a super ordinate and cast someone else into the role of a subordinate. A would-be super ordinate can make at least three grades or degrees of dominance-claiming gestures for this purpose. The lowest grade one, is where the would-be super ordinate issues an order to, or hurls an insult at, a would-be subordinate. In either case, the unstated presumption is exactly the same. The individual issuing the order *or* hurling the insult is a bit superior to the one to whom the order or insult was directed, and thereby deserves to perform the super ordinate role.

The moderate grade of dominance-claiming gestures is where a would-be super ordinate both issues a command to *and* hurls an insult at a would-be subordinate that adds insult to injury. Here, the unstated presumption is that the individual issuing the command and hurling the insult is not just a little better than, but is far superior to the person to whom the order *and* insult was directed.[2] Because the former individual stands head and shoulders above the latter one, there should be no question as to who should perform the super ordinate and subordinate roles.

The highest grade dominance-claiming gesture is where a would-be super ordinate threatens to, or actually physically violates, or annihilates a would-be subordinate. Here, the unstated presumption behind the would-be super ordinates' physically threatening actions is that they are members of a higher strata of life than their would-be subordinates. Thus, they not only deserve to perform the super ordinate role, but while doing it, to be totally indifferent to the physical or mental well-being of their would-be subordinate (see Shibutani, 1970).

During the second step in a dominance engagement, the would-be subordinate must resist being cast into the subordinate role. The way in which would-be subordinates resist their being cast into the subordinate role is to make their own dominance-claiming gestures. As in the earlier case of the would-be super ordinate, the would-be subordinate can make anything from the lowest to the highest dominance-claiming gestures for this purpose.

During the third and final stage of a dominance engagement, at least one of the two would-be super ordinates must decide to overcome the other ones' actual *or* anticipated resistance to performing the subordinate role. Of course, *truncated violent dominance engagements* may always occur. Here, based on past experience, would-be super ordinates anticipate that a would-be subordinate will resist their domination. Thus, they plan in advance to exert pressure on a would-be subordinate before she has any opportunity to resist their domination, giving these dominance engagements a distinctive, premeditated character.

If the pressure that a would-be super ordinate exerts on a would-be subordinate takes the form of brute physical force, then the dominance engagement becomes a violent one. However, not all dominance engagements are waged violently. They may be also waged non-violently. Whether dominance engagements are waged violently or non-violently, however, the goal behind them remains the same: it is to determine who will ultimately perform the super ordinate and subordinate roles in some common endeavor.

Of course, it is during violent dominance engagements that "violent persons" test their newly made mitigated violent resolution that they earlier formed during the defiance stage. For this to happen, however, the proper set of circumstances must be present. A would-be super ordinate must cast them into a subordinate role through making either the *ultimate or penultimate* dominance-claiming gestures. Next, the would-be subordinate must think that he has at least a fighting chance against his would-be super ordinate. The would-be super ordinate must also remain undeterred by the possible prospect that the would-be subordinate will physically resist his violent subjugation. Finally, no third party must intervene during the violent dominance engagement to prevent this would-be subordinate from putting his resolve to the full test.

As important as the operating circumstances surrounding a violent dominance engagement is its immediate outcome. There are several possible outcomes: a "major" or "minor victory," a "major" or "minor defeat," a "draw," or "no decision." In a major victory, the perceived subordinate scores a clear-cut win and in the process inflicts serious injuries upon the would-be super ordinate. A major defeat is simply the reverse. A minor victory or defeat is the same as major ones, except that no one is seriously injured. A "no decision" is where the engagement never progresses to the point that a "winner" or "loser" could be declared; it ends before any of the combatants could inflict serious injuries upon the other. In contrast, a draw is where an engagement does progress beyond that point, but still no clear winner or loser can be determined. Here, the combatants inflict equally grievous injuries upon one another. As in the case of all dominance engagements, the most common outcomes of violent dominance engagements are minor victories and defeats, as well as draws and no contests, while the least common are major defeats and victories. Before putative subordinates can move on to the next stage, they must achieve at least one, and usually more, major victories.

Case 69, taken from my second major study (1992, p. 67), illustrates a violent dominance engagement where an adolescent male suffers a minor defeat at the hands of his stepfather:

> *Case 69:* After dinner, we were sitting around the table talking about events in the newspaper. There was something in the paper about communist countries, and I said that I thought real communism would be a good idea. When my stepfather heard that, he got mad and said, "Why don't you move to fucking Russia?" I said, "If we lived in Russia, I would send you to Siberia." Then he blew his top and yelled, "Don't smart off to me," and hit me in the face with his fist, knocking me back in my chair.
>
> I jumped up and ran, but he chased me. When we got to my room, he grabbed me by the shoulders, threw me against the wall, and knocked me down. Then I decided I was going to fight and said, "This is it. I'm tired of taking all of your bullshit." He stared at me and said, "You are? Then why don't you do something about it, punk?" I said, "Okay, let me up and I will." As I got up, I reached for the knife I kept in my dresser drawer, but he kicked the drawer closed on my hand. I screamed and pulled my hand out of the drawer. Then he grabbed me by the shoulders and slammed me against the wall again, but harder. He knocked the wind out of me and I fell down on the floor gasping for air. He stood over me glaring and said, "You had enough yet, punk?" I said real low, "Yes." He said, "Are you sure you had enough, punk?" I got my wind back and said, "No, I'm not." He said, "Do you want some more of me, punk?" I quickly said, "No, no, no."

Case 81, also from my second major study (1992, pp. 70–71) illustrates a violent dominance engagement that takes place between non-family members. Here, a young, adolescent male scores a major victory during a violent dominance engagement with an older male:

> *Case 81:* My girlfriend and I were at a pizza parlor that had a pool table. I started shooting pool with an older guy who was there, and my girlfriend sat in a nearby chair smoking cigarettes and watching us. While we were playing pool, I noticed that this guy kept checking out my girlfriend. She was sitting in her chair backwards and he was staring a hole through

her pants. I knew what he was thinking, "This is one bitch I want to fuck bad." I tried to get his mind off her and back on pool, but he kept staring hard at her pants and shaking his head. So I let him know that she was my girlfriend, but he wouldn't take the hint and kept staring at her ass and shaking his head. The next thing I knew he walks right up to her and straight out says, "You sure got a real nice big ass." When she didn't say anything back to him, he said, "You know, you ought to leave that little young asshole and go out with me." I was getting really pissed off now, but before I could say or do anything, he reached down and squeezed her ass. When he did that, she jumped out of her chair and said, "Get your hands off my ass." He said, "Fuck you, you dirty little rag," and she said, "Get out of my face."

I got mad as fucking hell then. First he won't stop checking out her body in front of me, next he makes the remark about her ass, then he squeezes her ass, and now he calls her a rag. After he called her a rag, that was it for me. He had now finally gone too far, so I grabbed a pool stick, tightened my grip around the thick part as hard as I could, and swung it with all my might at his head. I broke the thin part of it across the side of his head, which knocked him off his feet. Then I quickly turned the stick around, jumped on top of him and started smashing him in the head with the thick end of the stick. I was fucking up the guy bad, blood was pouring out all over his head, neck and shoulders. Everybody in the pizza parlor then started screaming, "He's gone crazy, he's gone completely crazy. Call the police." My girlfriend started yelling at me "Stop, stop, stop. You're going to kill him!" I threw the bloody pool stick down on the floor, grabbed her by the hand, and we ran out the door.

Males and females differ dramatically in how they fare in violent dominance engagements. Females usually fare worse than males for a variety of obvious and not so obvious reasons. Because more males than females reach this stage of violence development, females are more likely to confront males than other females during violent dominance engagements. The greater physical size of males, their more frequent participation in physical contact sports and gangs, and their greater knowledge of, and access to, lethal weapons all give them a decided edge in winning dominance engagements against females. In fact, females can provide a ready source of "cheap" major or minor victories that budding violent males can use to advance their stalled violence development (Rhodes, 1999, pp. 286–312). Thus, females who reach the violent dominance engagement stage are much less likely than males to pass successfully through it.

Case 106, which is from the same study (1992) as the previous one, illustrates the case of a middle-aged, married woman who reached the stage of violent dominance engagements but was unable to complete it. Two things were primarily responsible for her failure to complete this stage of her violence development. One was the repeated major defeats that she suffered at the hands of her husband and the other was her aversion to using more lethal tactics to score a major victory over him. Thus, she ultimately had to resign herself to the fact that she lacked an aptitude for serious violence:

Case 106: My husband beat me severely 15 or 20 times. I tried to fight back a few times, but he overpowered me. I could never get him off me using my hands. He was a boxer and so much stronger than me that there was no way that I beat him straight up. When I did fight back, it only made matters that much worse because he would just beat me that much more. He finally beat me down so far that he broke me. At the end, I was so scared that I did not even think about fighting him back anymore. I would just beg for mercy and try to get away. I did not have the nerve to shoot or stab him while he was sleeping – that would have been murder. I was too weak and scared to kill somebody in cold blood like that.

Although violent dominance engagements may resemble what Goffman (1967, pp. 149–207) calls "character contests,"[3] they definitely are not analogous notions for three indisputable reasons. First and foremost, unlike character contests, violent dominance engagements do not demand that the combatants form a working consensus that violence should be the means used for the resolution of their dispute. To the contrary, in the case of violent dominance engagements, the combatants often operate on conflicting presumptions about the use of violence to settle dominance disputes. After one party ascertains for certain that the other party adamantly opposes the use of violence to determine who should perform the super ordinate role, the first party may still seek to force the second party's hand and make her participate in a violent dominance engagement against her will and better judgement, as in the case in which a person wielding a dangerous weapon presses forward to attack a defenseless person (Athens, 1985, pp. 423–425). If there is any doubt about the absence of consensus about employing brute physical force during dominance engagements, then a review of cases 21, 25, 35, 76, and 84 illustrating them in Part III should completely dispel it.

Second, unlike in character contests, dominance engagements are not fought to determine whose character is the strongest. Instead, they are fought to determine who is dominant and thereby should perform the super ordinate role in some joint activity. Thus, the real underlying issue behind violent disputes becomes obfuscated in the notion of character contest.

Finally, for the two reasons just mentioned, a dominance engagement not only provides a more precise explanation of violent disputes than character contests, but it also provides a more encompassing one. Violent dominance engagements can account for all the violent disputes that are supposedly committed during character contests, whereas character contests cannot account for all the violent disputes that take place during a violent dominance engagement (see Felson & Steadman, 1983; Luckenbill, 1977; Ray & Simmons, 1987; Savitz, Kumar & Zahn, 1991). When people prove their superiority during a violent dominance engagement, they may also display either a strong *or* weak character rather than always a stronger one. In the case where a large young adult male wins a violent dominance engagement over a smaller adult female, a young child, or frail senior citizen, he proves his sheer physical superiority over them, but often at the cost of demonstrating a weaker, more twisted character. Thus, depending on the circumstances and victim, a character contest can bring honor as well as dishonor because one can "save" or "lose face" when violence is used to win one (Athens, 1985, p. 427).

Virulency

The fourth and final stage of violentization is "virulency." Unlike defiance and dominance engagement, but like brutalization, virulency is a composite experience comprised of three elemental experiences. "Violent notoriety," the first elemental experience, refers to the recognition that former subordinates suddenly acquire from their major victory over a would-be super ordinate or former violent subjugator during a violent dominance engagement. Although previously spoken of as being incapable or only possibly capable of violence during such dominance engagements, these former subordinates are now spoken about as if they are not only capable of violence, but proficient in it.

The second elemental experience, "social trepidation," flows directly from the first. Unlike violent notoriety, however, social trepidation does not refer to how people talk about you in your absence, but how they act toward you in your presence. In contrast to the past, people now act more deferentially and cautiously toward the former subordinate. Moreover, they now take special pains not to challenge or slight him in any way because they fear igniting a violent dominance engagement that they could lose.

If this newly ordained super ordinate decides to embrace rather than reject his violent notoriety and the social trepidation that it generates, then he will undergo the final elemental experience, "malevolency." Overly impressed with his sudden rise from a lowly subordinate to a lofty super ordinate, he becomes arrogant. Blown up with a false sense of omnipotence, his former mitigated violent resolution made earlier during the defiance stage is replaced with an unmitigated violent one. He now resolves to gravely harm or even kill someone for any dominative provocation, however slight.

After making this new violent resolution, he is transformed from a person who would only resort to violence to resist his or an intimate's debasement or violent subjugation to a person who relishes any opportunity to violently subjugate others. Undergoing the malevolency experience marks not only the completion of the virulency stage, but the entire violentization process. At the end of this stage, a "violent" individual matures into an "ultra-violent" one and, in the process, discovers a complete "cure" for his earlier personal disorganization.

Ultra-violent criminals live and die by a motto that turns the golden rule on its head: "Do onto to others as they have done onto you, but do it to them first." This motto becomes the new principle on the basis of which they complete their personal *re*-organization (see for examples: Rhodes 1999, pp. 156–198; Shakur, 1993).

As is true in the violent dominance engagement stage, more males than females pass successfully through the virulency stage. We are much more apt to consider males more dangerous and to fear them more than females because in our present society, cold, ruthless acts of violence are more closely associated with males. That same gender bias makes it much easier for males than females to gain violent notoriety, engender social trepidation, and accept a malevolent identity. Thus, at least in the case of creating barriers to violence development, sexism seems to work to the distinct disadvantage of males and to the distinct advantage of females (Kipnis, 1999, pp. ix–xi). Cases 69 and 93 below, taken from my second major study (1992, pp. 76–79), provide examples of adolescent males who have finished the entire violentization process and become ultra-violent individuals:

Case 69: After the stabbing, my friends told me, "Hey man, we heard about what you did to Joe. It's all over school. Everybody's talking about it. You must really be one crazy ass motherfucker." My girlfriend said, "Wow, you stabbed that dude." Finally things came together and hit right for me. My girlfriend and all my other friends were impressed with what I had done. I didn't really care what my parents thought. Everybody acted like nobody better piss me off anymore unless they wanted to risk getting fucked up bad. People were plain scared to fuck with me. My reputation was now made.

I was in cloud nine. I felt like I had climbed the mountain and reached the top. I had proven to my friends and myself that I could really fuck somebody up. If something came up again, I knew I could hurt somebody bad. If I did it once, hell, I could do it again. It felt just like the first time I had gotten pussy. After I knew how it felt to get some, I knew I could get some more. Now I knew I could fuck somebody's world around, send them sideways, upside down and then six feet under. There was no doubt at all in my mind now that I was a bad son of a bitch, a crazy motherfucker. I could do anything, kill or murder somebody.

Now that I had reached the top of the mountain, I was not coming down for anybody or anything. The real bad dude who wouldn't associate with me before because they thought I was a nobody now thought I was a somebody and accepted me as another crazy bad ass. I became a go-getter. I would go after people's asses for pissing me off in any fucking way at all. I meant what I said to people and said what I meant to them. They better listen to what I said because I wasn't playing games any more, but for keeps. I was ready to kill anybody who walked the streets.

Case 93: After I busted that dude's head open, the principal kicked me out of school for the rest of the year. The students all spread around that I had fucked up a dude real bad and sent him to the hospital, so the principal had to get rid of me. Everybody, my people and close friends, thought I had gone too far on the dude. They thought he deserved an ass-kicking from me, but not to be put in the hospital. They said, "You shouldn't have done him like that. You went too far." It tripped me out as much as them that I could hurt somebody that bad.

But nobody in the school or around my neighborhood would fuck with me after that. People said, "James is crazy. Don't go heads up with a dude like that because he will fuck you up." Most people made sure that they gave me plenty of space and stayed mellow around me. They paid more respect and said "Hi" to me when I walked by.

People may have thought that I went too far on that dude, but I later knew what I did was right. It must have been right because nobody was giving me any shit any more. They didn't want to take a chance of going up against me and having the same thing happen to them. Before I put that big dude in the hospital, they would say things like, "James talks a lot of shit, but I bet he is not really bad." I showed them I was not all talk. I proved that I might not be big, but dynamite can come in small packages.

The way people acted made me come alive. It swelled up my head. I said to myself, "If I put that big dude's ass in the hospital, then I could put any other dude on the street there too." If any motherfucker out there talked or even looked at me wrong, I was ready to walk right up on him and see if he wanted to give me some. I was ready to throw down with everything that I had. If a motherfucker loses his teeth, then he lost some teeth. If he loses his eye, then he lost an eye, and he loses his life, then he lost a life. It didn't matter to me. The way I looked at it was that is just one less motherfucker this world will have to put up with.

III. VIOLENTIZATION AND THE COMMUNITY

The Basic Building Blocks of Communities: Dominance, Institutions, and Socialization

A society may be thought of in some sense as the physical space over which a major community is spread. As Robert Park (1952, p. 181), the journalist turned sociologist, explains, "A community has a spatial and geographical connotation. Every community has a location, and the individuals who compose it have a place of residence within the territory which the community occupies." I would amend Park's definition slightly to include place of employment, which is nowadays often different from an individual's place of residence.

A major community is one in which various minor ones operate (Park, 1952, p. 96). In any major community, however, there must be at least some common institutions that effectively operate across all the different minor communities that comprise it. A minor community is the more limited physical space across which at least some unique institutions, including those for the socialization of new members, effectively operate. Minor communities are not static entities, but may evolve or devolve over time. As the minor communities that comprise a major community evolve or devolve, so may the major community in which they are incorporated.

One minor community's borders end and another's borders begin where people organize at least some of their social experiences on the basis of some important, different institutions. A minor community's corporal diameter is only as broad or narrow as the domain of its unique institutions. Thus, the effective limits of a minor community's important distinctive operating institutions demarcate its real physical boundaries.

What are institutions? Institutions provide the foundation from which all communities are constructed, demolished, and reconstructed. When all is said and done, they boil down to the common principles by which the people who live in communities organize their social experiences (Mead, 1934, pp. 211, 260–263). However, there always exists a gulf between how the members of a community purport their institutions run and how their institutions run in the actual practice. Thus, it is always deeds rather than mere words that reveal an institution's real, as opposed to stated, common operating principles.

If a community is to continue across different generations, then its young members must always be socialized as to how the institutions in their communities operate. During their socialization in a community's practices, they receive at least some preparation in advance for later organizing their social experiences according to their community's real and ideal operating principles, which may often contradict one another (see Mead, 1934, pp. 264–265).

Institutions are not born from an act of providence or spontaneous social generation. To the contrary, they are always born from individual ingenuity. Thus, in any community, it is the individual community member and not the community as a whole from which new institutions always originally spring (Mead, 1934, pp. 192–222). Although born from individual ingenuity, institutions depend on social experience for their continual existence (Blumer, 1969, pp. 16–20; Mead, 1932, p. 165). Herbert Blumer (1969, p. 19) warned sociologists long ago that "it is the social process in group life that . . . upholds the rules, not the rules that uphold group life." If my phrase "social experience" is substituted for his phrase "group life," then his warning ratifies my earlier point.

Based on the diameter of the domain in which an institution effectively operates, three types of institutional social experiences can be distinguished: (1) "societal"; (2) "communal"; and (3) "idiosyncratic." *Societal* institutions are principles for organizing social experiences in which the effective domain of operation cuts across an entire major community, with the sole exception of a few of its minor communities. Thus, it is always societal institutions that demarcate the borders of a major community.

Communal institutions are principles for organizing social experiences in which the effective domain of operation stretches from one end to the other of a minor community, with the sole exception of a few individuals or groups within it. If a communal institution is contrary to a societal one for organizing some particular social experience, then it is, to borrow an old term from Evertt Hughes (1984, pp. 98–105), a "bastard" communal institution. Nevertheless, whether or not a communal institution is a bastard one, it may serve to define a minor community's borders.

Idiosyncratic institutions are principles for organizing social experiences that do not effectively operate beyond a relatively few individuals or groups within a minor community. Although the concept of an idiosyncratic institution may appear to be an oxymoron, it is not one because, as noted, all institutions start from individual initiative and later die from personal disuse. If an operating principle for organizing a social experience has only first appeared in a minor community, then it is an *incipient idiosyncratic* institution. If the principle has not only operated for some time but has previously been a communal institution in a minor community, however, then it is a *vestigial idiosyncratic* institution. In neither case do idiosyncratic institutions demarcate the borders of a minor, much less a major, community.

The institutions on which communities are based are not static axioms, but may evolve or devolve over time. Incipient idiosyncratic institutions may evolve into communal institutions and communal institutions may, in turn, later evolve into societal ones. Conversely, societal institutions may devolve into communal ones, and communal-wide ones may later devolve into vestigial, idiosyncratic institutions. Because the evolution and devolution of our institutions are always a contingent and problematic process, the evolution and devolution of our minor communities are also contingent and problematic processes.

Dominance is the universal principle on which all social experiences, institutions, and in turn, communities are ultimately based (Athens, 2002a, pp. 30–32). Dominance refers to the swaying of a social experience in accordance with our preferences. People dominate when they impose their view of an emerging social experience on other people, and thereby steer the course of its development. The issue of dominance emerges as soon as people begin to undergo together an experience of any length. During our social experiences, the unstated question that always lurks beneath the surface is "who will be the boss?" As Samuel Johnson quips, "No two people can be a half hour together, but one shall acquire an evident superiority over the other." (Athens, 1998, p. 675).

Dominance is also the universal principle on which all communities – past, present, and future – are organized. It is an ugly fact of communal existence from which there is no escape. Although the faces of the people who occupy the top and bottom rungs of any pecking order change, a dominance order of some type or another always remains. Because people want to raise their positions, or at least keep themselves from falling into lower ones, disputes over dominance invariably arise among the members of a minor community (see Morris, 1969, pp. 21, 41, 56: Simmel, 1950, pp. 273–276).

Although it is impossible to stop dominance disputes from ever occurring in any community, the nature of their expression can be organized in particular ways. In every community, the members create operating principles for organizing how dominance engagements are waged. Of course, these operating principles may vary in their form and degree of institutionalization from one minor community to another and vary in both of these ways in the same minor community at different times. Thus, in all minor communities, there can be found at least some form and degree of institutionalized dominance engagements, for which their young members always receive some socialization.

The people who rise to the top of a minor community's dominance order are usually those who repeatedly win dominance disputes under the prevailing rules of engagement for which they have undergone socialization in their minor community. Conversely, the people who usually sink to the bottom of a minor community's dominance order are those who repeatedly lose dominance engagements under the prevailing rules of engagement for which they have undergone socialization. Thus, people primarily rise or fall in their minor community's pecking order through their winning or losing of institutionalized dominance engagements that they have been socialized to employ. This provides the basis for the popular refrain that "life is a rat race" to which I would add that "like it or not, we all have to learn to live with" (Athens, 1998, p. 675).

The type of people who rise to the top and sink to the bottom of a minor community's dominance order is the single most revealing fact about it. The impact that top dogs have on the tempo and flavor of their minor community's life far exceeds their absolute numbers in their community (Wirth, 1928, p. 286). In every minor community, the top dogs display insignia of their dominance that distinguish them from the underdogs. Although the particular insignia that they wear may vary from one minor community to another and from one time to another in the same minor community, these badges of dominance all serve to indicate where they stand in their minor community's pecking order. The homes or apartments in which they live, the stores in which they shop, the restaurants in which they eat, the streets on which they frequently pass, and the typical clothes that they wear all operate as dominance insignia. Thus, based on the nature and degree of a minor community's institutionalization of dominance engagements, the socialization that their members receive to wage them and the kind of people that most often win and lose them and thereby rise to the top or sink to the bottom of their dominance orders, three types of minor communities that transcend racial, ethnic and religious lines can be demarcated (Athens, 1998, p. 678).

The Civil Minor Community

In civil minor communities, the "non-violent dominance engagement" is the predominant institution for settling dominance disputes. During non-violent dominance engagements, the opponents engage in psychological, economic, and legal warfare against one another. The weapons used to wage psychological warfare range from gossiping about, ridiculing, snubbing, avoiding, and deluding rivals to shunning, ostracizing, disowning, betraying and defaming them. The weapons used to wage legal warfare range from legally separating from and divorcing their rivals to filing various types of criminal complaints, and civil suits and injunctions against them to passing laws that outright discriminate against them. The weapons used to wage economic warfare range from refusing to hire and promote rivals to demoting and firing them to charging them more for services and products. Although these different means of waging dominance engagements may be used separately or in conjunction with one another, the goal behind them is the same. It is always to force rivals to relinquish their claims on a higher position and accept their lower position in the community's pecking order.

One should not mistakenly conclude from what has been said that non-violent dominance engagements are relatively benign social experiences. To the contrary, when the combatants unleash their most potent psychological, legal, or economic weapons on one another, non-violent dominance engagements can be extremely cruel. In fact, even non-violent dominance engagements where only psychological warfare is used can become vicious enough to belie the old schoolyard saying that "sticks and stones will break my bones, but words will never hurt me." The words spoken and actions taken during the use of psychological warfare may not break people's bones, but they can scar people's minds for life.

Among the three types of violent people considered, it is usually the marginally violent person who rises to the top and violent and ultra-violent persons who sink to bottom of the dominance order in a civil minor community. Marginally violent people confine themselves to the use of psychological, economic, and legal warfare to settle dominance disputes, except under the extreme circumstances where they need to defend themselves or intimate from an opponent who actually or threatens to physically attack them. On the other hand, violent and ultra-violent people will employ brute physical force to win a dominance engagement even when their opponent does not threaten to or actually physically attack them or an intimate.

In civil minor communities, violentization is an idiosyncratic form of socialization. To be sure, some children are brutalized, somewhat fewer become defiant and still fewer have serious violent dominance engagements, and almost none graduate into virulency and later become dangerous violent criminals. Thus, even in the most refined civil minor communities, at least some children pass through some of the stages of violentization, but their completion of the entire violentization process is rare.

It should come as no surprise that the willingness of violent and ultra-violent people to use brute, physical force during dominance engagements under much broader circumstances than only self defense make them "social misfits" in a civil minor community. They may live or work within the physical boundaries of a minor civil community, but they are not an integral part of it. The selves of violent and ultra-violent people who continue to live or work in a civil minor community may split apart at the seams because of their treatment as social misfits. The personal disorganization that accompanies their *selves*' division can led them to become violent or marginally violent people or else become permanently disorganized (Athens, 1995, pp. 574–578).

Case 84, taken from my second major study (1992, pp. 1–2), illustrates a violent dominance engagement that took place in a civil minor community where one ultra-violent adolescent male scores a major victory over an entire group of apparently marginally violent ones:

> *Case 84:* I was cruising around town with two friends of mine, when we suddenly got hit in the rear end by another car. After we stopped off the road, I looked back and saw three guys in the car that hit us. I asked my friends, "What in the hell were those guys trying to do, kill us?" One of my friends said, "I don't know what in the fuck they were trying to do. Let's get out and find out."
>
> When we jumped out, they were already out of their car. The rear bumper of our car was only bent up some, but I was mad because they could have hurt us bad. I said, "Why in the hell did you run into the back of our car?" They said, "Why did you stop in the middle of a block so fast?" I said "Look, you stupid dumb motherfuckers, you ran into us, we didn't run into you." Then they said, "We didn't run into you on purpose, you stopped so fast, we couldn't stop in time." After they said that, I really got pissed off because they didn't act like they were sorry. They didn't seem to give a damn whether they hurt us or not, which got me mad as hell at those stupid motherfuckers. So I said, "Well, if that's all you dumb motherfuckers got to say about it, let's go on and fight." They just stood there looking at me dumbfounded, which made my hatred for them explode. I said, "You're going to be sorry for the day you hit us, you dumb stupid motherfuckers, because now I'm going to kill all three of you." I decided to get something and really mess them all up bad. I looked in the car and grabbed a heavy steel crowbar. I told my friends, "Now I'm going

to do some real damage to them." Without saying another word, I started swinging the crowbar and smacked one of the guys hard right in the side of his head. I could feel his skull splatter open when I hit him. He fell to the ground with blood pouring over his face, neck, and shoulders. As I looked at him, he clutched his head and blood ran through his fingers and he screamed, "Please help me, please help me, my head is bleeding real bad. I'm going to bleed to death!" But I was still mad and could not care less whether he lived or died. All I wanted was to get the other two guys before they got away.

Then I turned and quickly hit another one hard across his arm twice while he was still staring at his crying friend who I had hit in the head. After I hit him, he looked at me and squealed, "Oh my arm, my arm, you broke my arm." Next I swung and hit the last guy hard in the leg, but I didn't get a chance to hit him solid again. Before I could hit him again and do some real damage to him, he started running with the guy I hit in the arm. I chased those yellow mother fuckers for maybe a half block before I suddenly began worrying about the police getting me. Then I ran back as fast as I could to our car satisfied that I did real damage to two of them. We jumped in the car and drove off fast.

Case 25, taken from my first major study (1997, pp. 7–9), also illustrates a violence dominance engagement that took place in a civil minor community. In contrast to Case 84, however, Case 25 provides an illustration of a *truncated* violent dominance engagement between a young adult, ultra-violent male and a young adult female who, at the very most, appears to be a marginally violent person:

Case 25: While I was an orderly working in the emergency room of a hospital, a young woman came in with a bad cut on her arm. She was about average in looks, but she had a better than average body with nice long, hefty legs and a nice broad ass. I showed her to one of the cubicles where patients were treated. I started a conversation with her. I asked her how she got hurt . . . .. From the way that she talked and acted, I got the impression that she was a woman who made men come after her. She was conceited and all wrapped up in herself. While we were talking, I couldn't stop wondering about how she would look nude. I tried to get something going with her, but her nose was too far up in the air. She acted like she was way above me. I wanted to bone her bad, although I knew that I wasn't going to get to first base with her. While I was sitting there thinking about boning her, the doctor walked in. After he stitched her up, she split.

While at work a couple days later, she came back into my mind. I figured that I could get her name and address from the outpatient log. My pistol was in my car. I started getting excited thinking about breaking into her pad and ripping her off. When I go off work later that night, I headed straight for her pad. She lived in a first-floor apartment. When I got there, I noticed a dim light coming from one of the rooms. I crept around and looked in the window of the room where the light was coming from. I could see her lying on the floor of her bedroom with only her panties on doing some kind of exercises. Her titties were changing shape as she exercised, and I got hard. I wanted to bone her right then and there and wondered what would happen if I just tapped on her window and pointed my pistol at her. I figured that she would start screaming and someone would call the police, so I decided to wait and not break in until after she went to sleep. After she finished exercising, she grabbed some clothes and went into the bathroom. I heard the shower running and went around to the bathroom window. I couldn't see a thing, so I came back to her bedroom window and waited. When she came out of the bathroom fifteen minutes later, she flipped the lights out and jumped into bed. While I waited for her to get sound to sleep, I fantasized about tearing off her nighties and panties and boning her good.

About two or three hours later, I decided it was safe to break in. I put my mask over my face and checked all the windows. Her kitchen window was unlocked, and I climbed through it. Without making any noise, I then tiptoed into her bedroom. I was standing next to her bed staring at her, trying to get up my courage, when she suddenly woke up on her own. When she saw me, she sat up and sucked in her breath. Then I grabbed her by a the shoulder, pointed my pistol between her eyes, and said, "If you make even one sound, I'll shoot you." I dug the horror that I saw start in her eyes and then spread all over her face.

I didn't want her to know that I was after her pussy, because she might panic and start fighting me, so I asked her how much money she had around the pad to throw her off the track. She said, "I only have $15 in my purse." Since I wanted to get her completely helpless, I said, "Don't lie like that to me. I'm going to tie you up and search for myself." Then she swore to me that was all the money that she had and begged me not to tie her up, saying, "Please don't tie me up. Please don't. . .," but I said, "I'm not going to take any chances with you; getting tied up is a lot better than getting your head blown off." Then I grabbed her sheet and tore it apart. I tied her hands to the bedposts. I tried to tie her feet too, but she kicked them away from me and asked, "Why are you tying me up like this?" I pointed my pistol at her head again and said, "Shut up and give me your foot."

After I tied her feet to the bedposts, I pulled the rest of the covers off her and started slowly rolling her negligee up around her neck. She started crying and said, "Please don't do that. Please don't, please . . .." I said, "Whatever I do to you is better than you getting shot, right?" I put my hand on one of her tits and kept rubbing it over her nipple. She started crying. After I cut off her panties with my pocketknife, I pulled down my pants. I got on top of her and drove my rod all the way up her. After I stroked my dick in and out of her four or five good times, I busted my nut. Then I got off her and wiped my dick off with her bedspread. Although it was all over in about a minute, she kept sobbing away. I told her that I was going to search the place for money and that she better not move. I went into the living room and then quietly split out the front door.

The Malignant Minor Community

In contrast to minor civil communities, in malignant minor ones, the violent dominance engagement is the predominant institution for resolving dominance disputes, so that in addition to the use of possible psychological, economic, or legal warfare, physical warfare can be used to settle dominance disputes. Of course, in a *civil major community*, the violent dominance engagements that are institutionalized in malignant communities would operate as a bastard institution. The weapons used to wage violent dominance engagements include fists, blunt objects, knives, handguns, rifles, bayonets, submachine guns, and bombs. Rivals are beaten, raped, stabbed, cut, burned, and shot until they relinquish their claims to higher positions and accept without complaint their lower positions in the community's pecking order.

Among the three types of violent people considered, it is the ultra-violent and violent persons who rise to the top and marginally violent persons who sink to the bottom of a malignant minor community's dominance order. As already noted, unlike in the case of marginally violent people, ultra-violent and violent people do not restrict themselves to the use of non-violent means of warfare during a dominance engagement, except under the extreme circumstances of defending themselves or an intimate from physical attack. If subjected to a physical attack or extreme degradation during a dominance engagement, a violent person will resort to physical warfare to prevent his own or an intimate's physical injury or his debasement. In the case of ultra-violent people, however, the threat of physical safety or personal humiliation is not necessary for them to resort to physical warfare. To the contrary, they will use brute physical force against an opponent during a dominance engagement for the slightest, dominative provocation.

Unlike in minor civil communities, where it is a rare for children to complete even the early stages of violentization, in minor malignant communities, it is relatively commonplace.[4] In fact, most of these children not only complete at least the first two stages of violentization, but also enter into third stage, so that at least this portion of the violentization process is institutionalized in their communities. Thus, it is taken for granted that children in malignant minor communities will be brutalized and become defiant and will later have violent dominance engagements, although they will not necessarily become virulent. Nevertheless, far more children become ultra-violent criminals in malignant minor communities than in civil ones.

Unlike in minor civil communities, where ultra-violent and violent people are the social misfits, in minor malignant communities, the marginally violent people are the social misfits. They are the ones who are physically present in this minor community, but not an integral part of it. If marginally violent people remain in malignant minor communities for too long, they may be sooner or later brutalized, which could split their *selves apart* at the seams. The personal disorganization accompanying their selves' division could become a prelude to them later becoming violent or ultra-violent criminals, or else becoming permanently disorganized individuals (Athens, 1995, pp. 574–578). A couple of cases also taken from my first major study (1997, pp. 10–11) illustrate violent dominance engagements that took place in malignant minor communities. In case 55, with the aid of a rifle, a young adult, ultra-violent male wins a major victory over three other ultra-violent young adult males:

> *Case 55:* A partner of mine said he might come over to my pad with some broads, so I hurried over to the liquor store right around the corner to get a case of beer. As I was walking across the parking lot of the store, this guy almost ran me over. I flipped him off.

The driver and his partners jumped out of the car and rat-packed me. They knocked me down, and the driver pushed my head into the dirt next to the cigarette butts. Then they went into the store. I just felt, "What a low fucking thing to do to somebody. They are just a bunch of yellow motherfuckers." In my mind, I suddenly thought, "I've got to get back at these dirty motherfuckers," and I ran back to my pad for my rifle.

I got back to the liquor store as fast as I possibly could and waited for them about twenty yards from the front door of the store. While I was waiting, I kept trying to decide whether I should shoot to wound the motherfuckers or kill them, and whether I should shoot only the driver or his partners too. Finally, his two partners popped out the door. I said to myself, "Fuck it, I'll shoot all of them." I fired two quick, wild shots but missed them both, and they got away. I decided then that I better put the barrel to the chest of the motherfucker who I really wanted – the driver – and make sure that I didn't miss him. I had stone hatred for him, and I righteously couldn't wait to see the look on his face when I blew him away. As soon as he popped out of the liquor store door, I charged right up to him, rammed the barrel in his chest, and pulled the trigger.

Case 32, taken from the same study as previous one (1997, pp. 50–51), illustrates another violent dominance engagement that happened in a malignant minor community. In contrast to case 55, in case 32, however, a cunning, ultra-violent, young adult female scores a major victory over an older, ultra-violent male:

Case 32: We were partying one night in my rooms at the hotel where I lived and worked. Everybody there was a regular, except for this one dude who I had rented a room down the hall. He just kind of drifted in, and X said that he knew the dude, so it was cool. We were all drinking wine, taking pills, and having a mellow time when I overheard this dude asking X who I was and saying that I was a bitch. I said, "Hey, who's the bitch you are talking about?" and he said, "You're the bitch." I thought to myself, "What does this dude think he's doing, coming to my party uninvited and then calling me a fucking bitch?" I said, "Don't you come to my party and call me a bitch." He said, "You are a bitch; I was high and you shortchanged me out of fucking $20 when I paid you for my room today." I said, "Man, you are crazy." He said, "Don't try to slick me, bitch; I'm hip. I'm an ex-con. I know what's happening, and X knows I'm good people, so don't try to run that game on me."

My friends were having a good time, I felt good, and I didn't want to spoil the mood for any problems behind $20, so I thought that I'd just pacify the chump and give him a lousy $20 and end it. I said, "Look, man, I didn't shortchange you out of any money today, but just to show my good heart, I'll give you $20. How about that?" He said, "Well, since you needed it so fucking bad that you had to try to run a game like that past me, then you can keep it, bitch." Then I thought that motherfucker was just messing with me. He was trying to make me out as a petty hustler and call me a bitch right in front of my friends. I said to myself, "Please, motherfucker, don't mess with me any more." I finally said, "Mister, I'm warning you, don't you fuck with me any more or I'll show you what a fucking bitch is." He just looked at me, laughed, and said, "I haven't seen the bitch yet who could kick my ass."

Then I told myself, "This man has got to go, one way or another. I've just had enough of this motherfucker messing with me. I'm going to cut his dirty, motherfucking throat." I went into my bedroom, got a $20 bill and my razor. I said to myself, "The motherfucker wouldn't stop fucking with me, and now he's hung himself," and I walked out of the bedroom. I went up to him with a big smile on my face. I held the $20 bill in my hand out in front of me and hid the razor in my other hand. Then I sat on his lap and said, "Okay, you're a fast dude. Here's your $20 back." He said, "I'm glad that you are finally admitting it." I looked at him with a smile and said, "Let me seal it with a kiss." I said to myself, "Motherfucker, now I'll show you what a fucking bitch is," and then I bent over like I was going to kiss him and started slicing up his throat.

The Turbulent Minor Community

In contrast to both civil and malignant minor communities, in turbulent minor communities, neither the violent nor non-violent dominance engagement is the predominant institution for resolving dominance disputes. In these minor communities, there is an odd mixture of ultra-violent, violent, and marginally violent types who all live or work together in the same physical space, but for whom there exist no common operating principle for organizing how they wage dominance engagements against one another. The ultra-violent and violent members of this minor community display a distinct penchant for waging violent dominance engagements, whereas the marginally violent members prefer to wage non-violent ones. To add to the overall confusion in these minor communities, by threatening to or actually engaging in physical warfare, the ultra-violent and violent members can literally force the marginally violent members to participate in violent dominance engagements to protect themselves or their intimates from imminent physical harm (Athens, 1977, p. 67; 1997, pp. 99–100).

The absence of any effective institution for organizing dominance engagements in turbulent minor communities creates a chaotic environment for its members to live and work. Although dominance disputes are endemic to communal existence, in these minor communities, no common operating principles exists to organize their expression. Thus, when a dominance dispute erupts among these community members, they are never quite sure what principles will be in operation. The ever-present danger of chaos breaking out during dominance engagements creates a minor community that Park (1952, pp. 89–90) aptly describes as one in which "the physical distances and social distances do not coincide; a situation in which people who live side by side are not, and – because of the divergence of their interests and their heritages – cannot, even with the best of good will, become neighbors."

Although the ultra-violent, violent, and marginally violent people are all competing against one another to gain the upper hand in a minor turbulent community, none have gained it as yet. In turbulent minor communities, everything is topsy turvy. The marginally violent members may rise to the top of the community's dominance order only to be suddenly replaced by ultra-violent or violent members. Conversely, the ultra-violent and violent members may rise to the top only to be replaced just as suddenly by marginally violent members. The marginally violent, violent, and ultra-violent all seek to climb their way to the top of their minor community's dominance order, but they operate on opposing principles for the winning the dominance engagements that are necessary for them to get and stay there. Thus, in turbulent minor communities, no one knows for sure how you get or stay on top of the dominance order.

As in the case of dominance engagements, there is no institutionalized form of socialization for resolving dominance disputes in minor turbulent communities. The lack of any such institutional socialization in these communities only complicates further the lives of the children growing up in them. What they learn at home may be at sharp odds with what they learn on the streets, at school, or later on the job and vice versa. Because some children have graduated from many more of the stages of the violentization process than others, the dominance disputes that invariably break out between them are much more unpredictable than those in either civil or malignant minor communities.

It is no surprise that the passage of children through most of the stages of violentization is more prevalent in turbulent than civil minor communities, and it is less prevalent in turbulent than malignant minor ones. More children from turbulent than civil minor communities graduate from the brutalization and defiant stages, but less children from turbulent than malignant minor communities graduate from these two stages. Similarly, more children from turbulent than civil minor communities graduate from the violent dominance engagement stage, but less children from turbulent than malignant, minor communities graduate from this stage. Thus, more children from turbulent minor communities become dangerous violent criminals than those from civil ones, and less children from turbulent minor communities become dangerous violent criminals than those from malignant minor ones.

Unlike in either civil or malignant minor communities, in turbulent communities, almost everyone appears to be a misfit to someone else. Because none of the three types – marginally violent, violent, or ultra-violent persons – have gained the upper hand, and because no form of dominance engagements or socialization has become institutionalized as a result, no common yardstick exists to help turbulent minor community members pick out those who do belong from those who do not belong in their community (see Blumer, 2000, p. 351). As Park (1952, p. 89) says, in communities such as these, "everything is loose and free, but everything is problematic."

Thus, there may be one saving grace to living or working in turbulent minor communities where anarchy exists, at least as far as the means used to wage dominance engagements are concerned. Their members are more immune than those from civil or malignant minor communities to the personal disorganization that can result from living or working in a minor community where most people use the same basic means of settling disputes over dominance. In the latter minor communities, their members can exact a heavier price on those who choose non-institutionalized means of waging dominance engagements.

Case 56, taken my first major study (1997, pp. 73–75), illustrates a violent dominance engagement among the members of a family who reside in a turbulent minor community. In this violent dominance engagement, an adolescent male scores a major victory over his stepfather, although at the cost of killing him:

Case 56: We has just finished supper, and my stepfather told my brother to wash the dishes, but he refused. My stepfather was drunk, and he started throwing dishes off the table. My mother tried to clear the table before he broke all the dishes, and he smacked her in the face. My brother got up and ran for the back door, but my stepfather cut him off and told him not to leave the kitchen. My mind was on getting out of there as fast as I could before he got on me. I got up from the table, but he pushed me back down in my chair and said, "You better not move from that chair until I tell you, or I'll beat you ass good just like I did on your birthday." My mother and brother cleared the dishes left on the table and started washing them. He just stood there glaring at us until the dishes were done. Then he told us all to go into the living room. He bolted the front door shut, and my brother turned on the TV. My stepfather then turned it off so hard that he broke the knob clean off, and he began yelling at my brother again about the dishes. Finally I asked my stepfather if I could please go to my room and lay down since I wasn't feeling well. He told me it was okay, so I went to my room.

A couple of minutes later he came into my room and said, "You know, you're sick, because you were the one who should have done those dishes." Then there was a crash in the living room, and he ran in there and checked it out. My baby brother had knocked over a lamp, and my stepfather smacked him for it. My baby brother started crying, and my stepfather told my mother, "You better shut that little bastard up." The fear of him that I felt inside then turned to cold hate and anger. The thought came in my mind to kill him. My .22 rifle then flashed in my mind. I got frightened just at the thought of it. I told myself that tonight I was going to kill him.

My mind turned back to my rifle. My stepfather had taken the bolt out of it and put it in his dresser drawer. I just sat the on my bed and tried to figure out a way that I could get into his room without him catching me. Then my mother said, "X, go get the baby's pacifier off the green dresser in my room." I hesitated. The thought of actually going into their room where my rifle bolt was scared me. My stepfather then yelled, "Didn't you hear your mother, boy? Go get that pacifier." I walked into their room. First I got the rifle bolt out of his drawer. I put it in my pocket and pulled out my shirt to cover it. Then I got the pacifier and went into the living room. When I walked by my stepfather to give my mother the baby's pacifier, I trembled, and he noticed it and thought that it was from fear of walking by him, but it was mostly from the rifle bolt and what I had in my mind to do. My looking scared must have satisfied him good because he told me that I could go back to my room and rest.

As soon as I did, I put the bolt in my rifle and got some shells out of my sock drawer. As I loaded the rifle, I started thinking about what would happen if I fired and missed him and what would happen if I shot and killed him. I wondered if I'd go to prison. Finally I decided that I should kill him, so I grabbed my rifle and walked in the hallway and then turned around and walked back into my room. I did this over and over again until finally I got up enough nerve to walk into the living room. My stepfather was sitting on the sofa. I pointed my rifle straight at him and just stood there looking at him. Finally he noticed me, and he jumped up, and I pulled the trigger. I got him in the side, and he fell back down on the sofa. I felt relieved. He looked up at me, and I pulled the trigger again. This time I hit him in the neck, and his whole body started quivering, and I pulled the trigger again and got him in the head. He then completely collapsed down on the floor. I felt tranquil. I knew that he was dead. I had to go to the school for boys behind it.

Case 21, which is taken from my same major study (1997, pp. 40–41) as the previous one, illustrates a violent dominance engagement in a turbulent community between two recently made acquaintances. In this case, a young adult, ultra-violent male wins a major victory over one who is at most marginally violent:

Case 21: I was at a neighborhood tavern drinking beer next to this guy who I knew was a homosexual. He was showing his billfold around and I began to think about hustling him. We were in the bathroom together several times and I tried to hustle him, but he acted sneaky (he didn't put up any money), so I punched him. He then left the tavern, threatening to call the police on me. I thought, that motherfucking queer, I should rob him and bust his fucking head. So I followed him. He went home. I knocked on his door, but he wouldn't answer. I got mad and kicked his door open. Then this guy, his boyfriend, who was shacking up with him, comes up to me. His boyfriend being there got me madder, so I punched the boyfriend. The boyfriend took off out the front door. I then caught that queer standing there watching and staring at me. This got me madder. I figured this was a good opportunity to rob him and mess him up too. I've gone this far, so I might as well go all the way and do a good job on him. I'm in trouble as it is. You can get just as much time for doing a good job as a bad one. I wanted to fuck him up. I started beating him.

Case 35, which is taken from the same major study as two previous cases (1997, pp. 39–40), illustrates a violent dominance engagement with strong racial overtones between complete strangers in a turbulent, minor community. In this case, a young adult white ultra-violent male wins a major victory over a young adult black male who, at most, is a marginally violent person:

Case 35: I was just cruising around with some friends of mine, drinking wine, smoking dope, and eating a few reds. We came to an intersection and slowed down to make a turn when this black dude in a Thunderbird coming the other way cut us off in the middle of the intersection while he made a turn. Then he drove by us with a big grin on his face throwing the bone. The friend of mine who was driving just turned and started going the other way, but I suddenly said to myself, "That dirty jive nigger flipping me off and grinning – now he thinks he's one bad nigger. Well, I'm going to get down with that black motherfucker." Then I grabbed the wheel and said, "Turn around and catch that nigger driving that Thunderbird." We started following him, but after he made a couple of turns, we lost him. He was too far ahead of us. I said, "Well, he's got to be somewhere in this neighborhood, so let's just keep driving around here until we spot that Thunderbird, because I'm out to book that nigger." I could still see his big grin when he shot us the bird, and it was driving me up a wall. There was just no way that I was going to quit looking for that motherfucker. I was outright determined to have his ass one way or another.

Finally I spotted his car in a driveway in front of a house, and I told X, who was driving, to pull over and park in front of the house. Then I snapped my shotgun together and loaded it. One of my friends said, "Hey, Y, what the hell is your trip?" I said, "It's just my trip," and jumped out of the car. I didn't care about anything but having that nigger's ass. All I thought was, "I'm going to kill this punk." I walked up to the house and knocked on the front door. He answered the door, but as soon as he saw it was me, he slammed it shut in my face. Then I kicked the door wide open and saw him making tracks out the back door. I ran through the house after him and jammed him as he was climbing over the back fence. I leveled the barrel of my shotgun at his head and said "Nigger, get off that fence." After he did, I said, "Head back into that house." I wanted to fuck him up in the house so nobody would see it, but when we got to the back door, he stopped and said, "Man, I haven't done anything to you. Please don't hurt me." His sniveling made me madder. I shoved the barrel into his back and said, "Man, go into that house." He still wouldn't go in but just kept begging me not to shoot him. This pissed me off even more. I lost all my patience and said, "Fuck it," and shot him right where he was standing.

Case 76, which is taken from my second major study (1992, pp. 2–3), illustrates another violent dominance engagement in a turbulent, minor community with strong racial overtones. In this case, however, an adolescent ultra-violent black male scores a major victory over a middle-aged white woman who is, at most, a marginally violent person:

Case 76: James and I got the munchies and were walking to the grocery store to buy some cupcakes. In the parking lot of the store, we saw a fancy camper. I said, "Check out that camper," and we started looking in its windows. James said, "That's a bad truck, man." As we were walking away, an old woman walked by us with a big man pushing her grocery cart. She said, "Keep away from my truck." I said "We were just looking at it." She said, "Keep your black asses away from my truck." After she told us to keep away from her truck, I got mad. After she added the part about our black asses, I got doubly mad and wanted to kill her old stinking ass on the spot. I said, "Kiss my ass, you old stinking bitch." The big grocery store man said, "Get out of here before I call the police." I said, "Fuck the police, they're not about anything. I'll kill that old bitch for talking about my black ass."

About 10 minutes later we saw her truck again in a parking lot behind a building. I said to James, "Look, there's that same damn truck. Now I can get that old bitch." We ran out to the truck, looked around, and then busted open the back door. I told James, "When that old bitch comes back, let's take her out some place where I can stomp her ass. I'm going to fuck her up bad." James only laughed. I was still hot from her referring to our black asses and acting like we were dirt for her to kick around. I wanted to get her old stinking ass bad for saying that to us. I had hate for that old stinking white bitch. James wasn't as mad about her referring to our black asses as I was.

We sat in her camper eating the food she had gotten while we waited for her to come back. I couldn't wait till she saw us. When she came back to the camper, we pulled a knife on her and told her to start driving. She said, "I'll do anything you want, but please don't hurt me." As we drove off, she said, "I'm sorry for what I said to you at the grocery store, please let me go." We didn't say a word until we told her to pull the camper into a vacant lot we drove past. After she parked the camper, she started crying and slobbering, "Please don't hurt me, please don't hurt me. I'm sorry, please . . .." I knew the old stinking bitch was only lying. Seeing her slobber like that only made me madder and hate her even more.

I jumped out of the camper, grabbed her by the shoulders and threw her out of the cab. She landed face first on the dirt. She got up on her hands and knees and started yelling, "Help, police, help police, help." I said, "Shut up, you old stinking bitch," and kicked her in the stomach as hard as I could and knocked all the wind out of that old bag. She rolled up in a ball in the mud gasping for her breath, and I kicked her again which straightened her out like a stick. I tried to lift her up by the clothes, but she was so muddy that she slipped out of my hands, so I grabbed her by the hair. James said, "Would you look at her ugly old face." After I looked at it, I got so mad, I smacked and backhanded her about twenty times. Then I threw her against the camper and she slumped down on the ground. James opened a can of pop and asked her, "Do you want some pop?" She said, "No, I only want you to let me go." I said, "I'm not going to let you go, you stinking old bitch. I'm going to kill you." I grabbed her by the hair again and slammed her head back and forth against the side of the truck until blood started running out from her hair and over her ears. Then I dropped her to the ground, kicked her over into the mud puddle and left her for dead. We got into her camper and drove off.

The Communal Change Process:
The Transformation of Civil, Malignant, and Turbulent Minor Communities

Civil, malignant, and turbulent minor communities are not static entities; they are in a constant state of evolution and devolution. Malignant minor communities may evolve into turbulent ones, and turbulent minor communities may further evolve into civil ones. Conversely, civil minor communities may devolve into turbulent ones, and turbulent minor communities may further devolve into malignant minor ones. Thus, turbulent minor communities are always in transition from either malignant minor communities to civil minor ones or from civil minor communities to malignant minor ones (Athens, 1998, pp. 684–686). They represent minor communities, in which, according to Park's (1952, p. 89) apt words, "the old order is passing, but the new order has not yet arrived."

Civil minor communities devolve into turbulent minor ones as violent dominance engagements become increasingly more prevalent within their borders. The increased prevalence of violent dominance engagements in civil minor communities leads to more of their members starting, although not necessarily finishing, the violentization process. The more civil minor community members who start and finish the violentization process, the more ultra-violent and violent people are ultimately created to initiate violent dominance engagements, not only against each other, but against marginally violent community members. If violent dominance engagements begin to rival the use of non-violent ones as the chief means for resolving dominance disputes and violent and ultra-violent people begin to vie with marginally violent ones for dominance in a civil minor community, then that community will devolve into a turbulent one.

The increased prevalence of violent dominance engagements in turbulent minor communities leads to more of their members not only starting, but also finishing, the violentization process. The more members of a turbulent minor community who start and finish the violentization process, the more ultra-violent and violent members are created to initiate violent dominance engagements against each other and against marginally violent community members. If violent dominance engagements or the threatened use of them becomes the predominant means of settling dominance disputes and violent and ultra-violent people come to predominate in a turbulent minor community, then it will devolve into a malignant one.

Malignant minor communities evolve into turbulent ones as non-violent dominance engagements become more prevalent within their borders. The increased prevalence of non-violent dominance engagements in malignant minor communities leads to fewer of its members starting and finishing the violentization process. The fewer members of malignant minor communities who start and finish the violentization process, the fewer ultra-violent and violent members are created to initiate violent dominance engagements, not only against each other, but also against marginally violent community members. If non-violent dominance engagements begin to rival violent ones as the chief means of resolving dominance disputes and marginally violent people begin to compete with violent and ultra-violent ones for dominance in a malignant minor community, then it will evolve into a turbulent one.

The increased prevalence of non-violent dominance engagements in turbulent minor communities leads to even fewer of their members not only starting, but also finishing the violentization process. The fewer members of a turbulent minor community who start and finish the violentization process, the even fewer ultra-violent and violent members are created to initiate violent dominance engagements against each other and marginally violent community members. If non-violent dominance engagements become the predominant means of settling dominance disputes and marginally violent people come to predominate in turbulent minor communities, then they will evolve into civil ones.

Thus, turbulent minor communities can emerge in a complex society in either of two ways. They may evolve from malignant minor communities as the institutionalization of violent dominance engagements steadily loses ground and the institutionalization of non-violent dominance engagements steadily gains ground until these two ways of resolving dominance disputes become on nearly equal footing with one another. Or else, turbulent minor communities may devolve from civil minor communities as the institutionalization of non-violent dominance engagements steadily erodes and the institutionalization of violent dominance engagements steadily grows until these two means of settling disputes over dominance reach parity with one another.

At this critical juncture in the history of a turbulent minor community, violent and non-violent dominance engagements compete with one another for institutionalization in the minor community. They are, in effect, both competing idiosyncratic institutions that are making a bid through their respective proponents' actions to become a communal-wide institution. If marginally violent people and non-violent dominance engagements come to predominate in the community, then it will become a civil minor one. On the other hand, if ultra-violent and violent people and violent dominance engagements come to predominate in the community, then it will degenerate into a malignant minor one. Of course, if neither of these three types of persons – ultra-violent, violent, and marginally violent – nor the two types of dominance engagements – violent and non-violent – become predominant, then the community can indefinitely remain a turbulent minor one.

Thus, minor communal change is always a *multi- rather unidirectional* process. There is no guarantee that malignant minor communities will later evolve into turbulent ones, and once they become turbulent minor communities, that they will ever evolve into civil ones. After malignant minor communities evolve into turbulent ones, they may further evolve into civil ones, indefinitely stay as turbulent minor communities, or devolve back into malignant ones. Likewise, there is no guarantee that civil minor communities will never devolve later into turbulent ones, and once they become turbulent minor communities, that will never devolve further into malignant ones, remain turbulent indefinitely, or evolve back into civil minor communities.

In short, as in the case of the dramatic personal change that takes place during the violentization process, the change of minor communities is always a precarious process. Whether a minor community ultimately changes from civil to malignant, from malignant to civil, or from civil or malignant to turbulent always depends on two mutually dependent factors: (1) the type of people who climb to and stay at the top of a community's dominance order; and (2) the nature of institutions for resolving dominance disputes that effectively operate within its borders.

IV. CONCLUSION

If we ever hope to experience widespread, domestic tranquility, then the present landscape of our complex societies must be drastically changed. Civil minor communities can no longer be limited to certain protected pockets or regions of a society, but must be extended to every corner of it. For this to happen, we must search for and promote programs that change malignant minor communities that exist anywhere in our society into civil ones. No matter the race, ethnicity, religious creed, or income of the members of a minor community, they should not be condemned to live and die within the confines of a malignant or even a turbulent minor community (Athens, 1998, pp. 684–686; 2000). Because the physical distances that separate civil, turbulent, and malignant minor communities are daily shrinking all across our society, the threat that ultra-violent or even violent people from malignant or turbulent major or minor communities will wander or settle into civil ones and create havoc and sorrow for all who live or work there only continues to grow. Thus, it serves the long-term interest of members from all our minor communities, including those from the most refined, civil ones, to support the search for and development of programs to help transform malignant minor communities into civil ones. Although I (1992, pp. 90–99; 1997, pp. 155–159; 2001; see also Rhodes, 1999, pp. 313–323) have touched on elsewhere about how such programs could be implemented on a societal-wide basis, they require much broader and further development on my part as well as on the part of many other well-qualified scholars before they can be profitably applied.

The dire need for developing and implementing programs of this nature should not be discounted. As in the case of minor communities, major communities are not static entities, but evolve or devolve over time by a similar dynamic that operates on a much larger scale. If more and more of the civil minor communities that comprise our present civil society degenerate into turbulent ones as ultra-violent and violent community members start competing with marginally violent ones for dominance and as violent and non-violent dominance engagements start competing for institutionalization within their borders, then we could all find ourselves living in a turbulent major community or society. If more and more of our turbulent minor communities degenerate into malignant ones as ultra-violent and violent community members climb to the top and drive marginally violent people to the bottom of their dominance orders and as violent dominance engagements come to prevail over non-violent ones within their borders, then violent dominance engagements will no longer be an idiosyncratic or even a bastard institution, but a societal one, and then we all could find ourselves living and working within one gigantic, malignant society. If we allow the latter development to become a reality, then our only recourse will be to work and live in sealed-off and heavily fortified minor civil communities or to find another civil society somewhere else on the earth in which to move.

Finally, although civil major and minor communities are always preferable to malignant or even turbulent ones, they are now far from perfect in their operation. The non-violent means that marginally violent people now use to win dominance engagements could stand considerable improvement. Otherwise, the most underhanded and expedient, marginally-violent people will not only continue to rise to, but also to stay at the top of the dominance orders in civil major and minor communities – a high cost to pay for preventing ultra-violent and violent people from monopolizing these positions in our society.

NOTES

1. Because I will be drawing on cases from more than one study for illustrations, it will be necessary for me to change some of the numbers of the cases from my studies so that the case numbers can run consecutively. Thus, the cases from my first study (1997 [1980]) will retain their original numbers (1–58), except for my two participant observation cases, which were originally numbered 1 and 2, but which will now be renumbered 59 and 60, respectively. The cases from my second study will be renumbered here (61–110). Of course, in addition to these 110 cases, I also drew on my life experiences that Rhodes (1999) describes in part I his book titled: *The Man Who Talks To Murderers*.

2. I created the notion of "dominance engagements" as a replacement not only for violent performances (1992, pp. 63–71), but also my four violent interpretations of the situation (1997, pp. 32–41). However, I am by no means casting my former ideas aside as ill-founded, but instead merely enfolding them within the notion of a dominance engagement. I should also point out here that a "violent subjugation," which is one of the elemental experiences that comprises brutalization, may be thought of as a violent dominance engagement that one has lost. My creation of the more encompassing notion of violent dominance engagement not only allows me to integrate all these formerly separate ideas of mine, but also, more importantly, to place greater emphasis on the interactional character of conflict and violence.

3. James Gilligan (1996, pp. 6, 47–85, 96–136, 184–185, 230–235, 267) adds some important new twists to Goffman's (1967) "character contest" by re-phrasing it in psycho-analytic terms and not requiring that it operate on the basis of consensus. Unfortunately, Gilligan neither examines Goffman's original development of this idea nor the considerable research that it has spawned over the last 25 years. Like Goffman (1967) and his later followers, Gilligan attributes violence ultimately to the need, although an unconscious one, for people to demonstrate the strength of their character and avoid the

shame and ridicule of displaying a weak character. Thus, some of my (1985) criticisms of Goffman and his followers (Felson, 1978; Luckenbill, 1977) would also apply to Gilligan. Moreover, in my opinion, all these authors ignore the following stricture from Sutherland (1973b, p. 10) : "The attempts by many scholars to explain criminal behavior by general drives and values, such as the happiness principle, striving for social status, the money motive, or frustration, have been and must continue to be futile since they explain lawful behavior as completely as they explain criminal behavior." To drive this point home, he adds: "They are similar to respiration, which is necessary for any behavior but which does not differentiate criminal from non-criminal behavior." I would argue that Sutherland's stricture applies equally well to cases of face-saving and character proving, as it does to those of striving for happiness and social status that Sutherland mentions in the passage that I quoted.

4. A number of criminologists have remarked to me that they believe that the real source of violence is our "pro-violent" culture rather than violentization. If our culture does cause violence, however, then it works *through, not independently* of the violentization process. Unlike cultural theories, violentization can explain by means other than mere exposure how a violent culture become implanted in and transmitted across people. It is inconceivable to me that people could subscribe to violent norms and values, but not brutalize each other. In fact, a malignant community is precisely where the violentization process becomes an integral part of a community's culture. Moreover, the theory of violentization can explain the violent dominance engagements that social misfits wage in civil communities, in which no violent culture exists. Thus, the theory of violentization can provide not only a more in-depth, but also a more *inclusive* explanation than a cultural theory of violence.

ACKNOWLEDGMENTS

I presented an abridged version of Parts I and II of this paper at the first annual conference of the European Society of Criminology held in Lausanne, Switzerland on September 6, 2001.

I thank Marshall Clinard, Priscilla Ferguson Clement, Nick and Effie Pavlou Janulis, and Richard Rhodes for their thoughtful suggestions for improving earlier versions of this essay. Jefferey Ulmer, the senior editor for the series in which this volume appears, also deserves my thanks. Without his unwavering support for this project, this volume of his series would have never seen its way into print.

REFERENCES

Athens, L. (1974). The Self and The Violent Criminal Act. *Urban Life and Culture*, *3*, 98–112.
Athens, L. (1977). Violent Crime: A Symbolic Interactionist Study. *Symbolic Interaction*, *1*, 56–70.
Athens, L. (1980). *Violent Criminal Acts and Actors: A Symbolic Interactionist Study*. London: Routlege, Kegan & Paul.
Athens, L. (1985). Character Contests and Violent Criminal Conduct: A Critique. *The Sociological Quarterly*, *26*, 419–434.

Athens, L. (1986). Types of Violent Persons: Toward the Development of a Symbolic Interactionist Theory of Violent Criminal Behavior. In: N. K. Denzin (Ed.), *Studies in Symbolic Interaction* (Vol. 7B, pp. 259–268). Greenwich, Conn.: JAI.

Athens, L. (1989). *The Creation of Dangerous Violent Criminals.* London: Routledge Publications.

Athens, L. (1992). *The Creation of Dangerous Violent Criminals.* Urbana: University of Illinois Press.

Athens, L. (1995). Dramatic Self Change. *The Sociological Quarterly, 36,* 571–586.

Athens, L. (1997). *Violent Criminal Acts and Actors Revisited.* Urbana: University of Illinois Press.

Athens, L. (1998). Dominance, Ghettoes, & Violent Crime. *The Sociological Quarterly, 39*(Fall), 673–691.

Athens, L. (2000). The 'Crime Line' Replaces the 'Color Line.' *Society for Symbolic Interaction Notes, 27,* 6.

Athens, L. (2001). Theories of Violence. In: P. Clement & J. Reinier (Eds), *American Boyhood: An Encyclopedia* (pp. 733–742). Santa Barbara: ABC/CLIO.

Athens, L. (2002a). Domination: The Blind Spot in Mead's Analysis of the Social Act. *Journal of Classical Sociology, 2,* 25–42.

Athens, L., & Starr, R. (2002b). One Man's Story: How I Became a Disorganized, Dangerous Violent Criminal. *The Sociology of Crime, Law and Society, 4,* 53–76.

Bailey, A. (2000). Review of 'Violent Criminal Acts and Actors Revisited.' *Contemporary Sociology, 29,* 547–548.

Blumer, H. (1969a). *Symbolic Interactionism: Perspective and Method.* Englewood Cliffs, N. J. : Prentice-Hall.

Blumer, H. (1969b). Collective Behavior. In: Alfred Lee (Ed.), *Principles of Sociology* (pp. 65–121). New York: Barnes & Noble.

Blumer, H. (1979). *An Appraisal of Thomas' and Znaniecki's "The Polish Peasant in Europe and America."* New Brunswick, NJ: Transaction.

Blumer, H. (1997). Foreword. In: L. Athens, *Violent Criminal Acts and Actors Revisited* (pp. 3–6). Urbana: University of Illinois Press.

Blumer, H. (2000). Mass Society. In: S. Lyman & A. Vidich (Eds), *Selected Works of Herbert Blumer: A Public Philosophy for Mass Society* (pp. 337–352). Urbana: University of Illinois Press.

Clinard, M. (1949). Criminal Behavior Is Human Behavior. *Federal Probation, 13,* 21–27.

Cooley, C. (1926). The Roots of Social Knowledge. *The American Journal of Sociology, 32,* 59–79.

Denzin, N. (1989). *Interpretive Interactionism.* Newbury Park, CA: Sage.

Dewey, J. (1929). *Experience and Nature.* La Salle: Open Court.

Felson, R. (1978). Aggression as Impression Management. *Social Psychology, 41,* 59–74.

Felson, R., & Steadman, H. (1983). Situational Factors in Disputes Leading to Violence. *Criminology, 21,* 59–74.

Gilligan, J. (1996). *Violence: Reflections on a National Epidemic.* New York: Vintage.

Goffman, E. (1967). *Interaction Ritual: Essays on Face to Face Behavior.* New York: Doubleday.

Hughes, E. (1984). *The Sociological Eye: Selected Papers.* New Brunswick: Transaction Publishers.

Kipnis, A. (1999). *Angry Young Men.* San Francisco: Jossey-Bass.

Kruttschnitt, C. (1994). Buddy, Can You Par-Digm? Three Predictive Models of Deviant Development. *Journal of Research in Crime and Delinquency, 31,* 328–336.

Lewis, D. (1992). From Abuse to Violence: Psycho-physiological Consequences of Maltreatment. *Journal of the American Academy of Child and Adolescent Psychiatry, 31*(May), 383–391.

Lewis, D. (1998). *Guilty By Reason of Insanity.* New York: Fawcett-Columbine.

Lewontin, R., Rose, S., & Kamin, L. (1984). *Not In Our Genes: Biology, Ideology, and Human Nature.* New York: Pantheon.

Lewontin, R. (1991). *Biology as Ideology: The Doctrine of DNA.* New York: Harper Perennial.
Lewontin, R. (2000). *The Triple Helix: Gene, Organism, and Environment.* Cambridge: Harvard University Press.
Luckenbill, D. (1977). Criminal Homicide as a Situated Transaction. *Social Problems, 25,* 176–186.
Mead, G. (1922). A Behavioristic Account of a Significant Symbol. *The Journal of Philosophy, 29*(January–December), 157–163.
Mead, G. (1932). *The Philosophy of the Present.* La Salle: Open Court.
Mead, G. (1934). *Mind, Self & Society.* Chicago: University of Chicago Press.
Mednick, S. (1977). A Biosocial Theory of Learning Law-abiding Behavior. In: S. Mednick & K. Christiansen (Eds), *Biosocial Bases of Criminal Behavior* (pp. 1–8). New York: Garner.
Mednick, S., Pollock, V., Volavka J., & Gabriella, W. (1982). Biology And Violence. In: *Criminal Violence* (pp. 21–80). Beverly Hills: Sage.
Milovanovic, D. (1991). Review of 'The Creation of Dangerous Violent Criminals.' *Criminal Justice Review, 16,* 110–113.
Montagu, A. (1985). The Sociobiology Debate: An Introduction. In: F. Marsh & J. Katz (Eds), *Biology, Crime and Ethics: A Study of Biological Explanations for Criminal Behavior* (pp. 24–33). Cincinnati: Anderson.
Morris, D. (1969). *The Human Zoo.* New York: Mc-Graw-Hill.
Park, R. (1952). *Human Communities.* New York. Free Press.
Ray, M., & Simmons, R. (1987). Convicted Murders' Accounts of their Crimes: A Study of Homicides in Small Communities. *Symbolic Interaction, 10,* 57–70.
Rhodes, R. (1999). *Why They Kill: The Discoveries of A Maverick Criminologist.* New York: Knopf.
Rhodes, R. (2002). *Masters of Death: The SS Einsatzgruppen and The Invention of the Holocaust.* New York: Knopf.
Savitz, L., Kumar, K., & Zahn, M. (1991). Quantifying Luckenbill. *Deviant Behavior, 12,* 19–29.
Schutz, A. (1973). *Collected Papers: The Problems of Social Reality, 1.* The Hague: Martinus Nijoff.
Shakur, S. (1993). *Monster: The Autobiography of an LA Gang Member.* New York: Penguin.
Shibutani, T. (1970). On the Personification of Adversaries. In: T. Shibutani (Ed.), *Human Nature and Collective Behavior: Papers in Honor of Herbert Blumer* (pp. 223–233). Englewood Cliffs. N.J.: Prentice-Hall.
Simmel, G. (1950). *The Sociology of Georg Simmel.* K. Wolf (Ed., Trans.). New York: Free Press.
Simon, D., & Burns, E. (1997). *The Corner: A Year in the Life of an Inner City Neighborhood.* New York: Broadway.
Sutherland, E. (1973a). Susceptibility and Differential Association. In: K. Schuessler (Ed.), *Edwin H. Sutherland: On Analyzing Crime* (pp. 42–43). Chicago: University of Chicago Press.
Sutherland, E. (1973b). A Statement of the Theory. In: K. Schuessler (Ed.), *Edwin H. Sutherland: On Analyzing Crime* (pp. 7–12). Chicago: University of Chicago Press.
Szasz, T. (1960). The Myth of Mental Illness. *The American Psychologist, 15,* 113–118.
Thomas, W. I., & Znaniecki, F. (1958[1917]). *The Polish Peasant in Europe and America* (2 Vols). New York: Dover.
Ulmer, J. (2000). Review of 'Violent Criminal Acts and Actors Revisited.' *Symbolic Interaction, 23,* 87–89.
Wirth, L. (1928). *The Ghetto.* Chicago: The University of Chicago Press.
Wolfgang, M., & Ferracuti, F. (1967). *The Subculture of Violence: Toward an Integrated Theory in Criminology.* London: Tavistock.
Zahn, M. (1992). The Making of Violent Men. *Contemporary Psychology, 37,* 365–366.

RECIPE FOR VIOLENCE

Matthew P. Dumont

The question, "Where are you coing from?" is a good one for science. In its most direct, idiomatic, and streetwise form, it would not have been an unreasonable one to pose to those "researchers" who chose to study the relationship between IQ and race. More recently, I have been tempted to ask the same question of my psychiatric colleagues who "demonstrate" the superiority of a drug while they discreetly wear the collar of its manufacturer. Maybe in some fairer future all scientists will be expected to state why they selected their hypotheses, what their values are, and what's in it for them.

One of the revelations of *Why They Kill: The Discoveries of a Maverick Criminologist*, by Richard Rhodes, the Pulitzer-Prize winning author of *The Making of the Atomic Bomb*, is that precisely where his subject is coming from is so essentially connected to the nature of his research. The issue of personal violence explored by Lonnie Athens, the criminologist who is the focus of Rhodes's book, is important to all of us. We live in a society so obsessed with it that we celebrate its perpetrators in the movies and kill them in reality.

But Athens, now a professor in the Department of Criminal Justice at Seton Hall University, had a more personal axe to grind. His father, Pete, was a brutal man whose sadistic values were played out endlessly against his wife and children. As Rhodes recounts:

> Pete was no less violent at home. "He'd grab my brother and me by the hair and smash our heads together, bloody our faces," Athens says . . . .. "He was a barbarian, a peasant from a Greek peasant family, an extreme patriarch." . . . He would fight anybody [and] Athens respected his determination. "He didn't go off every day. I don't want to give the wrong impression. But when he went off, he went *off*" (p. 11).

Violent Acts and Violentization: Assessing, Applying, and Developing Lonnie Athens' Theories, Volume 4, pages 43–52.
© 2003 Published by Elsevier Science Ltd.
ISBN: 0-7623-0905-9

Lonnie was on a path toward internalizing those values and becoming a dangerously violent person himself:

> He was one of those tough little kids who won't stop fighting, forcing a potential attacker to commit in advance to serious violence or avoid confronting him. In the eighth grade he chased everyone out of the gym locker room with a baseball bat. In the ninth grade, walking home from school, a bully stepped on his heel once too often and Lonnie was all over him, beating him, until the bully's sister bashed Lonnie with her purse, cutting his eye, and he ran off to find first aid (p. 22).

However,

> small stature as an adolescent saved him from the successful violent performances that he would later identify as crucial to the development of violent criminality. "I never had any serious major victory, never really . . . hurt anyone. It's fortunate that I never resorted to weapons [and that no one] called my bluff . . .. It bought me time to grow mentally (p. 26).

How? Why? And how did he change paths? Finding answers to these questions became his life's work.

He was a bright, angry, working-class kid with an anti-authoritarian instinct and a sensitive bullshit detector. Some of his teachers were scared of him or directed him, with more or less kindness, to the black-and-blue-collar destiny of his social class. Others (and we should be thankful for them) looked beyond his angry edge and saw the germs of genius.

Rhodes's description of the coming of age of this remarkable man reads like something out of Dickens. But it is not limited to his ascent to a doctorate and on-going struggle with academic brutality (I can think of no other word). More important for us is the story of his unfolding conceptual and ideological life. Athens says, "Except for those corporate executives whose decisions affect the safety and health of millions, the people I chose to study are the most dangerous people on earth" (p. 31). And yet, as an intimate of such dangerous violence, Athens approaches his subjects with a respect unusual in the most social of scientists. Coming from his own inside, he wanted to know the violent criminals he studied from *their* inside. He wanted knowledge *of* them, rather than knowledge *about* them.

For this reason, Athens very quickly became disenchanted with the statistical obsessionalism of most contemporary sociological research. He was not interested in collecting lists of attributes of people called criminals and milking correlations from a large number of them compared to controls. He noticed (as should we all) that such studies often overrate statistical differences that ignore the concept of *variance*, i.e. the measure of just how much of the reality under study can be explained by the differences found.

Rather than examine at a large number of subjects superficially, Athens chose to look at a smaller number profoundly. He thought it would bring him closer to the truth of the matter to study fifty people in depth than five thousand on the surface. He was eventually to focus on about one hundred "exemplary specimens," acknowledged perpetrators of the most heinous and brutal crimes. He interviewed them one-on-one in repeated sessions for a total of about nine hours each.

But where was he coming from as a methodologist? To Athens's credit – and Rhodes's for appreciating it – the foundations of his research, its epistemology, was fully evident. How do we look? How do we see? And how do we know that what we see is true? And, by the way, what is truth? Athens was influenced by the writings of G. H. Mead,[3] a philosopher and social psychologist sadly forgotten in this era of genome reductionism and survey research. Mead argued that it is culture, invisible, supremely powerful, and all-pervasive, that shows us how to see what we look at – a process of mental editing in which perception is sifted through filters of socially derived meaning. Our essence as human beings is the attachment of meaning to objects and people, and our behavior is determined by those meanings.

For example, a bit of mineral called "gold" or a piece of bread called "God" have meanings that have determined much of the course of human history. What we call "mind" and "self" are not stored programs of DNA but developing social processes that moor an individual to society through language, in which meaning resides. A personality is built up through social transactions involving a series of inner dialogues with a constantly expanding and increasingly more "generalized other." This becomes an acquired sense of community through which the individual incorporates the values of social institutions into a pattern of personal conduct.

Athens modified Mead's concept of the "generalized other" to a more intimate group of voices of past experience, which he termed "phantom others." He believes we carry on constant conversations with them, paralleling the conversations we have with people in the here and now. In his own recent book,[2] Athens expands on his research ideology, distinguishing between the positivist approach and his own "interpretative" one. In the latter, people are seen to be guided by their interpretation of events as monitored through "phantom voices." Positivists are interested only in objective factors they see as causative. They tend to separate themselves from objects of study, while "interpretivists" (I can't say it either) participate in the social world of their subjects so as to appreciate its properties. Positivists need operational definitions before they begin to collect data, whereas Athens identifies concepts only through the process of his inquiry. In short, he sees his work as art as much as science, an idea offensive to his number-crunching colleagues.

With the sensitivity and skill of a rare clinician, Athens built alliances with the dangerous, violent men and women he selected on the basis of their histories of criminal violence. He had to overcome his own fear of them, their distrust of him, the hostility of the correctional staff surrounding them, and the contempt of other criminologists. In the language of the sociological case study method, Athens's interviews demonstrated their validity through saturation, intensity of detail. He never asked *why* the crimes were committed. (A psychoanalyst among my teachers once told me never to ask a question the patient could not answer, "Why?" being chief among such questions.) What Athens wanted revealed was a self-narrative that moved between thought and event in so many different axes around a violent episode that a perfect sphere of understanding developed. He wanted to know how violent people thought of themselves and how they thought others thought about them. And, while his interviews took a peripheral and circular approach to each violent event (more like a fox than a hedgehog), he focused more on the acts themselves than their antecedents – on how they were *experienced*.

While lying is always a concern, Athens decided that it would be difficult for his interviewees to maintain a false consistency of both subjective and objective narrative throughout such detailed histories. His population cut across gender and racial lines but were not randomly selected. "The conclusions that I sought were not about a statistical distribution of characteristics but the social psychological processes at work in violent criminal acts" (Rhodes, p. 61). Most important, the common processes he identified had to be present in *all* the cases he studied.

We have all heard the catch phrases: "mad dog killer," "senseless act," "irresistible impulse," "didn't know what he was doing." But just because people move very quickly from thought to action does not mean that there is no thought. Athens concluded that there is *always* thought, that "violent people consciously construct violent plans of action before they commit criminal acts" (p. 67). They always know what they are doing and have some reason for doing it.

After analyzing his interviews, Athens found that the perpetrators of violent crime made one of four different interpretations of a situation before acting. One he termed the "physically defensive" interpretation, in which fear is the predominant emotion based on a conviction that the perpetrator himself was going to be attacked. In the second, which he called "frustrative," the intent of the perpetrator – a rapist or a thief, for example – is frustrated by the victim and anger is the prevailing emotional state. Third is the "malefic" interpretation of a situation, in which hatred is experienced toward a victim perceived as evil or contemptible. Finally, there is a "frustrative-malefic" interpretation, in which the victim's resistance leads the perpetrator to think of him as evil person who is intentionally being irksome. Here, the predomiant emotion is anger, which later turns to hatred.

Whatever the interpretation and accompanying emotion, the violent act is entirely *volitional*. It is never senseless to the actor, however senseless it appears to the victim or to the rest of us. The disposition to violence is associated with a self-image constructed through the feedback of "phantom voices," which guide the individual's interpretation of a particular event. Violent people see themselves as violent and are convinced that others also see them as violent. And whether they interpret a situation in physically defensive, malefic, frustrative, or frustrative-malefic terms, their preferred recourse is violence. Those with a nonviolent self-image may also resort to a violent response, though only when their internal dialogue informs them of a physically defensive situation.

The question remains: *How do violent people become violent people?* This was the central problem for Athens and, as described by Rhodes, its exploration forms the body of his work. Athens identified four stages in the development of what he calls "violentization." Their presence is both necessary and sufficient for the emergence of a violent person. They are not, fortunately, inevitable or incapable of being interrupted. The first stage is "brutalization," which most of us have been calling "abuse." But it is not just abuse, and abuse itself is not enough to predict violence. It involves "violent subjugation," "personal horrification," along with "violent coaching." The child is not only subject to beating or sexual brutality by someone, usually someone in the family, but also witnesses such behavior done to others. At the same time, the child is "taught" that this is the way it has to be – that in life you are either the abused or the abuser. The violent coaching can come from anywhere: home, school, community, or repeated exposures to the make-my-day-punk ideology of the media, which treat violence as a commodity.

The second stage described (and experienced) by Athens involves the internalization and generalization of a hostile and hypervigilant attitude that he calls "belligerency." Third comes a period of trying out, of "violent performance," which, when successful, paves the way for the final stage of "virulency." During virulency, the person is rewarded for his violent behavior with a reputation for toughness and deference. By the end of this last stage, the person perceiving threat or frustration, or sensing "evil" in another, is capable of acts of sadistic, unremitting, or lethal violence.

It is not easy to make a violent person. When you think of all the angry drunks behind the wheels of their SUVs, it's remarkable how relatively tame "road rage" actually is. Further evidence of this proposition is offered in *Why They Kill*, where Rhodes describes the interesting history of military personnel in battle who do not use their weapons, a phenomenon much more widespread than generals like to acknowledge. And, while we tend to think of modern urban life in America as violent, the actual murder rate (even before its recent decline) is historically low. As Rhodes points out, the homicide rate for all men in the United States was at a high of thirty-seven per 100,000 in 1994. For African Americans, the highest rate was forty-six per 100,000 in 1960. Compared to modern Western Europe, these rates are very high, but in seventeenth century England the murder rate was fifty per 100,000 and comparably high in Sweden, Holland, and France. One historian is quoted by Rhodes to the effect that, until the seventeenth century, "violence was the normative method of settling personal disputes in all classes of society" (p. 218).

What brought homicide rates down to their current historic lows was not a change in the mental health or genetic make-up of Europeans but the centralization of power in emerging monarchies, which created a royal monopoly of violence: "By the time of Elizabeth I, English homicide rates had dropped . . . as a consequence of a progressive shift of the burden of prosecution from the relatives of the deceased to some public authority" (p. 223). We don't generally think of Louis XIV of France as a progressive figure and civilizing force in society, but his "l'État-est-mois" arrogance may have saved more lives than anything else in French history. He proscribed dueling among the nobility and encouraged foppery, ridicule, and disdain as the upper-class method of establishing hierarchies, a tradition that persists on the Upper East Side of Manhattan. Civil violence is not good for business, so an increasingly powerful middle class was grateful for the court system put into place to stabilize and control disputes. And, of course, the prison and mental hospitals were established for the social control of violence among the poor (the distinction between them being as vague then as it is once again becoming).

It can be argued (and has been) that the extent of violence among young minority males in contemporary urban America is in part a function of their perception of a discredited and illegitimate central authority. Nevertheless, Athens maintains that, regardless of social class, racial, or political categories, violence will not emerge in the absence of the four stages of "violentization."

But what about the mentally ill? "Lonnie Athens," Rhodes tells us, "found no evidence that mental illness causes violent crime." Echoing Athens, Rhodes goes on to suggest the possibility that the distinction between the "criminally responsible" violent person and the one "not responsible by reason of mental illness" (p. 199) may be arbitrary and false. It might be argued that Athens was not in a position to generalize about violence among the mentally ill because he studied a population of incarcerated criminals who were found guilty and considered responsible. But, based on my own experience, I think Athens is right. I work on a locked unit of a state hospital with patients who are psychotic and violent. While I do not use Athens's systematic approach, I do talk to my patients about their violence. I find that no matter how impulsive, apparently unprovoked, or seemingly responsive to hallucinations and delusions is their behavior, they always know that they have perpetrated a violent act. Further, while it may require some patience to determine it, they always have a reason for their violent acts. There is the same range of defensive, frustrative, malefic, and frustrative-malefic interpretations of situations that Athens found in his subjects.

We can argue endlessly about whose fear, anger, resentment, or hatred is more or less rational than anyone else's, but that is always a capricious enterprise. From the point of view of social psychology, the mentally ill *experience* their acts of violence in the same way as do others who are violent. There is always an "internal dialogue with voices of past experience" and, whether they are remembered or hallucinated, there is the same ascription of meaning to an event, assessment of the victim's attitude, and *decision* to be violent. Despite the centuries of tradition in Anglo-Saxon law and all the obsessionalism of forensic psychiatrists, the whole issue of "insanity" versus "criminal responsibility" is meaningless except for the social class and racial discrimination that select one disposition over another. Rhodes recalls that Isaac Ray, one of the "fathers of psychiatry" (there were no mothers), distinguished the disease of kleptomania from the crime of theft on the basis of whether the perpetrators' social position renders their behavior as "peculiarly degrading," and whether their deprivation of liberty "deserves to be respectfully considered." In more recent times, John Hinckley, Jr., an affluent white man, was judged insane after shooting Ronald Reagan, whereas Sirhan Sirhan and Jeffrey Dahmer, both of lower social standing, were considered criminals, though exhibiting obvious signs of psychosis. But what, after all is said, is to be done?

Stating that "a theory with no policy implications is sterile" (Athens, 1997, p. 155), Athens proposes a program blending general prevention, selective rehabilitation, and selective incapacitation of violent offenders. He looks to the school as the place to foster the development of nonviolent phantom communities. Along with reading and writing, children should be taught about responsible membership in a community. He is convinced that a good school can undo the harm of a bad family. My own experience with the therapeutic communities that dominated the drug rehabilitation scene in the 1970s confirms this. The community-oriented moral education that they provided was able to transform some of the most morally bankrupt individuals imaginable into responsible citizens. Athens calls for a reformulation of public institutions, with a whole new set of purposes, values, and direction. But a social revolution of some kind would be necessary to break through the self-serving enterprises that law and psychiatry have built for themselves around the problem of violence.

Rhodes relied primarily on the earlier of Athens's two books (Athens, 1992). I read the later one[2] and ended up feeling like a critic of Boswell's *Life of Samuel Johnson*, wondering whether to recommend the book about the subject or the subject's own book. Both will be well worth your time. Rhodes is a bit more literary; in addition, he gives the historical dimension, a discussion of military violence, and the inevitably seductive case histories of pop figures whose violence was the stuff of front-page coverage – the likes of Mike Tyson, Lee Harvey Oswald, and Cheryl Crane (remember? Lana Turner's daughter, who stabbed her mother's stud to death and, by dint of typical Hollywood justice, was declared innocent). But Athens's own book (Athens, 1997) is readable, as well. It is short and crisp, written in the manner of someone who has an important story to tell but more important things to do. The interviews are more detailed and the theoretical issues of research methodology more thoroughly explained than in Rhodes's version. Nor does Athens slight the personal dimension: he describes his own experiences and the emotions involved.

There is about Athens an irresistible combination of honesty, simplicity, and depth that comes through in his writing. Richard Rhodes was so taken by the man and his work that he went from writing about the atom bomb to writing about Lonnie Athens. I was so taken by Rhodes's book that I wanted to read Athens's work myself, and then so moved by the work that I wanted to meet him. As expected, Athens is far from the tweedy, academic stereotype. The middle-aged man greeting me in the lobby of my upscale hotel is short, muscular, agile. He moves like a former bantamweight boxer who is ready to climb back in the ring. He wears a black T-shirt, has close-cropped greying hair, and carries a battered briefcase. If he looks out of place in this particular setting, it may be because he has always been somewhat out of place. Having evolved from potential killer to social scientist and scholar, he has devoted his life to understanding how dangerously violent people develop. His speech is a curious mixture of New Jersey and Virginia, a subtle drawl of the South kept from lingering by the pace of the North and the edge of prison. He is intense and perceptive; not too open at first, wanting to know where *you* are coming from.

He tells me that he started out suspicious of where Rhodes was coming from, as well. His initial assumption was that Rhodes, Pulitzer awardee or not, was only out to get some consultation, to "pick his brains for the price of a meal." Only later did he realize that *Why They Kill* was going to be mainly about him. He was pleased, of course, but he is quick to note the difference between a writer and a researcher, between the person who wants to be read and the one who wants to capture and understand some fundamental new truth about human behavior. He himself would not want to make the historical and ideological leaps in which Rhodes indulged.

"Personally," he says, "I don't like ideologues from the left or the right. I want things to speak for themselves and theories to be grounded in facts rather than deduced from our pre-set ideological positions." However, he is now becoming more interested in "macroscopic aspects of violence," and explaining how communities devolve from civil through turbulent to malignant status and evolve from malignant through turbulent to civil status depending on the concentrations of violent people in them.

Athens feels more than ever that schools should become the central and guiding institutions for the social development of people. It is, he says, what "saved" him. On the other hand, he is intensely frustrated by academic bureaucracy, in which, although he is finally tenured, he is treated as an outsider. He is still being told that, rather than pursue his own analysis of violence, he should incorporate his findings into some already "well established" framework, hitch his wagon to some social science star. Athens is not one to follow such advice, and he pays the price by being denied the grants, stipends, and other goodies guided by those stars. (In the floating crapgame run by academic élites, mavericks are allowed in the door, but the dice they're handed are always loaded.)

Nevertheless, Athens is very much a teacher, and he takes his role seriously. Further, that role is not limited to the classroom. He would teach judges, prosecutors, and probation officers how to distinguish the incipiently violent offender who is still receptive to rehabilitation from the malignantly violent ones who need to be kept from hurting people. This does not, he insists, require esoteric skills or personal charisma. A straightforward and systematic analysis of past social experience is all that is needed.

When I asked him about group violence, whether at soccer riots or revolutions, Athens remains true to his thesis. He maintains that only violent people act violently at soccer games, that they attend for the purpose of rioting. And he does not believe that being a revolutionary necessarily means that one is a terrorist. Yet, he is interested in how bureaucracies can transform the brutal into the mundane and particularly how "the military mimicks many of the stages of violentiztion process during its training regimens." Although Athens finds Stanely Miligram's work highly provocative, he ultimately dismisses it: "Obedience to authority is not blind as Miligram and his devotees would have us believe. For people to blindly follow authority, they would have to be robots. If people were robots, then preparing soldiers for warfare would be a lot easier because none of the stages of violentization would need to be incorporated into their basic or advanced combat training."

In short, *Why They Kill* and Lonnie Athens's work will not obviously be the final word on the subject of violence. More than one source of light is needed to illuminate that vast, dark, frightful room in the house of humanity. But his is a brilliant beam, and more than a few corners will be less shadowy, perhaps more habitable, because of the explorations of this bold and clear-sighted man.

REFERENCES

Athens, L. H. (1992). *The creation of dangerous violent criminals*. Champaign, IL: University of Illinois Press.
Athens, L. H. (1997). *Violent criminal acts and actors revisited*. Champaign, IL: University of Illinois Press.
Mead, G. H. (1964). *Selected writings*. New York: Bobbs Merrill.

ONE MAN'S STORY: HOW I BECAME A "DISORGANIZED" DANGEROUS VIOLENT CRIMINAL

Lonnie Athens and Randy Starr

> Perception without conception is blind; conception without perception is empty.
>
> Herbert Blumer (1931, p. 531) paraphrasing Kant's famous dictum.

INTRODUCTION

When I stumbled across Lonnie Athens' books (1992, 1997) on violent crime and criminals a couple of years ago, I experienced a revelation. It was the first time I had read anything on this topic that made any real sense to me. I have known a lot of "bad" guys and girls during my life, and have often been struck by the common denominators among them, yet up until reading Athens' two small books, I have never been able to pinpoint these common denominators. For example, while interacting with violence-prone individuals, I have often found myself knowing what they are going to say before they even say it. I used to see my knack of predicting their statements and actions as a "second sense" that I had acquired over the years. I have now come to believe, however, that it is much more down to earth than any magical power. It is based on my "tacit knowledge" of violent offenders and offenses (Polanyi, 1958), but tacit knowledge has its limits. Like a diamond in the rough, it must be carefully excavated, faceted, and polished using the right conceptual tools. To my delight, I discovered that Athens' analysis of violent criminal acts

Violent Acts and Violentization: Assessing, Applying, and Developing Lonnie Athens' Theories, Volume 4, pages 53–76.

and actors comes from an interpretive, naturalistic perspective (Athens, 1984; Blumer, 1969; Denzin, 1989a, b) rather than from a psychoanalytic (Abrahamsen, 1973; Menninger, 1966; Tanay, 1972), multi-factor (Kipnis, 1999; Lewis, 1998; Starr, 2000) or integrated approaches (Gilligan, 1996). It better explained and was more in sync with my tacit knowledge than anything that I (Starr, 2000, pp. 25–26) have written or read before (see Feyerabend, 1993, pp. 24–32). I have experienced Athens' (1992) four stages of violentization and his three types of violent individuals (Athens, 1986, 1997, pp. 145–146) over and over again, not only in my life, but through the lives of many unfortunate, violently inclined souls whose paths have crossed mine. Ever since I first read Athens' books, I have felt compelled to pass on my personal insights about the violence-related experiences that he describes.

Writing a narrative like this one, even with the help of a bonafide expert (see Rhodes, 1999), constituted a difficult challenge for me. First, I confronted the intellectual challenge of describing all the subtle nuances of Athens' ideas, which unless one has lived them, may be impossible to appreciate (Cuthbertson & Johnson, 1992; Johnson, 1994; Ulmer, 2000). Without his help, I could not have written my life story from a natural, interpretive perspective. During our collaboration, we help erase the *fictitious* line that has been traditionally drawn between the analyst and narrator in the life stories of criminals (see, for example, Shaw, 1930; Sutherland, 1937). Just as in the physical and social sciences, there are no brute facts, there are no raw narratives. Because the possible facts bearing on any scientific problem or surrounding any person's life are inexhaustible, they must always be selected and thereby constructed from some perspective, no matter how rudimentary or explicit that perspective may be (see: Blumer, 1931, 1969, pp. 24–25; Feyerabend, 1993, p. 11; Fleck, [1935]1979; Znaniecki, [1934] 1969, pp. 14–16).

Beyond the intellectual challenge, I also confronted a much bigger emotional challenge of re-examining my life from this new viewpoint, which proved to be a self revelation. I had to wrestle with my inner demons. It was like handling hot coals. Perhaps, to some extent, by sharing my story, I am paying society back for services rendered, at least in a token way. I am also trying to justify my existence. I am desperately trying to share the insights that I gained from my violence-filled life with the hope that something might be learned from it to help prevent other hapless souls from repeating it.

BECOMING A DANGEROUS VIOLENT CRIMINAL

In *The Creation of Dangerous Violent Criminals*, Athens (1992) describes the violentization process – the series of social experiences that all the violent beasts in our human tribe, including myself, have gone through (see also Athens, 2001). The first club to come down upon us, "brutalization," is three pronged: During "violent subjugation" and "personal horrification" we confront the constant threat of violence from authority figures. This club's third prong, "violent coaching," is where authority figures pound proviolent messages into our ears. The next club that is used on us is "defiance." During defiance, we come to the realization that there are certain times when we must gravely hurt or even kill our fellow human beings. This crucial insight on our part prompts us to move into a "mitigated violent phantom community" and develop into a "violent self." It is not until we are hit with the thorny club of "dominance engagements," however, that this insight gets put to trial by fire. The final club is "virulency." This is where we make the fateful decision to grab the club out of the hands of other people and wield it against them. Once we take hold of this club, we move from a mitigated to an "unmitigated violent phantom community" and develop into a "malevolent" self. Until I came across Athens' "violentization process," my life was a fucking riddle to ponder.

I was a violent boy and I have been a violent man. I grew up in a hostile and violent world. Violence and drunkenness were the norm, not the exception, in my family. Although not the norm in our neighborhood, my family was not the only one that suffered from these problems. We lived in what Athens (1998) calls a "turbulent," rather than a "malignant" neighborhood. Personal horrification, violent subjugation, and violent coaching were "gifts" that my parents bestowed on me. My father was a real cocksucker. The old man would often get drunk, go into one of his rages, break furniture, beat our mother, and sometimes go on to beat us kids. There were three boys in the family, no girls, and I was the youngest. It was either my oldest half-brother (who I will just call Spike) or me who usually ended up catching hell from the old man. That was in great part because we tended to side with our mother, especially once the old man started getting physical with her. The brother in between (who I will call Martin) typically managed to stay out of the old man's way. Martin had a knack for disappearing into the wood work at the first sign of trouble. He tended to mind his own business and keep his nose clean. Our Martin was the most benign member of the family. In contrast to him, we were a bunch of wild motherfuckers!

My childhood was brutal. When I was six or seven years old, Spike, who was about 14 years old at the time, defended our mother during one of her more heated altercations with our father. Spike, by the way, was the old man's stepson. Spike picked up a baseball bat and broke the old man's collarbone that night. I felt ashamed because our neighbors saw the whole fight unfold in our front yard. Spike's attack on the old man terrified me. Nevertheless, I was glad that Spike did it. For most of the decade to follow, Spike spent most of his time committing an assortment of petty crimes. He was a two-bit hoodlum, but I always admired him for his bravery. Talk about negative male role models, hey? Spike's biological father allegedly murdered his pregnant wife with a shotgun and then killed himself. The old man loved telling that story when he got drunk. I do not know if it is true or not, but I always believed it.

Later that year, Martin and I had one of our many spats while trying to kill some birds with a pellet gun. We argued over who would take the next shot. I got pissed off at him for hogging the gun, so I busted the back of his head with a rock the size of my fist. He dropped to his knees and cried. Our parents did not get too upset about it. The old man gave me an ass-whipping, but not a very bad one. It was no big deal. I violently subjugated Martin and then my old man violently subjugated me. That's the way things worked in my household.

When I was eight years old I watched my mother beat another woman bloody. The fight started when the woman accused my mother of messing around with her husband. As my mother loved to say, "That woman stepped on the wrong person's toes." The two of them were drunk and I witnessed the whole brawl. Their fight terrified me. My mother looked like an enraged baboon as she screamed and slammed the woman's head against the floor. I was afraid that my mother might kill the woman and worried about what might happen to my mother if the woman died. "Stop, Mother!" I screamed. "You're going to kill her!" Although it was a frightening experience, some good came out of it. It made me respect my mother more. By the next day, the two of them had kissed and made up. My mother had personally demonstrated to me how you win a dominance engagement with someone.

The old man, on the other hand, was always getting into trouble with the law, mostly for domestic violence and barroom brawls. In one of these bar room fights, he ended up with a broken leg – a compound fracture. I felt sorry for him. It was serious enough that he was put in traction and pins had to be placed in his leg. He was out of work for a year and we had to go on welfare. I was about nine years old, which would have made him about 35 at the time. I felt ashamed, both because he had lost the fight and because we went on welfare. His violent dominance engagements with other people continued. When he lost them, I kept feeling sorry for him.

My childhood (and early adult) memories of violence are far greater than you probably could ever imagine. On bad days, the flashbacks of the violence that I experienced as a child and as a young man make it hard for me to keep up with my daily duties. Bits of blood, bone, and flesh still cloud my mind. It is as though I keep seeing a horror movie that some director made by piecing together different ugly scenes from my early life. The best thing about my childhood was that it was short! All that brutalization has taken a heavy toll on me. I am always afraid that if I forget what happened to me, history would repeat itself. I do not want to kill again, but I know that I am capable of doing it if the "right" situation was to arise. I still have violent thoughts from time to time, but I now try harder to restrain them (Athens, 1997, pp. 42–53).

When I was seven years old or so, my drunken father beat me until I could not scream anymore, while my mother, aunt and uncle stood by passively. They thought that the old man had a right to beat me because they said I was "his property." I thought he might kill me that night. I can still smell the stench of cheap whiskey on his breath. It was not until my aunt and uncle's German shepherd tried to bite my dad that he redirected his wrath at the dog. My uncle and aunt stopped him before he hurt their dog. I surmised from that incident that it was okay to beat a kid half to death, but wrong to hurt a dog. Violent subjugation was the main meal for the night, and it was my tiny ass that everyone feasted on!

Another time, I was returning with my parents late at night after they had been drinking heavier than usual. I was 10 or 11 at the time. The old man outdid himself that night. As our car approached a pack of dogs, he hit the accelerator and plowed into them. Thud! Thud! Thud! The old man laughed that insane laugh of his as my mother and I gasped. It was another spoonful of "personal horrification" that I had to swallow.

There was one Christmas (I was 12 or 13) when the old man got drunk and tried to humiliate me by making me take off his boots, which I refused to do Earlier that day, while drunk, he bumped into the Christmas tree, knocked it over, and busted several ornaments. His bullshit really put a damper on our holiday spirit. After he threatened me, I ran into the basement, one of those that had adjacent crawl spaces where there was only dirt instead of a finished floor. I hid there until he got tired of looking for me. I often hid in that part of the basement. Sometimes I would also hide from him under our front porch, from where I peered at the outside world through the lattice slats. My old man was a dumb, loud, and vulgar son of a bitch. He was hell bent on scaring the shit out of all those around him, especially if they were smaller or weaker than him.

Once, when I was in my early teens, Martin (who was about three years older than me) jumped me while I was lying down on the couch and watching television. He pinned my shoulders down with his knees and then punched me in the face. He said that I had gotten "smart" with him and had to be put in my place. He caught me totally off guard. Letting your guard down was not a smart move in my household. My anger exploded! Moments later, I returned from the nearby kitchen with a butcher knife. I felt 10 feet tall as I backed him into a corner. My elation was short lived, though. After he grabbed a wooden club and we squared off, our mother stopped us from coming to blows. We had a Cain and Able relationship. This incident probably marked my entrance into the "defiance stage" (Athens, 2001); I had taken enough crap from Martin.

It was not until the next day that the old man addressed the matter with me. He was sober, which made him sheepish. He seemed to fumble for words as he tried to explain to me why it was wrong for brothers to attack each other with lethal weapons. The old guy was a complete hypocrite. He could beat the fuck out of anyone that he wanted, but no one could touch any member of the family without his permission. Do something to piss him off, the old prick would tear you a new asshole, but do something to piss someone else off, he would ignore it. I finally figured out my old man's logic. He was the king of the roost. The king of the roost not only makes the rules, but can change them anytime that he wants without consulting anybody. His motto was, "Fuck with me and I'll kick your motherfucking ass."

A couple of years later, however, when that prick Martin was home on leave from boot camp, he started bullying me around. We had never been fond of one another. I kicked the fucker's ass, and if our old man had not stopped me, I might have killed him. I had gotten him into a death lock choke hold and was squeezing the life out of him. While Martin had been training in some faraway pansy-assed, army boot camp, I had been training in the streets and in our house with the old man. During this dominance engagement with Martin, I had one of my best "violent performances" so far in my life (Athens, 1992, pp. 63–71). I knew that if I kept trying long enough, I could do some noble ass kicking myself. Martin made the near fatal mistake of underestimating his little brother's capacity for violence. I was now meaner than he was. My victory in this "dominance engagement" against Martin would pave the way for even bigger and better ones later (Athens, 2001).

I grew up constantly feeling vulnerable, like I was just seconds away from being knocked on my ass. I felt like a little fish who was always on the verge of being eaten by one of the larger fish in his family. My old man was a great white shark always on the prowl for smaller prey to swallow. Tension always ran high in our household as we wondered who would get swallowed next. I always worried that it would be me, but the day would soon come when the other fish, including him, would have to keep a watchful eye out for me.

When I was 14 years old, my old man gave me the most severe beating of my life. I really thought the fucker might kill me. He beat my back and the back of my upper thighs with a three-foot-long bamboo stick. (I guess I was lucky that he did not have a two-by-four board handy.) After the bamboo stick broke apart, he pounded me with his cuffed hands on the sides of my head. I begged for him to stop, but he didn't until I was close to passing out. Disoriented and crying, I crawled to a nearby corner. He had crossed the line with me this time. He made me feel like a hunk of worthless meat. I got a big chip on my shoulder from this beating. I was steaming mad at my mother because she did not move a finger to help me. She just stood by and watched that mean fucker beat me half to death without saying a word or doing a thing! My mother lost a lot of points with me that day, points that she never won back. At that moment, I hated her almost as much as I hated him.

I was never quite the same after that particular beating. My father had left me badly bruised, both physically and mentally. He had snapped something in my mind. Whatever childhood that I had left in me was gone. I became more leery of people and explosive. The rule that a son should respect his father because his father is his father was now thrown out the window. I was determined never to let him or anybody else beat me like that again. He had poked at me enough through my cage with his stick. A killer was born that day. If I was fucked with bad, I was ready to kill or be killed. He had turned me into a rabid dog. The hands-on nature of his brutalization program was a success. In fact, it had worked far better than anyone, including my old man, could have ever anticipated. That was the very last time that I would allow my old man to violently subjugate me without a fight.

A couple of months passed before we got into it again. One night he came home drunk and ornery, like he did most Friday and Saturday nights. He did not know that I was a bit drunk and ornery myself that night. He insulted my mother first and then it was my turn: "You're a bastard. Spike's father also fathered you. You fucking bastard," he said. I went nuts. I blind-sided him and took him to the ground even though he outweighed me by a 100 pounds. While he was trying to get up, I pounded the hell out of his head. I was 14 years old, with a couple shots of whiskey in my belly, the adrenaline pumping through my body, and a lifetime of scores to settle with my old man. I started smashing windows out of the house, a couple with objects I threw, a couple with my bare fist. I even tossed a chair through a window. I felt blind hatred toward him. My old man just seemed to have disappeared and all I could see amidst the broken glass was a nearby office building, and I wanted to bust its windows out with my bare fist, too. I was finally ready to fight this no-good bastard to the death. If my mother and my two friends who had been spending the night had not stopped me, I might have killed him. I spent that night at my maternal grandma's apartment. There was blood was all over me. It felt like a moral victory to me. I had finally made a statement to my father and drawn my line in the sand: I wanted it to make clear that to cross that line with me from now on out would place your life at risk. Having my two friends see me go nuts like that magnified the impact of the occasion. I could see their respect for me grow in their eyes. My first "minor victory" over my old man was a golden moment for me. It fits under what Athens (1992, pp. 66–68) describes as a "violent personal revolt" during which you score a "sweet victory" over a past violent subjugator. Whatever you call it, in my case, it was long overdue.

After that night, things were never the same in my house. I now represented a threat to the pecking order, which increased the tension in the air. Ironically, through this act of defiance, I had gained some measure of control over my environment. I had not only matched the prevailing standards of violence in my family, but had exceeded those standards. Goddamn it! I had exceeded their wildest expectations. I was never the same again. Looking back on this incident, it marked my birth as the black sheep in the family. I wore the title well, even taking satisfaction and security in knowing the others were much less likely to push me around now. I took great satisfaction in knowing that at the still-tender age of 14, I had won a violent dominance engagement against my father. I still had more work to do before I could graduate to that fourth level of violentization, known as "virulency." I had won a "minor victory" over a long-dreaded subjugator, but I had not yet become a "dangerous violent criminal." As Athens (2001) reminds us, there is a difference.

During the next couple of years I was involved in so many fist fights with other kids, my old man, and brother Martin that it seems like a blur looking back on it now. I would guess that I got in as many as two dozen fights. Although I took my share of hard hits, I never backed down from a dominance engagement. I took pride in having a thick skull. I would pick fights whenever I got the chance. I would beat up a kid one day, only to have his big brother or friend to beat me up the next. I did not care. Violence had long since become the name of the game for me. I would hurt others and others would hurt me. It was the understanding of life that I had. The messages of my violent coaches echoed in my mind. Physical pain became a primary defining point of my life. I used to practice seeing how long I could hold my hand over a burning flame, how deep I could cut myself with a pocket knife, and I even held a burning cigarette against my arm. Sometimes, I repeatedly hit myself on the head with a stick, so that I could just to get used to pain. I was furthering my earlier boot camp training.

When I was 13 or 14 years old, a kid picked a fight with me. I kept trying to back down because I knew he was in a gang. I figured that I could not win for losing. If I kicked his ass, then his gang boys would kick my ass. At the end of the school day he caught up with me in the stairwell and forced my hand. He wanted me to go to a nearby park, where his gang members were gathering to watch us fight. His guys were supposed to be there to help him when he needed it. Well, none of his friends were around at that moment and two of mine were hanging close to me. He took a step or two down the stairs ahead of me. I punched the prick in the back of the head two or three times, whipped a choke hold on him, and started choking the living shit out of him. He bit me in the side of my chest, and I gnashed my teeth into the top of his head. The two of us were both screaming out in pain like a couple of piglets. Somewhere along the line I shoved my thumb into one of his eyes. We ended up on the balcony, which was one flight of stairs above the ground floor, about a 10- to15-foot drop. I was beating that motherfucker to a pulp, slamming his head into the wall and screaming my brains out. Then, I tried to throw him over the guardrail, but my two friends stepped in and pulled me off him. I ate up the fear and exultation in their eyes. I had earned another notch in my belt by winning another dominance engagement.

The three of us took off running, higher than holy fuck on adrenaline. These two guys were really ecstatic about how I had tried to kill that guy. I had earned a ton of respect from them, which made everything that I did worthwhile. I left knowing that no fucker in his right mind would want to go out of his way to screw around with me anymore, at least not one on one. I was a bad-assed motherfucker who was riding high! "Fuck him and his pussy-assed gang member buddies!" I shouted. If I had to, I would take them all on.

Once, when I was a freshman in high school, a kid whipped my ass very badly. The "fight" lasted for over an hour and our classmates got bored watching it. I would not stop taking blows. The school staff finally broke it up, which was a lucky break for me. I was later handcuffed and driven to jail in the back of a squad car. Why would I not stop fighting? I do not think that it even crossed my mind to give up. My mother taught me that when you get into a fight, you fight to win! Once again, my violent coaching had worked. Two months later I got into another fight with this same kid. I was looking forward to a rematch with him. When I got one, I was determined to fuck him up bad (or kill him if I had to), and was ready to stab or cut him if I could not whip his ass with my hands. I brought a knife with me that night because I was not about to take another ass-kicking from this same guy. As it turned out, I won my rematch with him without the knife.

The day before my 16th birthday I attacked a carload of kids, who were all older than me. I was beaten until I had double vision, yet kept coming back for more. As they sped off, I threw a couple pieces of broken brick at their car. I missed! It had all started when one of them flirted with my girlfriend. The way I saw it, that was a no-no. You cannot let guys get away with flirting with your girlfriend in front of your face. While fighting with this pack of kids, I felt indestructible even though I was getting the shit kicked out of me. I was willing to take yet another beating, because it seemed to me that it was the right thing to do. I had to keep trying to win the dominance engagement. While the biggest guy of the bunch was beating on me, I felt like a sack of potatoes that was being tossed around.

Shortly afterwards, I had my last fist fight while still in high school. I really did not want to fight this one kid who I had always respected. Besides, I was not really in the mood for unloading on anybody, but his insistence that we fight changed my mind. He had a reputation of being quite a boxer, so I knew that I would have to get down and dirty with him to win. We started fighting right there in the classroom. He out-boxed me, as I had both feared and expected. The speed at which he threw his punches dazzled me. I out-fought him street style, by pounding his head into the wall, smashing his face into my knee, and putting my foot into his nuts a couple of times. I did what I had to do. When I finally let go of him, he was wasted. He looked like a wilted flower that someone had pissed all over. I dropped out of school after winning that dominance engagement. I had chalked up a badly needed "major victory" to offset my earlier "major defeat." The last thing that I remember about high school was the little old janitor mopping up the kid's blood from the floor. I was glad that I taken this kid out before I left. I badly needed this "major victory" to offset the "major defeat" (Athens 1992, pp. 64–65) that I had earlier suffered. What the fuck, the prick got just what he deserved for fucking around with me bad. The big dog eats the smaller dog and the smaller dog eats the littler one still, right? When I got home, I told my mother about my fight at school. She was proud of me for beating the shit out of such a tough guy. For a long time afterwards, she would tell people about my fight at school.

I dropped out of high school while in the tenth grade. After quitting school in January 1967, I got a job as a bag boy at a local supermarket. It was around this time that the old man and I had our last big fist fight. Who swung first? I do not really remember anymore. I hit him a few times that night, but I took more hard hits than I gave him. He struck me once so hard in the center of my forehead that I saw a flash of red light! I knew that I had to change quickly the direction that this fight was heading before I got seriously hurt. I squatted down like a football player and tackled him with all my might. I managed to push the big fucker backwards across the floor and shove his stinky ass into a large sofa chair. I pounded him in the face and head until he promised that he would quit. However, as soon as I stopped, the prick came back at me. It looked like it was either him or me. He was a real chicken shit when it came to knives; I knew where to find one if I needed it.

The brawl ended when he ran me out of the house with a shotgun. Before he got his shotgun, I was chasing him around the house with a sword and threatening to kill him with it. I was having a fucking ball until my mother screamed, "Run, Randy, run! He's getting his shotgun!" Bare fisted, I punched a windowpane out of the back door, slashing my forearm. My adrenaline was pumping so hard I was oblivious to the pain. When I got outside, I smashed the windshield of my old man's prized possession, a red 1963 Chevy Impala, Super Sport, with the handle of my sword. Although still terrified, I screamed out in glory! Our household was like a fucking zoo full of wild, dangerous animals, and I was one of them. I had finally attained Athens' (1992, pp. 74–75) exalted state of "malevolency."

A few weeks after that, I stole my old man's work car and ran away from home with my childhood sweetheart. Believe it or not, I was afraid to steal his favorite car. At the time I figured that, if I could just lay low until I was 17, I would be able to join the fucking Marines. Then I would go over to Vietnam and kill some "gooks," "Charlies," "bad guys," or whoever else I could lay my hands on. The violence and madness of my family life was becoming too much for me to bear. To make a long story very short, a month later the two of us were back in our hometown, where we got married. Our teenaged marriage started a whole other story that had to do more with sex, shoplifting, and stealing cars than with violence.

First married at 16 and a father at 17, I became an abusive husband by the time I turned 18. Thus, the family tradition of violence continued, but this time I was the bad guy. Unlike my father, however, I never beat my son. As I started acting more and more like my old man, I started hating myself more and more. I physically and mentally intimidated my young wife by breaking furniture and yelling at her. As the years passed, I played the role of the household intimidator more and more until my life had in Athens' (1992, pp. 75–76) words, "gone full circle" from the hapless victim of brutalization to ruthless brutalizer. I had gotten the message from my old man while growing up: "If a man and a woman argue, the man ain't a man unless he wins every argument." That reasoning may be faulty, but that was the reasoning that I operated on 24 hours a day, seven days a week. It had become part and parcel of my "unmitigated violent phantom community" (Athens, 1997, pp. 145–146).

Several weeks after getting married, my then-wife and I moved in with my parents, which fortunately lasted only a few miserable weeks. We had a hard time making ends met and the harsh reality of our economic situation came crashing down on us. It was a real ball-breaking experience. I appreciated that my mom and especially my old man were letting us stay with them while I saved up enough cash for us to get our own place. Things were different now. Before, I had gotten away with being a smart-mouthed, punk kid who stuck his nose in his parent's business and always came running to his mother's defense whenever the shit hit the fan. But not anymore, because I now knew that it was dead wrong to bite that hand that feeds you. It was my old man, and not my mother, who was providing the roof over our heads and the food in our mouths.

But peace could not prevail for too long in our household. All hell broke loose when my mother's older sister and younger brother and their spouses came to visit my parents. We newlyweds were trying to stay out of the way, but one thing led to another and we found ourselves in the middle of a fight. My drunken mother kept nagging my old man. She just kept egging him on and would not stop. She was performing the role of the poor, beleaguered wife to the hilt for the rest of us. She would not give it a rest because she knew that one of us, most likely me, would risk life and limb if my old man laid a finger on her. Sure enough, he slapped her and she slapped him back, and then he slapped her back even harder. My old drunken relatives kept saying, "Why don't you help your mother? What kind of son are you?" I tried to explain to them that it was none of my business and that I was keeping my nose out of it, but they would not buy it.

The fight turned uglier. My mother's younger brother pulled out his pocket knife, like he always did whenever trouble started. Then someone started shouting that my dad was getting his shotgun. The next thing that I knew I was squaring off with my uncle. He was holding an opened knife and I had a large glass pop bottle in my hand. I asked him to put the fucking knife away. Fortunately, he listened to me for once. I can provide no better proof than this incident that my family was a "malignant community" unto itself (Athens, 1998). Hell, almost everyone in my family had either Athens' (1997, pp. 145–146) "mitigated" or "unmitigated violent phantom others" swimming around in the their heads. I know that most of us were violent sons of bitches!

Moments later we found ourselves gathered in a parking lot next to the house. My aunt's husband was still trying to talk some sense into my old man. Then – boom! The old man punched him in the face, but the guy did not swing back. He was less of a fool than the rest of us. After someone called the police, a couple of squad cars pulled up. The cop in charge started threatening to arrest the whole bunch of us, which scared the shit out of my new bride. An ambulance had also been called for my uncle, who had been punched by my old man. Blood was streaming down the side of his face. While we were all trying to convince the police officers that this was only a family misunderstanding and nothing for them to get too concerned about, I noticed that my mother was nowhere to be found. I wondered where the hell she could be? Then I spotted her peering out from a window in the house. It suddenly dawned on me that she was the one who had called the cops. I could not believe it. She was the loudmouth who everyone was fighting over, but she was the only one who was not out there talking to the cops! I felt like she had tricked us all. That was a real eye opener for me. Before that incident, I must confess that I had been blind to her manipulative ways. I had always seen her as the poor, helpless, and innocent victim of my old man's brutality. I never saw her that way again after that. I knew that it took two to tango. After the police left, everyone else went their separate ways except for the old man, my mother, and the two of us dumb-ass teenage newlyweds. Less than an hour after all the high drama had ended, the old man and my mother were acting like nothing had ever happened. Can you believe it? What a violent bunch of motherfuckers!

SELF DISORGANIZATION

As the years rolled by, I continued to beat down my young and vulnerable wife both physically and mentally. Although she bore the great brunt of my malevolence, she was not the only one upon whom I inflicted it. Like my father, I worked in the construction field for the most part. I usually got assigned jobs in which I worked alone. Once, when I was 25 years old, I got into a really bad fight with a co-worker. Back then I was always lifting weights and occasionally taking martial arts classes. The fight began with an exchange of profanity. I called him a dirty name, and then he called me dirty name back. After I challenged him, he shoved me. That gave me the excuse to unload everything that I had on him. I beat the hell out of this poor guy and ripped the hair out his head. I shoved his face, head, and entire torso through a glass window. I could have cared less whether I killed him. His blood and hair were all over me. I was really trying to fuck this guy up bad! After I was finished with him, he had to be treated at a nearby hospital. I was not arrested or even fired for what I did to him, although I could have served time behind bars for felonious assault. After winning a major victory during this dominance engagement, I gained a great deal of respect from the bunch of roughnecks with whom I worked. If I had known they were going to be so impressed with me for beating the hell out of this guy, I would have done it sooner.

At this point in my life, I was a confirmed "dangerous violent criminal, " so what Athens (1992, pp. 72–79) calls "violent notoriety," "social trepidation," and "malevolency" were all natural states of being for me. I know that I was much more violent than most people with whom I came into contact. I had become a misfit even in the rough-and-tumble blue collar community where I lived and work. It was in 1974, when I was 23 years old, that I first sought psychiatric treatment. In a nutshell, I was having trouble adapting to the world of work and married life. I found all the responsibilities and demands overwhelming. I worked hard, but I did not seem to be getting anywhere. To make matters even worse, I started drinking a lot while taking prescription and street drugs. Unfortunately, several years of outpatient treatment, one week of inpatient treatment, and multiple diagnostic labels, had all netted zero (see also Starr, 2000, pp. 27–44). Every day I became crazier and crazier. I did not care about anyone or anything. I told my then wife that I was thinking about becoming a hit man for the Mafia because I had the perfect disposition for it. My physical neglect and poor hygiene were apparent to everyone. I had become a stinking, dirty motherfucker. I would not bathe, brush my teeth, shave, comb my hair, or change my clothes. I went for days without sleeping. Both suicidal and murderous thoughts raced through my mind.

Looking back, I now realize that I was experiencing what Thomas Szaz (1960) calls a serious "problem in living." The "unmitigated violent phantom" community around which I had organized my life for so long was starting to show signs of "crumbling" (Athens, 1995). Life as a dangerous, violent criminal takes its toll on the meanest of men, and I was no exception. It was doing a real number on me. Living up to the demands of an unmitigated violent phantom community in a "civilized" or even "turbulent" society (Athens, 1998) isn't all that it is cracked up to be. In fact, it is a damn lot harder than most people who have never done it may think. Even with all his millions, sexy women, and fame, I pity Mike Tyson (see Rhodes, 1999, pp. 167–174). I cannot speak for Mike, but I can tell you one thing for sure: I was beginning to come apart at the seams. I had fallen face first into what Athens (1995, pp. 573–574) describes as the "fragmentation stage" of dramatic self change.

During the mid- to late seventies, I made threatening phone calls to my parents and my brother Martin. I became increasingly convinced that the three of them were to blame for my miserable fucking life. On the surface, it may have seemed to others that we were getting along well with one another, but I still harbored a lot of anger toward them. I had not talked about these feelings in a long time, but they were definitely there. I started treating my family as if all the shit they had done to me when I was an adolescent had just happened the day before. The extent of my pent-up anger for them shocked us all, but brutalization isn't something that one can easily or quickly forget.

One time, when I was about 22 years old, I was at Martin's house. We did not get together too often, and when we did, it was usually tense. While working out, we began to do some gymnastic tricks. I fell and banged my head hard on the floor. When I stood up, I saw stars and then briefly passed out. As I regained consciousness, I started having a minor seizure and my breathing became labored. As I gazed up, I saw Martin standing over me with a down-right evil grin on his face laughing his fucking head off. He was in seventh heaven. After that, any remaining shred of trust or goodwill that I ever had for him vanished. Martin had been extremely foolish that day. His laughing at me was a very dangerous move for him to make toward a wild, violent brother. Apparently, he did not recognize that I was a dangerous person. He did not realize who he was fucking around with. Maybe none of them had.

When I was 23 years old, the old man, while drunk, challenged me to a fight. Yeah, it was like the old fucker was handing me a gift or something. With his hands behind his back, he lurched forward, taunting me. "I'll give you a hundred to one odds that I can kick your ass, even if I am a lot older than you," he said. On one hand, I knew he was drunk and just horsing around, but on the other hand, I despised this man for bullying me around my whole life. Here he was itching for another fight with me to prove once and for all who was king of the hill. I could not believe that he was attempting to physically intimidate me in front of my wife and child. His audacity first shocked and then incensed me. I stood up and offered to take him up on his challenge. After I accepted his challenge, however, he quickly tried to fence mend with me. I refused to buy any of it and urged my wife and young son to leave my parent's house with me. I stopped the car at a park few blocks away, and got out. As my wife drove off with my son, I ran to the middle of a park and threw myself to the ground, crying, screaming, and pounding my fists into the grass. My rage and anger overwhelmed me. I felt like I was going to explode! I still could not believe that he had the nerve to challenge me to a dominance engagement in front of my wife and child. We never returned to my parent's house after that night. Later, during phone calls, I learned that my family felt that I had overreacted. "Besides," they said, "he was drunk." Not exactly a good reason for me to want to kill him. Like Martin, he had not realized who he was fucking around with.

In the old man's defense, I will share what little I know about his childhood relationship with his father. I was told that his father died of throat cancer when I was just a baby. As I recall, my grandfather was a World War I veteran. He supposedly once told my old man's older brother, "You better take care of your damn dog, or I'll tie it to a tree and shoot it." According to the story, his older brother did not heed his father's warning, and my old man's dad shot the dog dead! My grandfather was apparently a hard and violent man and he apparently made my dad a hard and violent man, and in turn, my dad made me a hard and violent man. In Athens' (1992, pp. 85–86) lingo, it is called the reproduction of brutalization across generations.

I told my relatives, friends, and even several community-based mental health workers that I wanted to kill my family, but they brushed off my threats as just a lot of hot air. "You're just saying that to get attention," they said. A psychiatrist told me, "You are a romantic; you would never kill anyone." My malevolent self and the unmitigated violent phantom community on which it was based had cracked apart completely by now. I was crying out for help, but unfortunately, I never received any effective treatment. If I had, then maybe I would have completed the dramatic self-change process that I had embarked, become a civilized person, and never have taken a human life. What would have been effective treatment, though? I had already received both in and outpatient treatment, and an arsenal of prescription drugs, including Thorazine, Haldol, Stelazine, Valium, Ritalin, and Congetin. Perhaps the only effective treatment for what was ailing me would have been putting a bullet through my head? I sometimes wished that someone would have done it.

One afternoon in 1978, I went berserk. Two or three days before, I had stopped taking my Valium and my nerves were on edge. I had been hooked on this drug for more than a year. With no booze and no pills, I could not deal with my life. After some petty argument with my wife had set me off, I destroyed our two car garage and then I destroyed our car with a sledgehammer. The neighbors gathered around in disbelief as I performed for them. My poor wife and 10-year-old son witnessed this whole ugly event. I was mad at the world and did not know any other way to strike back at it.

About a month or so later, I killed a dog. Yes, it was me who killed a dog this time. Which came first, the chicken or the egg? Does it really matter? At the time, I saw it as a mercy killing. Now I see it for what it really was – murder. I still do not like to talk about killing the dog, though. It happened about a year before I murdered a human being. Was it merely a practice run for the "real thing?"

THE DEADLY ENGAGEMENT

It was the night before my 29 birthday, October 27, 1979. I returned to my parent's house for the first time since that night my father challenged me to a fight in front of my wife and child and I vowed never to return. I had heard through the grapevine that they were getting a divorce. Great, I thought, now they are finally getting divorced after all the hell that they put me through as a child. I hoped to find both of them at home because I had a serious bone to pick with them. On October 24 and 25, I had seen a shrink who hypnotized me to grease the wheels for my regressive therapy. While under hypnosis, he had me relive all the childhood abuses that I had suffered at the hands of my parents. That journey through the past left me wanting to confront them both about the awful childhood that they had given me and the violent nut into which they had made me. I was a fucking time bomb waiting to explode.

When I got there, however, only my mother was home. After she invited me into the house, she sat on the sofa. It was my opportunity to let her know that I saw her as an accomplice in my father's brutalization of me. I also wanted her to finally acknowledge that I was the real victim in our family, not her, because I was the helpless child while she was the grownup. My mother did not want hear any of it. She was not ready for an encounter session with me about how she and the old man had fucked up my life. All she wanted to do was engage in some superficial, sugar-coated, chit chat like "glad to see you," "happy birthday," and "how are you?" Finally, her saying that she loved me while trying to embrace me was the straw that broke the camel's back. How could a mother who really loved her son do what she did to me and allow my father to do what he did to me? For her to say that she loved me given everything that had happened was an insult to my intelligence. It enraged me to the point that I exploded on her. I kicked her in the face, next in the body. While I was kicking her, she asked me, "Why are you doing this to me?" Her asking me that question at that moment only added insult to injury. She knew very damn well why I was doing it. I pulled out my pocket knife and stabbed her with it. After that, I ran to the kitchen and got another larger knife to stab her with. Finally, after I knew that she was already dead, I stomped and stabbed her some more.

During my attack on my mother, I had perfectly formed what Athens (1997, pp. 36–38) calls a "frustrative-malefic interpretation." If she would have only admitted that she and my father had wronged me and asked for my forgiveness rather than acted as if they had never done anything bad to me, then I maybe I would have never formed my frustrative-malefic interpretation or I could have restrained myself from attacking her after I formed this interpretation. However, she would neither admit any wrongdoing on her part nor ask for my forgiveness. My anger and frustration boiled into rage, then turned suddenly into cold hatred, and I stomped and stabbed her to death. I found out later that I had broken numerous bones in her body, from the top of her head to the tips of her toes. According to the autopsy, I had beaten, stomped, and stabbed her 47 times. At first, I was totally numb to the magnitude of my crime's brutality, although now it haunts me.

INCIPIENT SELF RE-ORGANIZATION

After my arrest, I spent the next several weeks in the maximum security cellblock of the county jail. While serving time there, my unmitigated violent phantom community, which before my mother's death had been on the verge of a complete melt down, had sealed *almost* completely back together. I watched fellow inmates verbally, physically, and sexually attack one another. My reputation as a dangerous criminal spared me from such brutal treatment at the hands of other inmates. In fact, the cruel and ruthless behavior that I witnessed there was so horrific that I will never forget it for the rest of my life. Many of the guards winked at the inmates' violent subjugation of each other. I was able to survive in part because the other dangerous, violent inmates respected me. For a while, I bonded with a handful of the "baddest" guys on the cell block. Through our shared lust for violence, a love of sorts was born. I can vividly remember a couple of the inmates' out-of-tune rendition of the late seventies' pop song, "We are family, my brothers, sisters and me . . ." Those of us who were facing murder charges bonded together the most, because we faced the common plight of possible life in prison. We were pumped and primed to kill. The state of virulency abounded. That county jail, or at least its max unit, was the living embodiment of Athens'(1998) "malignant" community.

One of our cellblock's main sexual predators, who was facing charges for home invasion and murder, asked me, "What are you going to do if one of these guys tries to stick a dick up your ass?" I quickly figured out that he was testing me. My answer was, "He would never get away with doing that to me because I'd kill the motherfucker." He then asked, "But what if the other guys hold you down while he shoves it in?" I said, "Then, I'd kill them all one by one, the next day, or the next week, or however long it took." My answers must have impressed him because he never asked those questions again. I marveled at the insatiable appetite that some of those guys had for violence, but their sexual perversion sickened me. One night, while a bunch of us were watching television, two of them took turns butt-fucking some poor guy on the cellblock's floor. It all happened just a couple of feet from me. The trick was to mind one's own business, but it was a hell of a trick to pull off. I can still hear the guy moaning and groaning as they shoved their dicks up his ass. If I had not been transferred later to a nut house, then who knows what I would have done? It was certainly not out of the realm of possibility that I could have stooped to fucking punks. I know for sure that I would have become even more malevolent. Sooner or later, I would have had to kill or hurt somebody badly or else let them shove a dick up my ass. These were the only two choices that you had in there. If forced to make that choice, there is no doubt in my mind that I would have chosen to kill somebody before I let them fuck me in the ass.

DIAGNOSED AS INCURABLY INSANE

It has been more than 22 years since these words rang in my ears: "Put your hands up, now!" A sandy-haired, stocky female police officer delivered this command to me in a deadpan voice as she and two or three other uniformed officers aimed their revolvers at me. I think that off to the side somewhere there were some more officers, who had not drawn their weapons yet, but I can't be sure now. It felt as if a powerful magnet had slowly pulled my arms straight up into the air. The same cop who told me to put my hands up also handcuffed me. A leather restraining harness was then quickly strapped on me, which they connected to the cuffs. These are the snapshots of my arrest still in my mind now. The images of these cops busting me seemed surrealistic at the time. The scene moved in slow motion and had a dreamlike quality. I needed for someone to bring me back to reality. A simple and direct command was then issued to me: "Put your hands up, now!" That was all that it took.

Yeah, that is all that she said, but the pure simplicity and directness of her command made it that more effective. Under those circumstances, a more drawn out and complicated command would have proven less effective. "Put your hands up, motherfucker," for example, definitely would not have worked. No threats or insults were made nor were they needed. No one, for example, added, "...or we will blow your fucking head off, you crazy bastard!" Any insult tagged on the end of that command definitely would have set me off. As in the case when I killed my mother, I would have undoubtedly formed a "frustrative malefic interpretation" and attacked those cops. My sense was that they wanted to end the event, my arrest, non-violently, if at all possible. I also knew, however, that these cops were determined to bring me in dead or alive. Fortunately, for everyone concerned, the cops were the guys in white hats that night, or the one wearing the black hat would have been dead meat. The last thing that I needed was to have another murder charge added to my record for killing a cop in the line of duty.

Later, back in my maximum security cellblock, I quickly noticed that the jail house guards, unlike the police who arrested me, did not carry guns. The deputies who escorted inmates from place to place were a different story, however. They were armed and dangerous. On four separate occasions, I was taken to see a psychologist and a psychiatrist whose jobs were to determine my mental sanity. It was during the last of these four trips that I came within a hair of attacking an armed deputy. The court-appointed psychologist's office was only a short distance from the county jail. While I was being escorted to his office, there was a shift change so another deputy had to be assigned to do the job. The second deputy seemed more concerned about the "ins and outs" of the shift change than with the killer in his charge. I certainly had not become benign after serving a couple of months in jail with some of the most low-life motherfuckers who had ever walked the face of the earth. On the contrary, I was more dangerous than ever. The primitive savage in me detected weakness on his part. I smelled vulnerability from his awkward gait and general demeanor.

I wondered if I should jump him. It suddenly dawned on me that I had an opportunity for suicide by cop. That was one way to beat a long prison sentence.

Even though the deputy's superior had denied my earlier request to the first deputy to undo my cuffs, I conned the second one into doing it for me. I told him that I needed to go take a piss. I was cuffed to the chair in which I was seated. Not only did he uncuff me from the chair, but he failed to recuff my hands together as he walked me down the hall to the nearby restroom. I kept thinking about attacking him. Unfortunately, he had only undone my left hand from the cuffs, leaving my right hand still secured. I did not feel confident enough to take out an armed deputy with only my left-hand. I kept thinking to myself that if I only had my right hand free instead of my left, then I could have at least tried to punch out this poor guy, get his gun, and shoot him. Although I was a crazy son-of-a-bitch, my mind operated perfectly when it came to calculating when I should attack people. Guess I was not all that sold on opting for the self-destruct mode that night, after all.

After we arrived at the office of Dr. Champion, one of the two mental health experts who had been assigned to evaluate me, he went off on the deputy because I was not handcuffed properly. "This is an extremely dangerous man!" he said. When I heard Dr. Champion's remark, I smiled to myself. If I could have gotten my hands around his throat at the time, I could have strangled the life out of him just for the fun of it. We both knew it, too. Although I respected him for his professional savvy, this would not have stopped me from killing him on the spot if I had the opportunity. In his report to the court, Dr. Champion diagnosed me as suffering from "schizophrenia with depressive, psychopathic, sociopathic, and anxious features" and concluded that I was "an extremely dangerous person who appears to be incurably insane and not appropriate for community-based mental health treatment." In line with this diagnosis and conclusion, he recommended to the court that I "should be placed in a secure mental institution probably for the remainder of . . . [my] natural life." His recommendation to court came as no shock to me. His remarks to the deputy made it obvious to me from the very beginning he thought that I was a violent nut who should be locked up in a crazy house with the key thrown away. On the basis of Dr. Champion's evaluation and court testimony, along with other evidence, I was found not guilty by reason of insanity for killing my mother. After later undergoing treatment for almost five years in various mental institutions in the state of Illinois, I was judged to be no longer a threat to others or myself and released back into the community. In fairness to Dr. Champion, I should acknowledge that he ultimately supported the court's decision to grant my conditional release, although he had previously opposed it (see Starr 2000, pp. 79–86).

CONCLUSION

I now must confess. I was not born with the name Randy Starr. My birth name was Dale Johnson. I legally changed my name several years after my conditional release from the state's custody in late 1984 (Starr, 2000, pp. 85–86). When I killed my mother on the night of October 27, 1979, I also was not truly insane, which raises the question of what exactly was my mental condition at the time of my crime? Although I did not recognize it at the time, I was a dangerous violent criminal who was caught in the throes of dramatic self change. I had an ultra-violent self and lived in an unmitigated violent phantom community. As I earlier noted, however, the unmitigated violent phantom community in which I inhabited had started to crumble under my feet and I fell into a severe self crisis, for which I held my family, especially my mother, ultimately responsible.

Did my severe self crisis constitute criminal insanity? As I have already stated, I do not believe now that I was really criminally insane because I understood what I was doing when I killed my mother, I did not fall under the power of an irresistible impulse to kill when I did it, and knew that killing her was definitely wrong, at least in the eyes of the law. If the self crisis into which I had plunged did not constitute criminal insanity, then did it constitute a severe mental illness, such as psychosis? I never experienced any breaks from reality where I thought I was Jesus, Moses, Buddah, Stalin, Saddam Hussein, or Superman or that I lived on Mars, Jupiter, or in Medieval Europe or ancient Mesopotamia. If my self crisis was an illness, it was like no other illness from which people suffer such as cancer, pneumonia, streep throat, near-sightedness, or tuberculosis. I was not aware of any toxic agent, gene, or germ that could have created my unmitigated, violent phantom community or later splintered it triggering my self crisis (see Szasz, 1960, 1961). In any case, it was not the disorganization of my self that made me kill, but rather the "violent phantom others" who continued to populate my disintegrating phantom community. Some violent voices in the chorus of my phantom community still came through loud and clear. Although I was unhappy with myself, what I had become was an ultra-violent person that was ready to kill himself or anybody who crossed him.

I found Athens' (1995, pp. 573–580) contention that the undergoing of self disorganization is a normal part of dramatic self change to be a revelation almost on par with that of "violentization." After my unmitigated violent phantom community had began to break apart, I had not yet come close to developing a suitable "anti"- or even "non-violent" replacement (Athens, 1986) for it that was still several years down the road for me. According to Athens (1995), whenever the process of dramatic self change becomes thwarted for any prolonged period, people find themselves becoming discombobulated. What distinguished my case of *thwarted* dramatic self change from most people's, however, is that I was a dangerous violent criminal. Despite the crumbling apart of my unmitigated violent phantom community, some "violent phantom others" continued to inhabit it.

I believe now that I could have been most accurately described back then as a "disorganized, dangerous violent criminal." It was only because my ultra-violent self was undergoing division when I committed my heinous homicide that I was *open* to treatment, and, thereby, a viable candidate for rehabilitation even though I was *still* a dangerous person. If my ultra-violent self and the unmitigated violent phantom community around which it revolved had remained intact, no amount of treatment could have ever helped me. Thus, when the Honorable Judge Rodney Scott found me "not guilty by reason of insanity" for killing my mother, he should have found me *"guilty but in need of and susceptible to treatment."*

Unfortunately, no such verdict existed then nor exists now, but I hope that such a verdict may one day come into existence, so that judges will no longer have to find people like me, who knew right from wrong, "criminally insane" to insure they get the treatment that they not only need, but can greatly benefit from. I am living proof of the value of providing this verdict option to judges in the special case of *disorganized, dangerous* violent offenders because while living outside the confines of a mental institution for almost 20 years, I have not been arrested for, much less convicted of, any serious crime. I hope to devote the remainder of my life to helping create and carry out rehabilitation programs especially designed for changing disorganized, dangerous violent criminals, a special category of offenders, among which I once included myself into "marginally violent people," the category into which I would now place myself. According to Athens (1986, 1997, pp. 145–146), a marginally violent person will only commit a grievous act of violence to defend himself or someone else from serious physical harm or death. I believe that the key to creating such programs is finding an effective way to change people with *divided, mitigated or unmitigated violent phantom communities* into people with *united, nonviolent ones* (see Athens, 1997, pp. 139–142).

ACKNOWLEDGMENTS

We presented an abbreviated version of this paper at the annual meeting of the "Scientific Study of Social Problems" held in Chicago on August 15, 2002.

Randy Starr would like to thank his friends and colleagues: Lonnie Athens, Dr. Champion, Kathleen Elftmann, Jonathan Heggen, Dennis Hill, Diana Meyers, Peggy Pendell-Frantz, Karen Ponce, Diane C. Pierson, Marianne Suwanski, Darek Williams and last but not least his wife, "Sweetie" Starr, as well as all the other unnamed people who accept him for who he is now. Lonnie Athens thanks Heidi V. Whittaker for her invaluable suggestions, and expresses his admiration for Randy Starr, who had the courage to re-examine his formative years from a new vantage point in the hope of lifting more blinders, which not only benefits him, but others as well.

REFERENCES

Abrahamsen, D. (1973). *The Murdering Mind*. New York: Harper and Row.

Athens, L. (1984). Blumer's Method of Naturalistic Inquiry: A Critical Examination. In: N. Denzin (Ed.), *Studies in Symbolic Interaction* (Vol. 5, pp. 241–257). Greenwich, Conn.: JAI.

Athens, L. (1986). Types of Violent Persons: Towards the Development of a Symbolic Interactionist Theory of Violent Criminal Behavior. In: N. Denzin (Ed.), *Studies in Symbolic Interaction* (Vol. 7b, pp. 367–389). Greenwich, Conn.: JAI.

Athens, L. (1992). *The Creation of Dangerous Violent Criminals*. Urbana: University of Illinois Press.

Athens, L. (1994). The Self as a Soliloquy. *The Sociological Quarterly*, 35, 521–532.

Athens, L. (1995). Dramatic Self Change. *The Sociological Quarterly*, 36, 571–586.

Athens, L. (1997). *Violent Criminal Acts and Actors Revisited*. Urbana: University of Illinois Press.

Athens, L. (1998). Dominance, Ghettoes, and Violent Crime. *The Sociological Quarterly*, 39, 673–691.

Athens, L. (2001). Theories of Violence. In: P. Clement & J. Reiner (Eds), *Boyhood in America: An Encyclopedia* (pp. 733–743). Santa Barbara: ABC-CLIO.

Blumer, H. (1931). Science Without Concepts. *The American Journal of Sociology*, 36, 515–533.

Blumer, H. (1969). *Symbolic Interactionism: Perspective and Method*. Englewood Cliffs, N.J.: Prentice-Hall.

Cuthbertson, B., & Johnson, J. (1992). Exquisite Emotional Sensitivity and Capture. In: N. Denzin (Ed.), *Studies in Symbolic Interaction* (Vol. 13, pp. 155–166). Greenwich, Conn.: JAI.

Denzin, N. (1989a). *Interpretive Interactionism*. Newbury Park, Cal.: Sage.

Denzin, N. (1989b). *Interpretive Biography*. Newbury Park, Cal.: Sage.

Feyerabend, P. (1993). *Against Method*. London: Verso.

Fleck, L. (1979[1935]). *Genesis and Development of a Scientific Fact*. Chicago: University of Chicago Press.

Gilligan, J. (1996). *Violence: Reflections on a National Epidemic*. New York: Vintage.

Johnson, J. M. (1990). Review of Athens' 'The Creation of Dangerous Violent Criminals.' *Symbolic Interaction*, 13, 293–295.

Kipnis, A. (1999). *Angry Young Men*. San Francisco: Jossey-Bass.

Lewis, D. (1998). *Guilty By Reason of Insanity*. New York: Fawcett-Columbine.

Menninger, K. (1966). *The Crime of Punishment*. New York: Viking.

Polanyi, M. (1958). *Personal Knowledge*. Chicago: University of Chicago Press.

Rhodes, R. (1999). *Why They Kill: The Discoveries of a Maverick Criminologist*. New York: Knopf.

Shaw, C. (1930). *The Jack Roller: A Delinquent Boy's Own Story*. Chicago: University of Chicago Press.

Starr, R. (2000). *Not Guilty By Reason of Insanity*. Chicago: Recovery Press.

Sutherland, E. (1937). *The Professional Thief*. Chicago: The University of Chicago Press.

Szaz, T. (1960). The Myth of Mental Illness. *The American Psychologist, 15*, 113–118.

Szaz, T. (1961). *The Myth of Mental Illness: Foundations of a Theory of Personal Conduct*. New York: Harper.

Tanay, E. (1972). Psychiatric Aspects of Homicide Prevention. *American Journal of Psychiatry, 128*, 49–52.

Ulmer, J. (2000). Review of Athens' 'Violent Criminal Acts and Actors Revisited.' *Symbolic Interaction, 23*, 87–89.

Znanieki, F. (1968[1934]). *The Method of Sociology*. New York: Octagon.

THE GREAT CEREBROSCOPE CONTROVERSY

Richard Restak

By the year 2010, the neuroimaging capabilities of the amazing Cerebroscope promised to bring satisfying scientific certainty to criminal trials – and freedom to hundreds of Death Row inmates. And why stop there? Wouldn't it be very helpful to know if job applicants – or applicants to college – had safe, normal brains?

In this serious spoof, neurologist and best-selling writer on the brain Richard Restak looks back from the future, wishing that we had scrutinized more carefully the first suggestions, in 1999, that brain scanning could reveal "the Mark of Cain." Then perhaps neuroscientists would have rejected the role of expert witnesses on moral and social issues, and saved the good name of brain science as the second decade of the twenty-first century began.[1]

DECEMBER 2010

Looking back now with the wisdom of hindsight, most reasonable people would agree that we should have anticipated the impact of the Cerebroscope.

As we know, researchers working at five research centers in 2005 developed a scanner capable of revealing subtle and heretofore hidden aspects of brain processing. Thanks to this new and revolutionary technology, neuroscientists could study the brain in "real time" and in exquisite detail as people made decisions, reminisced, or thought about important topics.

After several months' experience with the Cerebroscope, a young post-doctoral student made an astounding and controversial observation. As part of

Violent Acts and Violentization: Assessing, Applying, and Developing Lonnie Athens' Theories, Volume 4, pages 77–91.
© 2003 Published by Elsevier Science Ltd.
ISBN: 0-7623-0905-9

a research grant jointly funded by the Justice Department and National Institutes of Health, this student performed Cerebroscopic recordings ("Cerebrograms") on every prisoner in the nation awaiting execution for capital murder. In each instance, she noted abnormalities, sometimes very subtle, in their frontal lobes.

Upon publication of what became known as the "Cerebroscope Death Row Study" in the *Journal of Neuroscience*, the director of the American Civil Liberties Union's Capital Punishment Project got in touch with this young neuroscientist. (At her request I omit her name here because, as she told me when I called her for an interview, "I only reported the findings. I don't want to be attacked all over again.") Months later, based on the publication and wide dissemination of the Cerebroscope Death Row Study, all executions were put on hold. What's more, lawyers for many of the prisoners requested that their clients be re-tried. In the interval, these clients should be transferred to mental hospitals, the lawyers argued, because the Cerebroscope findings established that they were not responsible for their crimes; they met the requirements for a plea of "not guilty by reason of insanity."

Within a year or so of its introduction, the Cerebroscope, with new technical refinements, began to serve as a kind of brain fingerprint to identify people likely to commit even relatively minor crimes, such as petty theft or cheating on income tax returns.

Additional enhancements of the Cerebroscope led to applications entirely outside the criminal justice system, such as cheaper and easier screening of job applicants. Applicants with frontal lobe or other Cerebroscope "abnormalities" not only didn't get the jobs; personnel departments began referring their names to law enforcement officers for observation and monitoring.

"NORMAL" ABNORMALITIES

As the Cerebroscope became cheaper and more generally available, neuroscientists recognized the need for obtaining a larger baseline of "normal" Cerebrograms. Gathering this information involved testing hundreds of thousands of people picked at random from the general population. An important but initially puzzling finding emerged.

The Cerebroscope detected in significant numbers of people drawn from the general public abnormalities similar to those described earlier in death row prisoners. While in many cases the abnormalities weren't quite as prominent as those of some prisoners, the frontal areas nevertheless seemed to show some deviation from "normal."

In fairness, no one could have anticipated this development. Prior to the national testing in 2007, no one had ever carried out a large-scale study estimating the prevalence of brain abnormalities in the general population – not abnormalities detectable by a test as sensitive as the Cerebroscope. Neuroscientists and others expressed uncertainty about what conclusions to draw.

Had neuroscientists developed an instrument sensitive enough to detect "lesions" that had escaped surveillance by earlier less sensitive scanners? Or were the "lesions" just normal variations that, once again, could only be revealed by the super-sensitive Cerebroscope? And, while deciding these questions, what should be done about people in the general population with abnormal Cerebrograms? Despite never having committed a crime, should they be considered, along with the job applicant rejects, as possible or even as probable violent criminals?

In a sensible effort to avoid new controversy, neuroscientists and the Cerebroscope manufacturer shifted their emphasis to less contentious applications. A paper published in *Science* on September 12, 2008, reported on the usefulness of the Cerebroscope as a predictor of academic achievement. Within months of the Science report, Harvard became the first of the Ivy League universities to drop the requirement for a written exam for acceptance. Instead, prospective students had only to submit their Cerebrograms.

While this seemed like an eminently practical application of the Cerebroscope, the issue of frontal abnormalities raised its ugly head once again. A surprising number of applicants turned out to show abnormalities on their Cerebrograms. Once again, the findings were often subtle: the frontal areas not quite "normal" but yet not clearly "abnormal" either. Not certain how to interpret these findings, the admissions committees of most schools decided that their respective institutions should play it safe, rejecting candidates with the suspicious Cerebrograms. If left at that, things probably would not have gotten so out of hand. Unfortunately, some committees went a step further. They added to their rejection letters a "tactfully worded suggestion" that unsuccessful candidates might wish to seek a neuropsychiatric evaluation.

Not surprisingly, the uproar that ensued on the college and university front (remember the intense and sometimes hostile focus groups on campus a year or so ago composed of prospective students, parents, and faculty?) brought into sharp focus several questions that everyone concerned with the Cerebroscope had been ducking for too long: What was the appropriate response to an abnormal Cerebrogram? And, getting back to the original findings on death row prisoners, was it possible on the basis of any brain test to make confident assertions about a person's state of mind, motives, intentions, and culpability when he or she killed another human being?

The need to address these questions became urgent after editorials in the *New York Times, Washington Post,* and *Los Angeles Times* suggested neuroscientists were overstepping their bounds. How dare they arrogate to themselves determinations such as who might later commit a criminal act, who should be hired for a particular job, or how universities should go about choosing their students? The *Times* editorial even made an unfortunate comparison between the then current president of the Society for Neuroscience and the late actor Peter Sellers in his role as *Dr. Strangelove*.

LOOKING BACK AT 1999

Responding to the ensuing uproar and growing animus toward neuroscientists and neuroscience, the NIH this month established a commission to make recommendations. The commission's chairman, a professor of the history of science at Princeton University, is making the unusual but intriguing suggestion that the Cerebroscope controversy should be examined from a historical perspective. Instead of letting the advanced technology of the Cerebroscope shape our responses, he urged, we should put ourselves back to the time before the Cerebroscope existed. What would have been the best approach to take a decade earlier (in 1999) to a claim that brain-imaging abnormalities might someday explain why people kill others?

For the "1999 perspective" he is distributing the transcript of a panel discussion held that year about violence and the brain. What follows are selected statements of three panel members on what had been referred to in 1999 as the "neurologic defense." Also included are thought-provoking comments by a neuroradiologist, a lawyer, and a psychoanalyst who attended the discussion. Here are excerpts from that 1999 panel.

Moderator: Before we get into the neuroscience, let's hear from a man who has interviewed and studied more violent people than anyone else alive. Lonnie H. Athens is a criminologist with two qualifications for understanding and explaining violence. First, he speaks from experience: As a young child Athens regularly suffered violent beatings at the hands of his father. Second, Athens, in his capacity as one of the nation's foremost criminologists, spent more than 30 years interviewing hundreds of violent people. In those interviews, Athens discerned a pattern. Violent people are violent because they incorporate the attitudes and values of other violent people they have been exposed to. This "phantom community," as Athens puts it, is the "hidden source of emotions like fear, anger, hate and love. It also provides a skewed interpretation of people and situations that serves to justify violence in the eyes of the violent offender."

As I understand it, Mr. Athens believes that violent criminals, as a result of early exposure to violence, interpret their world differently from their non-violent neighbors and that their violence emerges from these different inter-pretations. Mr. Athens and his research inspired the new book by Pulitzer prize winning author Richard Rhodes, *Why They Kill: The Discoveries of a Maverick Criminologist*. Mr. Athens, perhaps you could elaborate for us.

Athens: "Engaging in violence is not only a matter of having nothing to lose, but also a matter of having something to gain. People who have a greater commitment to a violent social world than to a non-violent one perceive they have less to lose and more to gain by engaging in violence. The more committed a person is to a violent social world than a nonviolent one, the more violent he or she will likely be. Violent people consciously construct violent plans of action before they commit violent criminal acts. Just as people who have never read a physics book do not make earth-shattering discoveries in natural science, people who have never had any prior violence-related experiences whatsoever do not suddenly commit heinous crimes."

Moderator: What you're saying seems sensible regarding people living in neigh-borhoods or communities where violence is a way of life. But what about violent people who don't grow up under such circumstances? What about the so-called "good" children from "good families" who later turn out to be violent?

Athens: "People who commit heinous violent crimes always have some violence-related experiences in their backgrounds, although such experiences may sometimes be deeply hidden from others and not apparent without a thor-ough and painstaking investigation of their biographies."

Moderator: What about the relationship of violence to mental illness? I believe you wrote something about your father and why, despite his violent tempera-ment, he was not suffering from a mental illness.

Athens: "He wasn't illogical. There was a logic to his violence. So I never really believed in the mental illness model of violence. I knew you could be mentally ill and not violent. And I knew you could be violent and not mentally ill. There's no one-to-one correspondence." Richard Rhodes in his recent book describing my work, *Why They Kill,* wrote that " 'crazy' is a value judgment. Athens's work demonstrates from evidence that people who commit violent criminal acts have reasons for doing so that they believe to be significant, not trivial or senseless – reasons they do not usually share with mental health professionals."

Moderator: So I take it that you would not agree that there is a "Mark of Cain," a tell-tale neurologic sign by which potentially violent people can be identi-fied? Or that a person's brain organization predetermines their propensity for violence?

Athens: "Since human beings are normally aware of at least some of the contingencies that confront them in any situation, they can always exercise some degree of control over their conduct. At bare minimum they can decide whether to pursue or avoid a particular course of action."

The author Richard Rhodes summed up my opinion: "Athens's discovery that violent criminals know what they are doing when they decide to act violently means that murders are never senseless from the murderer's point of view; that motives however 'trivial' and 'apparently unimportant' they may seem to psychologists, do inform violent criminal acts; that violent criminals do not 'snap' but make decisions and act on them; that in every case where a violent criminal is willing to discuss his violent criminal acts honestly it is possible to know why he committed them."

Moderator: The next two speakers will get us into the neurobiology of violence. Each differs in background and experience; each holds fundamentally different views about violence and the brain.

Adrian Raine is a leading researcher on the biosocial basis of violent behavior and the author of a recent paper "Murderous Minds: Can We See the Mark of Cain?" published in the Spring 1999 issue of *Cerebrum*, a journal on brain research for professional and general audiences.

Raine: "My colleagues and I scanned the brains of 22 murderers and compared them with the brains of 22 nonmurderers. We found a select deficit (a lack of activation) in the prefrontal cortex in the murderers. When we increased our sample from 22 to 41 murderers we confirmed the significant reduction in prefrontal activity and found the brain structure known as the left angular gyrus functioned more poorly in the murderers."

Moderator: What did you conclude from that? Would you summarize your conclusions as you did in *Cerebrum*?

Raine: "We think poorer functioning of the prefrontal cortex predisposes an individual to violence while damage to the angular gyrus has been linked to deficits in reading and arithmetic. Such cognitive deficits could predispose to educational and occupational failure, in turn predisposing to crime and violence."

Moderator: Of course, the vast majority of people who fail at school and work aren't violent. But go on with your presentation.

Raine: "Our specific pattern of findings, involving the prefrontal cortex, corpus callosum, angular gyrus, amygdala, hippocampus and thalamus suggests a unique PET 'signature' of the brains of some murderers."

Moderator: You say only "some murderers"?

Raine: "We do not yet know if violent offenders in the community who commit serious nonlethal violent acts also have prefrontal dysfunction, nor have we established causality [in our sample of murderers]."

Moderator: As you heard, I asked Professor Athens about violent people from "good" homes vs. "bad: ones. Could you comment as well, please?

Raine: "We identified 12 murderers as having experienced significant psychosocial deprivation and 26 as having experienced minimal deprivation. While the deprived murderer shows relatively good prefrontal functioning, the nondeprived murderer shows the characteristic lack of prefrontal functioning. At first these findings seemed unexpected, but from another perspective they made sense. If a seriously violent offender comes from a bad home, it is plausible to seek the causes of his violence there. If he comes from a good home biological deficits become a more likely explanation."

Moderator: Mr. Athens suggested that those from either the good or the bad home became violent on the basis of their personal experience with violence. So far I haven't heard you address the issue of a violent person's earlier experience with violence; nor did you address it in your *Cerebrum* article, which I read earlier today. It sounds like you're saying, at least in regard to violence, that environmental experiences exert a determining influence in a deprived environment while in a more privileged one biological effects take precedent. I'm a bit confused at the logic here, but please go on. Your conclusions from all of this?

Raine: "The political, legal, and moral questions raised by this research are complex and worrisome, but they are too important to ignore. The question that law courts ask when dealing with a defendant is 'did he do it?' But the more important question – one that courts rarely ask – is 'Why did he do it?' The violent offender is like a jigsaw puzzle. Decades of careful psychosocial research have identified some of the pieces (e.g. child abuse, delinquent peers, and gangs). Recently we have begun to identify the biological pieces (low physiological arousal, high testosterone, birth complications, and low serotonin). Now brain-imaging research is beginning to identify the brain mechanisms. The challenge is to uncover more neurobiological pieces and put them together with the social pieces to fill out our picture of the violent offender."

Moderator: Thank you, Prof. Raine. The next panelist is Richard Restak, a neurologist and neuropsychiatrist. He has written on the relationship of brain damage and criminal responsibility in *The Sciences*, the *Archives of Neurology*, and the *Washington Post*. Dr. Restak has also appeared as an expert witness in many cases involving capital murder and the death penalty. Dr. Restak, your comments.

Restak: Of course brain damage can cause violent behavior. Or perhaps it would be more correct to say, "brain damage can be associated with violence." But certain distinguishing features identify brain-damage-related violence. Such violence usually involves sudden, explosive, and often unprovoked attacks. Afterwards, the attacker frequently speaks of "losing control" or suddenly being overwhelmed by aggressive, even murderous impulses. The technical term for this condition is "episodic dyscontrol syndrome." The name is an apt description of its two distinguishing features. So far, no one has presented a convincing instance of a person with a damaged brain who, as a necessary consequence of that damage, carried out a coldly premeditated act of violence.

It's also true that violent criminals show a higher incidence of some factors associated with brain damage – head injuries, abuse, seizures, attention deficit disorder, low IQ scores, and subtle neuro-psychological deficits – than do people in control groups. More significant, however, most people with these afflictions do not commit violent criminal acts. Nor does the presence of any of these factors in a person's past necessarily imply in a particular instance any appreciable impairment of that person's ability to control violent impulses toward others. This is especially true with regard to crimes like serial killing or stalking that involve premeditation or are carried out over extended periods of time.

At the maximum, brain damage – in the frontal lobe or elsewhere – has the potential to decrease a person's threshold for sudden impulsive violence. While this may be mitigating in some instances, it is neither exculpatory nor explanatory in others. Most violent people are neurologically normal.

As an example of where the neurologic defense (more appropriately termed "the neurologic excuse") can lead, consider Prof. Raine's comments about abnormalities in the left angular gyrus. This same brain area is abnormal in people with dyslexia – the basis, I assume, for his comment about "deficits in reading and mathematics." Yet very few dyslexics are violent. So what should we tell the parents of a dyslexic kid? "Your son may turn out to be a murderer?"

Nor do I think that Prof. Raine's sample of 41 "referrals from defense attorneys" qualifies as a large enough sample. And why just referrals from defense attorneys? Because "their clients will die unless mitigating circumstances such as an abnormal PET scan revealing brain abnormalities can be found," Prof. Raine tells us. This hardly sounds like the statement of an objective scientist. Why didn't Prof. Raine contact prison wardens and others and try to study death row prisoners not engaged in active efforts of appeal or in a search for "mitigating circumstances"? They would have formed an interesting control group. And while we're on that subject, who constituted his control group of non-murderers? Other incarcerated criminals? Volunteers? Surly graduate students?

A careful reading of Prof. Raine's article reveals that it is as much about why we should eliminate the death penalty as it is about violence and brain abnormalities. "Will we look back aghast at the execution of seriously violent offenders? Will we view execution of prisoners as we now view the burning of witches?" Prof. Raine doesn't fudge in his response to that question. "I would like to think so." While Prof. Raine has every right to hold this particular view, should he employ his status as a neuroscientist to promote it?

When it comes to evaluating violence, and criminality in general, neuroscience is a newcomer compared to criminology, sociology, and psychology. As a result, we should be careful not to let personal opinions about highly controversial and polarizing social issues like the death penalty determine our professional judgments. Is the death penalty a barbaric practice that should be eliminated from a humane and enlightened society? Perhaps it is. There is no easy answer to that question; we are entitled to our personal opinion about it. But we're not entitled to use our scientific credentials to advance personal political agendas on capital punishment. To do so devalues the present and future contributions neuroscience can make toward clarifying when and under what circumstances legitimate brain impairment may limit the control of violent impulses.

Moderator: You sound rather critical of both motives and techniques. Let's talk about your experience with death penalty cases.

Restak: I have testified both for the defense and the prosecution in murder cases where brain damage was raised as a defense.

Moderator: You have appeared as an advocate for the neurologic defense and, on other occasions, as an opponent of that same defense? Isn't that somewhat inconsistent?

Restak: I don't think so. In some instances brain lesions in the frontal lobe or elsewhere result in perceptions, feelings, and behaviors that can compromise a person's autonomy. In other cases, lesions are of dubious relevance. As I implied a moment ago, attacks of sudden uncontrollable rage that proceed from temporal or frontal lobe damage could explain a killing that took place in a burst of fury or temper. But that same damage would be incidental to offenses such as a planned murder preceded by months of stalking.

Besides, as Prof. Athens pointed out, violent people come from violent backgrounds. Head injury with frontal damage would not be unexpected in such settings. If such a person goes on to commit murder, his frontal injury, while perhaps a consequence of the violence done to him, isn't necessarily a sufficient explanation for his own subsequent violent actions. So in answer to your question about my experience as a witness, the neurologic findings are sometimes relevant and sometimes irrelevant. A violent person may have some form of frontal impairment and yet that impairment doesn't provide a forensically satisfying explanation of why that person kills his spouse or hires someone else to kill her. Each case must be looked at individually

A currently favored defense holds that frontal damage renders a person less anxious about acting violently, or less able to foresee the consequences of violent actions. In a recent issue of Nature Neuroscience, Raymond J. Dolan, a cognitive neurologist in London, suggests on the basis of some instances of damage to the orbitofrontal cortex that "knowledge acquisition relevant to moral and social behavior has a neuro-biological substrate dissociable from that of other forms of knowledge acquisition." If that proves correct, "we will need to reappraise the societal challenges posed by psychopathy and related disorders which currently (and inconveniently) linger in a hinterland between psychiatry and criminal services."

Aside from the fact that, as Dolan readily admits, "such patients are exceedingly rare,: a person with an orbitofrontal lesion isn't prevented from foreseeing the likely consequences of his actions. Although he – or she (although such criminals are almost exclusively men) – may "display profound and pervasive difficulties in social behavior," it doesn't require a lot of social savvy to foresee that killing somebody is wrong and likely to lead to some serious personal consequences. Perhaps this is one of the reasons why the vast majority of people with orbitofrontal lesions have never harmed anyone.

In addition, a person with frontal damage may satisfy the requirements for insanity by one legal criterion but fail to meet other, more stringent requirements. Let me give a specific example. On January 22, 1997, Mir Aimal Kansi, a Pakistani native recently arrived and seeking asylum in the United States, bought an AK-47 style assault rifle and ammunition at a Chantilly Virginia gun store. Three days later, Kansi stepped out of a car outside Central Intelligence Agency headquarters in Langley, Virginia, and shot five people as a protest against U.S. foreign policy towards Muslims in the Middle East. Two of the victims, CIA employees, died; three others were seriously wounded.

At Kansi's much-publicized trial, I argued that Kansi "was significantly mentally impaired from brain damage his whole life" and, as a result of this impairment, lacked the ability to anticipate the consequences of his acts. "He was impaired by his lack of empathy and caring about other people," I concluded.

My testimony was based on my examination of Kansi, which turned up frontal lobe findings along with abnormal MRI and SPECT scans that showed frontal abnormalities. The legal standard in Virginia, the McNaughton Rule, holds that a person is not responsible for criminal acts when, because of a "disease of the mind," he does not know the "nature and quality" of his acts or does not know they are "wrong."

On cross-examination I was asked, "When Kansi walked up to those cars and fired at point blank range, do you believe he knew that his actions were wrong and that as a result of those actions the people in the car could suffer death or serious injury?" I answered truthfully and affirmatively to both parts of that question. Frontal lesion or not, Kansi knew the nature of his action and its likely consequences and therefore did not meet the McNaughton standard for a determination of not guilty by reason of insanity. The jury found him guilty of first degree murder and sentenced him to death.

Would Kansi have met less stringent criteria for the "insanity defense," such as some version of the "irresistible impulse" standard? I believe that he would. But "insanity," as in the Kansi case, is a legal and not a medical determination. The jurors in one jurisdiction applying one standard found him guilty; jurors in another jurisdiction applying a different standard for "insanity" might well have reached a different conclusion and Kansi would not now be awaiting execution. While in each instance my testimony would have been the same, the difference in outcome might literally have been a matter of life vs. death. The legal system, not neuroscience, determined Kansi's guilt. It's helpful to remember that when we think we have "scientific proof" of an accused person's "innocence."

Moderator: We have time for three comments from the audience. First, an expert on neuroradiology will comment on whether or not we can look forward someday to a brain imaging device that might settle some of the differences of opinion we have heard thus far.

Audience Member: "I'm Edward Bullmore from the Institute of Psychiatry in London. In a recent issue of *Human Brain Mapping* we wrote of an instructive and perhaps analogous episode in the history of astronomy. In the late sixteenth century, a new-fangled imaging device became available for the first time, thanks to technological developments in optics. Astronomers were able to look at the planets through a telescope, but what they saw when they looked at the planet Saturn was both unpredicted and the subject of disagreement between [sic] them. The planet was obviously not always a perfect disc, as had been expected, but it was not obvious how it should be regarded instead. Different astronomers mapped it as a circle flanked by two smaller circles, or two triangles, or one or two crescents. Strangely, its appearance was also noted to change between observations by the same astronomers.

"This phenomenal inconstancy was ultimately resolved not by the development of much better telescopes, but by the development of a much better theoretical model of the observations. Christian Huygens understood that Saturn was constantly surrounded by rings and that its inconstant appearance viewed through a telescope was the result of a confounding interaction between the different orbits of Saturn and Earth around the sun. The point of this story is that a major technological development does not automatically clarify phenomena. It may even introduce new sources of bias."

Moderator: You seem to be saying that imaging devices can't make up for mistaken or muddled theories. No imaging device presently exists that will enable any scientist to read another person's intentions and, if I understand your astronomical analogy, imaging devices alone aren't going to give us the answer why some people kill others.

You, sir, would like to make a comment? Please step up to the microphone.

Audience Member: I am professor of law at the University of Pennsylvania, and I'd like to make a comment on something that seems to be largely absent from the discussion so far. As Dr. Restak briefly reminded us, judges and juries, not neuroscientists, make the final determination about insanity and responsibility. There is good reason and precedent for this. No test, no matter how reliable, will ever serve as the sole basis for deciding about *mens rea,* i.e. the state of mind and intention of an alleged murderer.

Remember the lie detector test? No one seriously believes anymore that the lie detector or any instrument can measure with certainty – the kind of certainty required in a court room – whether or not a person is telling the truth. If used at all – and lie detector evidence isn't even admissible in some courts – the test provides only a small segment of the total evidence considered by the judge and jury.

Would tests demonstrating a so-called "Mark of Cain" be admitted as evidence in a murder trial? That would depend on how much influence such a test might have on jurors' opinions. If the judge felt that the jurors would proceed – as some of you neuroscientists appear to be doing, incidentally – by using the test as ultimate determinant of guilt or innocence, I doubt the test results would be admitted.

In addition, technology is advancing at such a pace that this year's pet testing procedure (I mean no pun here) will be replaced in a year or so by something even more powerful. As a consequence, there simply isn't enough time to gather the necessary database. You have tons of testing done on people afflicted with various illnesses but so far no really large database – I'm talking hundreds of thousands of people here – on the average neuropsychiatrically normal American. Do you have any statistics to prove that if you scan a large enough cohort of people you will not uncover a significant number with "abnormal" findings? Of course you don't; such studies have never been done.

But even if you neuroscientists invent some incredible instrument that, as we laymen put it, can "read minds" you still can never be certain of why that person acted as he or she did. Courts don't necessarily make that determination either, but at least the legal process approaches the problem in a far more sophisticated way than relying on some magic machine to decide everything. If thats sound harsh, I don't intend it to. But most of you have never been in a courtroom in your life and haven't a clue about the law, court procedures, rules of evidence, and so on. To become an expert on these you'll have to do more than watch Court TV. And even in those televised cases, nobody comes running into the courtroom brandishing some imaging report that, alone, necessarily determines an accused person's guilt or innocence.

One final point. The track record of neuroscientists on social issues leaves much to be desired. Remember the psychosurgery fiasco of the 1940s and 1950s? Granted, the doctors involved in the 50,000-plus psychosurgical operations would not qualify today as neuroscientists according to the contemporary definition of that term. But the general public doesn't know enough about neuroscience to make such fine distinctions and tends to group all of you into the general class of "brain doctors."

Thank you.

At this point an elderly, slightly built man stepped to the microphone and spoke briefly with a soft Viennese accent.

Audience Member: Even though I am a psychoanalyst and not a neuroscientist, I can identify with what you are now facing. We encountered a similar challenge and failed miserably. Maybe I can help you avoid a similar mistake.

Sigmund Freud in his later years turned his attention away from what he knew best – patients and clinical issues – to concentrate instead on war, religion, politics, and other subjects far removed from psychiatry or psychoanalysis. Soon other psychoanalysts did the same. Almost overnight we became the authorities on everything. The public turned to psychoanalysts for child-rearing advice;

businesses sought the advice of psychoanalysts on how to deal with personnel and management issues; governments applied psychoanalytic ideas to arrive at "profiles" of world leaders such as Freud's own study on Woodrow Wilson.

Soon our entire profession was adrift in social and political issues on which we were not expert at all. Worse, we could never agree among ourselves on a particular issue. Was Hitler psychotic? A malignant narcissist? A megalomaniac? You could take your pick from dozens of characterizations and back up your opinion with the statements or writings of some psychoanalyst somewhere.

In time, the public caught on to our uncertainty and lack of depth in these areas. The credibility of our profession plummeted. Twenty years ago, after all, a panel discussing an issue like you're discussing today would have had at least one psychoanalyst on it. Today I consider myself fortunate to be here as an observer.

At this time, when it's vitally important to maintain public enthusiasm and funding for brain research, does it really make sense for neuroscientists to become identified in the public's mind not as scientists but as advocates on controversial and contentious issues like capital punishment or proposed biological "markers" for criminality and violence?

Finally, if some of you decide, as individuals, to become involved in the neuro-forensics of violence and crime, don't do so as an ideologue. Don't allow your political and social persuasions to influence your expert opinions. Stick to what you know. Avoid the temptation of believing neuroscience can provide explanations for everything.

At this point, the moderator of the 1999 panel called the discussion to a halt. His final comments, made a decade ago, can be recognized today, in 2010, as prophetic in regard to our present situation:

Moderator: You have heard the main arguments for and against the view that neuroscience is in a unique position to understand why people kill and therefore should play a major role in influencing the disposition of violent criminal offenders.

Think about what Athens, Raine, and Restak have said. Try to decide what conclusions seem reasonable. What position on all of this should you take? In essence, can neuroscience really make the kinds of distinctions required under the law to separate the mad from the bad? Is there any reason to think that it will ever be able to do so?

I'm convinced that it is important to reach a consensus now about the appropriate role, if any, for neuroscience in our legal system. Let's do so now, while the technological and ethical questions are still manageable.

NOTE

1. In the 1999 "panel discussion," the comments by Lonnie Athens, Edward Bullmore, Adrian Raine, and Richard Rhodes are direct quotations from their published writings.

VIOLENT SOCIALIZATION AND THE SS-Einsatzgruppen*

Richard Rhodes

I. INTRODUCTION

Athens derived his violent socialization model of violence development (Athens, 1992) retrospectively, using analytic induction, Humes's "method of universals" (Athens, 1997, pp. 115–120). This methodology establishes causality by identifying what is unique in the background of an exemplary population – in this case, violent criminals – while its requirement that all members of a class but no nonmembers exhibit a complete set of the identified unique features provides for falsification. Models derived by analytic induction, unlike models derived by quantitative statistical methodologies, are logically unaffected by the n of the population studied (an n of 1 has been sufficient historically in medical research to identify the cause of a disease) but their universality is tested by every new case. Since it has long been hypothesized among social scientists that serious personal violence has multiple causes, Athens's choice of a methodology that demands universality sets a high standard. Not only violent criminals (the usual population for studies of serious violent behavior and the population Athens studied) but also police officers and military combatants who

---

* This review is based on Richard Rhodes, *Masters of Death: The SS-Einsatzgruppen and the Invention of the Holocaust,* Alfred A. Knopf (2002), where complete citations may be found.

Violent Acts and Violentization: Assessing, Applying, and Developing Lonnie Athens' Theories, Volume 4, pages 93–106.
ISBN: 0-7623-0905-9

use force voluntarily without provocation (in so-called acts of police brutality and military atrocity) must have experienced and completed violentization or the model is falsified.

The purpose of this review is to test Athens's model by applying it to the notorious episode of Nazi SS and German police direct mass killing of Jewish men, women and children on the Eastern Front during the Second World War. Historians and social scientists alike have been baffled by the apparent willingness of police officers and soldiers who appear to be what historian Christopher Browning notably called "ordinary men" to commit such heinous and sustained acts of violence. Extreme anti-Semitism and Nazi ideology have been invoked to explain the savagery of these men. Both belief systems were clearly influential in the narratives of rationalization the men were offered by their leadership or formulated among themselves. Both belief systems, however, were common to many other individuals among the German forces who did not participate in mass killing and were repelled by it, including some members of the killer organizations who are said to have resisted participation by committing suicide, breaking down psychologically or even accepting alternative assignment to the German front lines, where high casualty rates made such assignment tantamount to a death sentence. If Athens's violent socialization model can explain how so-called ordinary men can be induced to massacre unarmed and unthreatening civilians by the hundreds of thousands, then its universality will be extended and supported.

II. A TEST CASE: THE SS-EINSATZGRUPPEN

No more heinous atrocities have ever been reported than those perpetrated by the Einsatzgruppen ("special task forces," hereafter EG) of the Nazi Party Schutzstaffel ("defense echelon," hereafter SS) under the authority of *SS-Reichsführer* Heinrich Himmler on the Eastern Front during the Second World War. Although EG mass killing of Jewish civilians by direct shooting into ditches and killing pits has been overshadowed by the more novel killing system of the death camp gas chambers, the EG and their allied cohorts (German Order Police battalions and auxiliaries recruited from among occupied populations, especially in Lithuania and the Ukraine), numbering in total ~50,000 men, were equally if not more efficient, murdering > 1.3 million victims in eighteen months across eastern Poland and the western Soviet Union. Small EG units of only a few hundred men organized and carried out the killing of as many as 17,000 people per day (as at Babi Yar, outside Kiev, the best-known EG massacre), a rate the death camps seldom matched. Historians conventionally assign the shift in 1942 from direct shooting to massacre in gas chambers to a desire on the part of the SS leadership for increased efficiency. The historical record indicates, however, that it was not in pursuit of increased efficiency but primarily in response to the psychosocial effects on the perpetrators of immersion in direct mass slaughter – effects consistent with and predicted by Athens's model – that led Himmler to order a change in killing technology.

The SS was a highly-indoctrinated paramilitary political cadre that evolved in the late 1920s from Adolf Hitler's personal bodyguard. As an organization within the Nazi Party, it operated extralegally and was answerable only to Hitler as the Party *Führer*; Hitler's dual role as *Führer* and *Reichskanzler*, and Himmler's dual role as *SS-Reichsführer* and Chief of the German Police linked it to the German state. The ~3,000 members of the EG (the core group of intended killers) assembled in the spring of 1941 in preparation for the German invasion of the Soviet Union *(Operation Barbarossa)* were drawn from the regular SS, SS and regular German police formations and the SS army (the Waffen-SS), all organizations made up entirely of volunteers. The EG leadership was recruited from high-ranking bureaucrats within the *Reichssicherheitshauptampt* (Reich Security Main Office, hereafter RSHA), an internal SS security agency headed by Himmler's second in command, *Obergruppenführer* Reinhard Heydrich, most of whom were lawyers, physicians and educators, many with doctoral degrees. Heydrich was assigned direct responsibility for EG operations. The EG would operate in parallel with the much more numerous (~20,000) forces of the German Order Police (regular civilian police), which Himmler commanded through Order Police Chief Kurt Daluege. In late summer 1941 several battalions of Waffen-SS assigned as Himmler's private army were shifted to killing duties as well and local auxiliaries were recruited, bringing the total force of SS killers on the Eastern Front to ~ 50,000.

Einsatz units had followed the Wehrmacht (the German Army) into Austria, Czechoslovakia and Poland when Germany had invaded and occupied those countries successively in 1938 and 1939. Einsatz units secured occupied territories in advance of civilian administrators. They confiscated weapons and gathered incriminating documents, tracked down and arrested people the SS considered politically unreliable – and systematically murdered the occupied country's political, educational, religious and intellectual leadership to reduce political resistance to German control. By the end of the Second World War, for example, Poland had lost to such systematic "decapitation" 45% of its physicians and dentists, 57% of its attorneys, > 15% of its teachers, 40% of its professors, 30% of its technicians and > 18% of its clergy. Jews were rounded up and ghettoized in Poland after 1939 and before *Barbarossa* and Jewish leaders and intelligentsia murdered, but the Einsatz units in Poland did not undertake extensive mass killing of Jews.

Although the Wehrmacht itself had conducted mass executions while it was still fighting to subdue Poland in autumn 1939, Wehrmacht leaders were disturbed by the continuing massacres of the Einsatz units in Poland. A memorandum by Eastern territories commander Johannes Blaskowitz indicates that Blaskowitz had implicit operational familiarity with the violent socialization process that Athens first made explicit, and predicts effects consistent with Athens's model:

> It is wholly misguided to slaughter a few ten thousand Jews and Poles as is happening at the moment; for this will neither destroy the idea of a Polish state in the eyes of the mass of the population, nor do away with the Jews. On the contrary, the way in which the slaughter is being carried out is extremely damaging, complicates the problems and makes them much more dangerous than they would have been if premeditated and purposeful action were taken . . ..
>
> The effects on the Wehrmacht hardly need to be mentioned. It is forced passively to stand by and watch these crimes being committed . . ..
>
> The worst damage affecting Germans which has developed as a result of the present conditions, however, is the tremendous brutalization and moral depravity which is spreading rapidly among precious German manpower like an epidemic.
>
> If high officials of the SS and the police demand and openly praise acts of violence and brutality, then before long only the brutal will rule. It is surprising how quickly such people join forces with those of weak character in order, as is currently happening in Poland, to give rein to their bestial and pathological instincts . . ..They clearly feel they are being given official authorization and that they are thus justified to commit any kind of cruel act.

In Athens's terminology, Blaskowitz's memorandum argues that the mass killing of noncombatants, accompanied by violent coaching from "high officials of the SS and the police," was moving "precious German manpower" (presumably German soldiers) from marginally violent to substantially violent identities: from men prepared to use violence only if physically threatened (a stage to which soldiers are typically violently socialized through military indoctrination to prepare them for combat) to men prepared to use violence even when not seriously provoked. As a military leader, Blaskowitz considered such men to be "bestial and pathological," brutalized and morally depraved.

When the members of the EG recruited for duty on the Eastern Front assembled for training at Pretzsch, a town on the Elbe River 50 miles SW of Berlin, EG leaders expressed similar concerns from their different perspective about the potentially traumatizing effects of the duties to be assigned. One recruit recalled hearing from the newly-appointed chief of EG A, Dr. Franz Walther Stahlecker, that "we would be putting down resistance behind the troop lines, protecting and pacifying the rear army area (the word 'pacify' was used very frequently) and hence keeping the area behind the front clear . . . Stahlecker also told us we would have to conquer our weaker selves and that what was needed were tough men who understood how to carry out orders. He also said to us that anyone who thought that he would not be able to withstand the stresses and psychological strains that lay ahead could report to him immediately afterwards." No surviving record confirms that any of the recruits at Pretzsch took Stahlecker up on his offer. The offer indicates, however, that the EG and SS leadership, like the Wehrmacht leadership, was aware that mass killing would challenge its subordinates' socialization.

Four EG (designated A – D and subdivided into 16 Sonder- and Einsatzkommandos, hereafter SK and EK, that operated independently) followed the Wehrmacht into Soviet-occupied eastern Poland and the USSR after *Barbarrossa* began early on the morning of 22 June 1941. Their immediate assignment was decapitation and pacification, similar to their predecessors' assignment in Poland, but they were also expected to encourage and support "spontaneous" local pogroms against Jews.

Thus in Kaunas (in present-day Lithuania) an advance detachment of EG A released violent convicts from prison and encouraged them to public displays of mass killing during which, guarded by Lithuanian irregulars whom the SS had recruited, they beat Jewish male victims to death with iron bars while Lithuanian civilians and off-duty Wehrmacht soldiers watched. A military photographer who observed one such public massacre by one man working alone (the so-called Death-Dealer of Kaunas) estimated that the man beat to death 45–50 men in less than an hour, the victims released to him one at a time by the irregulars onto the apron of a garage. The irregulars under SS guidance also rounded up large numbers of Jewish families in Kaunas – justifying doing so by claiming that Jews had been shooting from their windows at German troops – separated men from women and children and confined them separately within the walls of one of the fortresses that surrounded the city, where eventually the men were brought under machine-gun fire and slaughtered, the women raped and robbed; but after a week of confinement, the women and children were allowed to return home.

Fomenting local pogroms proved difficult, however – the occupied populations were less enthusiastic than the SS leadership about murdering their neighbors – and by early July the EG and the Order Police turned to direct killing, moving their operations away from populated areas and out of sight. Significantly, the first killing orders specified only Jewish male victims "between 17–45 years of age convicted of looting," a restriction that limited the class of victims to men of military age who could be construed to be dangerous to the killers, consistent with Athens's observation that people socialized to be marginally violent (a class which includes soldiers and police) are prepared to use serious violence only when physically threatened. (Since the intended victims were accorded neither an investigation nor a trial, their supposed "looting" was simply a cover.) Even killing this limited class of victims was expected to disturb the rank-and-file perpetrators in the EG and Order Police; an early killing order specifies group bonding activities and regular violent coaching to support and advance their violent socialization:

> Battalion and company leaders are to pay special attention to the pastoral care of the participants in this action. The impressions of the day are to be dispelled through evening gatherings with comrades. In addition, the men are to be instructed regularly on the necessity of this measure, resulting from the political situation.

An Athensian interpretation of these early SS restrictions on categories of victims is corroborated in the postwar trial testimony of Walter Blume, a police colonel and lawyer who led SK 7a of EG B. Blume claimed that when he began requiring his men to participate in the mass killing of Jewish male victims, he told them, "As such it is no job for German men and soldiers to shoot defenseless people, but the *Führer* has ordered these shootings because he is convinced that these men otherwise would shoot at us as partisans or would shoot at our comrades . . ... Our women and children will also be protected if we undertake these executions. This we will have to remember when we carry out this order." Blume testified that he ordered his unit's executions to proceed in "military style," with three men simultaneously shooting each victim lined up on the edge of a killing pit, an arrangement which dilutes personal responsibility for killing by making ambiguous which executioner's bullet is lethal, thus mooting successful violent performances and limiting violent notoriety.

Hitler and Himmler's requirements changed in mid-July 1941, however, when success in dominating the Russian army and advancing toward Moscow convinced Hitler that the war in the East would soon be won. On 17 July, Hitler decreed that Himmler's authority in police matters in the occupied territories was fully equivalent to his authority in Germany itself. In Germany Himmler was responsible for identifying and eliminating internal enemies; from the Nazi perspective, the equivalent of internal enemies in the East was first of all the Jews. Hitler's decree implemented his mid-July decision to eliminate the Eastern Jews. In the weeks after 17 July, Himmler traveled extensively conveying his orders to widen the scope of killing to his subordinates from Riga to Odessa.

Widening the scope of killing meant killing not only Jewish men but also Jewish women and children, a fact Himmler acknowledged in a 1943 speech:

> Then the question arose, What about the women and children? I decided to find a perfectly clear-cut solution to this too. For I did not feel justified in exterminating the men – that is, to kill them or have them killed – while allowing the avengers, in the form of their children,

to grow up in the midst of our sons and grandsons . . . For the organization that had to carry out this mission, it was the most difficult that we have received to date.

This "avenger" argument, which recurs in war, attempts to justify the killing of noncombatants by invoking the understanding common to groups where violence is controlled through clan and familial retribution that clan and family are responsible from generation to generation for retributive justice. In effect, it attempts to shift noncombatants into the same class as combatants and thus support a preemptive physically defensive interpretation of their slaughter. At his 1948 trial, Otto Ohlendorf, a Ph.D. economist who led EG D, made this specific point to justify his group's murder of Jewish children:

I believe that it is very simple to explain if one starts from the fact that this order did not only try to achieve a security but also a permanent security because for that reason the children were people who would grow up and surely being the children of parents who had been killed they would constitute a danger no smaller than that of their parents.

Another way the SS justified its mass slaughters was to frame them as retribution for supposed Jewish killing of Germans. A massacre on 15 September 1941 of several thousand men, women and children at Uman, southwest of Kiev in the Ukraine, was rationalized in this way. Himmler personally issued and signed the killing order, recalled by a Wehrmacht officer in postwar trial testimony:

Soldiers of the *Waffen-SS!*

In the forest of Vinnitsa, District of Kiev, six of our best officers were found assassinated, hanging on a tree.

The details are as follows:

They were found naked, with their legs pointing upward, their bodies slit open and their intestines showing.

As a result of this case, I have decided upon the following measures: As it may be taken for granted that this action was carried out by Jewish partisans, I hereby order that in the District of Kiev 10,000 Jews – irrespective of sex or age – are to die for each of the six officers mentioned above.

Even the child in the cradle must be trampled down like a poisonous toad.

May each one of you be mindful of his oath and do his duty, whatever may be demanded of you.

We are living in an epoch of iron during which it is also necessary to sweep with iron-made brooms.

Himmler personally observed an EG mass execution in Minsk on 15 August 1941, during which ~ 100 victims, including two women, were shot. Higher SS and Police Leader Erich von dem Bach-Zelewski, an eyewitness, testified after the war that Himmler was shaken by the murders. Himmler's chief of staff, *Gruppenführer* Karl Wolff, claimed to know "from [Himmler's] own mouth" that the *Reichsführer* had never seen a man killed up to that time. "Himmler was extremely nervous," Bach-Zelewski recalled. "He couldn't stand still. His face was white as cheese, his eyes went wild and with each burst of gunfire he always looked at the ground." Women were still a new category of victim in mid-August, and according to Bach-Zelewski "the members of the firing squad lost their nerve" and shot badly when the two women were laid down to be murdered. As a result, the women were injured but did not immediately die. Himmler panicked. "*Reichsführer* Himmler jumped up and screamed at the squad commander: 'Don't torture these women! Fire! Hurry up and kill them!'"

Bach-Zelewski claimed that after the massacre he challenged Himmler to reconsider direct killing, saying, "Look at the men, how deeply shaken they are! Such men are finished for the rest of their lives! What kind of followers are we creating? Either neurotics or brutes!" Himmler was visibly moved, and immediately called the men to assemble around him. Bach-Zelewski paraphrases Himmler's speech:

> Himmler first wanted to emphasize that he demanded from the men a "repugnant" performance of their duty. He would certainly not be pleased if German men enjoyed doing such work. But it should not disturb their consciences in the slightest, because they were soldiers who were supposed to carry out every order unquestioningly . . . He alone bore the responsibility before God and the Führer for that which had to happen.
>
> They surely had noticed that even he was revolted by this bloody activity and had been aroused to the depth of his soul. But he too was obeying the highest law by doing his duty and he was acting from a deep understanding of the necessity of this operation. We should observe nature: everywhere there was war, not only among human beings, but also in the animal and plant worlds. Whatever did not want to fight was destroyed . . . Primitive man said that the horse is good, but the bug is bad, or wheat is good but the thistle is bad. Humans characterize that which is useful to them as good, but that which is harmful as bad. Don't bugs, rats and other vermin have a purpose in life to fulfill? But we humans are correct when we defend ourselves against vermin . . .

Himmler was himself incompletely violently socialized; the godson of a Bavarian prince whom his schoolteacher father had tutored, he had pretensions to nobility. Having gained power by winning appointment as head of Hitler's brutal and distinctly unnoble secret police, he compensated by structuring the SS as a nobility of "blood," complete with a restored medieval castle and heraldic shields and other paraphernalia copied from the traditions of the Teutonic knights. To rationalize the SS's heinous assignment to murder millions of noncombatant men, women and children, he formulated the arguments, several of them self-contradictory, that Bach-Zelewski summarized from his speech in Minsk. As they helped Himmler cope, so also he thought they might help his subordinates cope, encouraging but also limiting their violent socialization: They were only following orders; the responsibility was not theirs but his and the *Führer's* (thus Himmler and Hitler appropriated their subordinates' violent notoriety without putting themselves at personal risk); any repugnance they felt was cause for congratulation, since it affirmed that they were civilized; life at every level struggled for survival. Himmler hoped to shift his killers one category beyond the defensive violence of military combatants: he wanted them to kill unthreatening victims without compunction whenever they were ordered to do so, but he did not want them to take pleasure in killing. In Athens's terminology (Athens, 1997, pp. 146–147), he wanted them to be violent, using their violence instrumentally from a conscious sense of duty, but not ultraviolent, using their violence expressively, for its own sake.

Many of the men of the EG and Order Police were killers with previous experience in the vigilante groups *(Freikorps)* that plagued postwar Germany, in the SS concentration camps and/or in occupied Austria, Czechoslovakia or Poland. Others were relative novices, only marginally violent, as were perhaps a larger number of young Waffen-SS fresh from training. Men under command observation who have not been fully violently socialized can pull the trigger and kill when ordered to do so, but those without sufficient violent experience are liable to break down just as people break down following other traumatic social experiences for which they are unprepared.

Even among persons with violent experience, there is a sharp and commonly recognized distinction (recognized by police and military authorities and in the law, as well as in Athens's findings) between those who use violence only defensively and those who use it without provocation. These three kinds of perpetrators-novice, defensive and malefic-can all be identified among EG, Waffen-SS and Order Police operatives. Christopher Browning, looking at postwar Order Police trial testimony, similarly identifies three types: a "significant core of eager and enthusiastic killers . . . who required no process of gradual brutalization to accustom themselves to their murderous task"; "a middle group that followed orders and complied with standard procedures but did not evince any eagerness to kill Jews"; and "a significant minority of men who did not participate in the shooting of Jews" and whose "nonparticipation was both tolerated and brushed aside as inconsequential." EG members could not so easily choose not to participate, since mass killings were their primary duty. *Obersturmführer* Albert Hartl, head of the staffing section of EG C, clearly distinguished the two extreme types (malefic and novice) in his postwar trial testimony:

> *SS-Gruppenführer* Thomas [who commanded EG C] was a doctor by profession; he was very preoccupied with the psychological repercussions of the *Einsatz* on his people. From my conversations with him I know that these effects took many different forms. There were people whose participation awakened in them the most evil sadistic impulses. For example, the head of one firing squad made several hundred Jews of all ages, male and female, strip

naked and run through a field into a wood. He then had them mown down with machine-gun fire. He even photographed the whole proceedings . . . [Participation] also had the reverse effect on some of the SS men detailed to the firing squads. These men were overcome with uncontrollable fits of crying and suffered health breakdowns. Thomas once told me that a very common manifestation in members of these firing squads was temporary impotence. It also happened that one member of the *Einsatzgruppe* who had participated in mass shootings one night suddenly succumbed to a type of mental derangement and began to shoot wildly about him, killing and wounding several men . . . A number of SS officers and men were sent back to serve at home "on account of their great weakness."

A staff officer with EG A in Riga reported similar problems. "After the first wave of shootings," the officer testified, "it emerged that the men, particularly the officers, could not cope with the demands made on them. Many abandoned themselves to alcohol, many suffered nervous breakdowns and psychological illnesses; for example we had suicides and there were cases were some men cracked up and shot wildly around them and completely lost control."

A German war correspondent stationed on a minesweeper in the harbor at Liepaja (present-day Latvia) in July 1941, described witnessing a massacre and observing both extremes: "I saw SD personnel weeping because they could not cope mentally with what was going on. Then again I encountered others who kept a score sheet of how many people they had sent to their death."

With the order in late July 1941 to begin killing women and children, which made it more difficult to rationalize the killing as the defensive execution of enemy partisans, some defensive killers also broke down. Robert Barth, a member of EK 10b (EG D), witnessed such behavior during a mass killing at Cherson, in the Ukraine, on 20 September 1941:

> About six kilometers from Cherson there was an anti-tank ditch. The Jews, among them women, children and old men, were brought up to the ditch in trucks. There they had to surrender their valuables and good clothing, then they were driven into the ditch where murder commandos had been posted to shoot the unfortunate victims. For the most part, *Waffen-SS*, regular police, Russian auxiliaries and members of the security service of the Gestapo and criminal police were employed for these shootings. Ghastly scenes took place during these shootings. Several members of the killer gangs had to be relieved, as their nerves had broken down completely. Even before they had started on their sanguinary jobs, the killer gangs were issued liquor and cigarettes before carrying out the shootings.

"When [such breakdowns] happened," an EG A staff officer testified, "Himmler issued an order stating that any man who no longer felt able to take the psychological stresses should report to his superior officer. These men were to be released from their current duties and would be detailed for other work back home. As I recall, Himmler even had a convalescent home set up close to Berlin for such cases. This order was issued in writing; I read and filed it myself . . . In my view this whole order was an evil trick; I do not think I would be wrong to say it bordered on the malicious-for after all, which officer or SS man would have shown himself up in such a way? Any officer who had declared that he was too weak to do such things would have been considered unfit to be an officer."

Himmler's experience at Minsk in August 1941 had alerted him to these problems. After the massacre, he had inspected a small mental hospital outside Minsk. Ordering Arthur Nebe, the EG officer accompanying him, to "release" the mental patients-that is, to have them murdered-he began a search for alternatives. "Himmler said," Bach-Zelewski testified, "that today's event had brought him to the conclusion that death by shooting was certainly not the most humane. Nebe was to think about it and submit a report based on the information he collected."

Nebe tried locking the mental patients into a concrete machine-gun emplacement and dynamiting it, which was gruesomely unsuccessful; his men had to pick body parts from the surrounding trees. For a less personal killing technology, Himmler turned to the euthanasia murder program that had recently stalled in Germany because of public protests at the mass killing (by gassing in gas chambers with pure carbon monoxide) of ill and disabled German citizens, many of them children. Dr. August Becker testified to the connection:

> Himmler wanted to deploy people who had become available as a result of the suspension of the euthanasia program, and who, like me, were specialists in extermination by gassing, for the large-scale gassing operations in the East which were just beginning. The reason for this was that the men in charge of the *Einsatzgruppen* in the East were increasingly complaining that the firing squads could not cope with the psychological and moral stress of the mass shootings indefinitely. I know that a number of members of these squads were themselves committed to mental asylums and for this reason a new and better method of killing had to be found. Thus in December 1941 I started working in [the RSHA, where my superior] explained the situation to me, saying that the psychological and moral stress on the firing squads was no longer bearable and that therefore the gassing program had been started.

Gassing first took the form of gas vans: moving trucks made gas-tight and fitted with pipes that conveyed their exhaust gases into the compartment where victims were packed, a killing system that had first been tried on a smaller scale by the euthanasia murder program. The gas van backed up to a loading facility; the victims were forced into the compartment; the doors were closed and locked and the engine started; and by the time the truck had driven to a dumping site (usually a pit dug in a nearby forest), the victims were dead. The EG generally resisted switching to the van system, historian Ronald Headland reports:

> According to eyewitnesses, the first use of gas vans for killing Jews took place in Poltava [in the Ukraine] by *Sonderkommando* 4a in November 1941. It is also known that

Einsatzkommando 5 received a gas van shortly before Christmas 1941 and that the other *Einsatzgruppen* received vans after the New Year . . . The gas vans do not seem to have been used with the enthusiasm hoped for originally. They were introduced, apparently on Himmler's order, for the killing of women and children in "a more humane" fashion. In general the vans were not popular with the *Einsatzgruppen*. According to the testimony of Erich Naumann, the leader of *Einsatzgruppe* B, his *Einsatzgruppe* did not use the vans, but forwarded them on to *Einsatzgruppen* C and D. The vans kept breaking down and were not always reliable. The poor state of the roads [in the Soviet Union] limited their use and the unloading of the corpses at the burial pits presented too great a mental strain on the members of the *Einsatzkommandos*.

A more successful stratagem the EG employed to reduce trauma to EG perpetrators was to assign most or all of the direct killing to ethnic auxiliaries recruited for the work. Much of the systematic slaughter in Latvia and Lithuania, for example, was carried out by auxiliaries like those recruited in Kaunas in the early days of "spontaneous" pogroms. Ukrainians were recruited in prisoner-of-war camps where the Wehrmacht notoriously provided neither food, water or shelter to Russian POWs, who died by the millions of starvation and exposure. Nationals of occupied countries were used as auxiliaries because the SS considered them expendable.

In the spring of 1942, the EG increasingly turned to fighting Soviet partisans, while death camps that used captured Russian tank and submarine engines to generate carbon monoxide for stationary gas chambers were constructed and brought on line in eastern Poland to handle the Polish and Western Jews. (Only Auschwitz-Birkenau used the prussic-acid insecticide Zyklon exclusively; Majdanek, outside Lublin in eastern Poland, used at various times either Zyklon or pure bottled carbon monoxide.) The death camps were staffed with a small number of SS supervisors and larger numbers of guards, usually Ukrainian; Jewish prisoners were forced to handle corpse removal and burning. These arrangements, in contrast to direct Einsatzgruppen killing, limited trauma to the German perpetrators. Routine extermination of Polish Jews began at Belzec on 17 March 1942; by the middle of June, when the rail transports were temporarily stopped to build new gas chambers, about 93,000 people had been murdered. In the late spring of 1942 the transports began moving from the Third Reich to the East.

Himmler met with Hitler on 16–17 April 1942, after which he traveled to occupied Poland and ordered the removal of Reich Jews from Lodz to the death camp at Chelmno. Transports left Lodz beginning on 4 May 1942, and by the middle of May, more than 10,000 people had been delivered to their death. The first Vienna transport to Minsk, to a stationary gas-van killing site on a former collective farm east of Minsk at Maly Trostinets, left on 5 May 1942; seventeen more transports followed. Construction of the death camp at Sobibor, northeast of Lublin near the Bug River, began in March 1942, and routine operation followed beginning early in May; 100,000 victims were gassed there in the first two months.

In mid-July 1942 Himmler accelerated the killing schedule, ordering the "resettlement" of the entire Jewish population of central Poland-that is, their murder-by the end of the year. Treblinka, a death camp built northeast of Warsaw beginning in late May or early June 1942, with an engine-exhaust gas chamber, began receiving transports from the former Polish capital on 22 July; within three months 200,000 people had been gassed there, with tens of thousands more to follow.

By the end of 1942, the Einsatzgruppen and their cohorts had largely fulfilled their mission. EG A had murdered according to its own reports 249,421 Jews. EG B counted 126,195, surely only a fraction of its total in Byelorussia. EG C and D had murdered 363,211 between September and December 1942 alone. Adding in other agencies and including the full period of the war, the historian Raul Hilberg estimates that > 1.3 million Jewish men, women and children were murdered in the East after *Barbarrossa* by direct shooting.

Ultimately, EG and Order Police perpetrators either broke down or they adjusted and adapted. Most of the killers became at least the hardeyed men of Himmler's vision, malefic but obedient. Himmler's fantasy was not fulfilled, however; they did not remain uncorrupted. "Members of the [border police] were, with a few exceptions, quite happy to take part in shootings of Jews," a Krakow police official testified. "They had a ball! . . . Nobody failed to turn up [for such assignments] . . . I want to repeat that people today [i.e. after the war] give a false impression when they say that the actions against the Jews were carried out unwillingly. There was great hatred against the Jews; it was revenge, and they wanted money and gold. Don't let's kid ourselves, there was always something up for grabs during the Jewish actions. Everywhere you went there was always something for the taking. The poor Jews were brought in, the rich Jews were fetched and their homes were scoured." While Himmler himself, as late as January 1942, was still dithering over whether to have a transport of Jews from Western Europe shot in Riga or to "chase them into the swamp somewhere," some of his minions chose to become virulent to a degree unimaginable outside of genocides.

"There was, for example," writes historian Leon Poliakov, "the police constable who afterwards at Lvov used to kill Jewish children to amuse his own children; or another who used to bet that he could cut off the head of a ten-year-old boy with a single saber stroke . . . We find the interpreter for the superintendent of police in the region of Slonim, one Metzner, using this terrible phrase in his testimony: 'The action was the work of a special SS commando that carried through the exterminations out of idealism, without using schnapps.'" In Trembowla in the western Ukraine, a survivor remembers, "the Gestapo man, Szklarek, always took part in the actions to liquidate the Jews. Once he ordered a little Jewish girl to lace her shoe, and when the child bent down, he shot her." Nor has malefic violence ever found plainer expression – and explanation – than in this testimony of SS-Hauptsturmführer Lothar Heimbach: "A man is the lord over life and death when he gets an order to shoot three hundred children – and he kills at least one hundred fifty himself."

III. CONCLUSION

The experiences and difficulties of the SS-Einsatzgruppen and Order Police on the Eastern Front during the Second World War test and strongly support Athens's violent socialization model of violence development. The SS leadership systematically extended the range of EG victims by categories that Athens's model predicts would maximize virulency. It used group bonding and many kinds of violent coaching to enhance violent socialization. Pervasive recourse to alcohol analgesia, psychological breakdowns and occasional suicides among EG forces support Athens's hypothesis that unless participants are socialized to serious violence they will experience their participation as traumatic. Passage through virulency into extreme maleficence characterized by violence applied enthusiastically as a form of self-expression, predicted by experienced German military leaders as well as by Athens's model, surprised and disconcerted the less-experienced SS leadership. They responded by developing more impersonal forms of killing – the death camps and gas chambers of the Third Reich – and by relegating most direct killing to expendable auxiliaries recruited from occupied populations. Athens's violent socialization model evidently applies to the training and activities of military and police and of mass killers as well as of violent criminals.

REFERENCES

Athens, L. H. (1992). *The Creation of Dangerous Violent Criminals.* Urbana: University of Illinois Press.
Athens, L. H. (1997). *Violent Criminal Acts and Actors Revisited.* Urbana: University of Illinois Press.

THE SHORT COURSE FOR MURDER: HOW SOLDIERS AND CRIMINALS LEARN TO KILL

Joshua Sanborn

INTRODUCTION

Scholars in many different disciplines have recently regretted the absence of sustained and disciplined inquiry into the production of violence (Keane, 1996, p. 7; Abbink, 2000, p. xii). The more that this statement is made, the less it tends to be true, but it remains the case that most writers struggle to come to terms with the phenomenon. It is still safe to say that the majority of social scientists treat violence either as a fully dependent variable (dependent on social conflict, on brain chemistry, etc.) or as an atavistic outlier unsusceptible to traditional academic methodologies (Athens, 2001). It is one of the great strengths of Lonnie Athens' theory of violentization that it avoids these unsatisfying treatments of violence. For him, as for many scholars who treat the subject seriously, violence is neither wholly dependent on social (much less biological) circumstances nor completely divorced from those circumstances. It is both contingent and driven by its own internal dynamic (Athens, 1989).

In this essay, I would like to probe this enigmatic relationship between the contingent and self-contained aspects of violence by drawing a parallel between the violentization of criminals and the violentization of soldiers. The observation that there are certain homologies between the "training" of soldiers and the "training" of criminals is not new. Sociologists and criminologists repeatedly

Violent Acts and Violentization: Assessing, Applying, and Developing Lonnie Athens' Theories, Volume 4, pages 107–124.
Copyright © 2003 by Elsevier Science Ltd.
All rights of reproduction in any form reserved.
ISBN: 0-7623-0905-9

make this claim (though they nearly always then bracket it in order to focus on criminal behavior) (Archer & Gartner, 1984, p. 98). Students of military organizations have traditionally been more reluctant to draw the connection, but studies of "brutalized" soldiers are now mainstream. Outside of the academy, an explicit linkage between criminal behavior and soldier behavior is awkward to make in a society in which so many members are either veterans or related to veterans, but the taboo on criticizing warriors weakened sufficiently in the post-Vietnam era to allow several influential pop-culture portrayals of the de-civilizing effects of military service to be made. Films in particular have been a powerful vehicle in this regard. Indeed, "decivilization" might be taken to be the fundamental theme of the whole Vietnam *oeuvre,* from *Apocalypse Now* to *The Deer Hunter* to *Full Metal Jacket.* These films were all more or less direct moral indictments of the war and the United States army. Soldiers were both the victims of moral collapse and its midwives.

Though raising moral issues regarding the impact of warfare upon soldiers and the societies they live in is both important and necessary, these moral questions are not my focus here. Instead, I hope to compare the violentization of criminals with the violentization of soldiers with as much precision as possible, pointing out not only the common aspects, but, just as importantly, the limits of the parallel and the reasons for those limits. In all of the discussion below, I understand violence to be not only a destructive social force but a constructive one as well. My assertion that violence is "constructive" is a descriptive, not a normative, claim. Social relations can be (and often are) centered around practices that are harmful to other human beings. This is true not only for members of criminal gangs but also for members of legal and broadly supported organizations. The very notion of national citizenship itself is inextricably linked to soldiering and to violent performances. The citizen-soldier is a powerful model in all modern national political systems (Sanborn, forthcoming). Failing to recognize the constructive aspects of violence means failing to recognize the power of the phenomenon and the complex methods that are necessary to deal with it.

Before undertaking the explicit comparison between the creation of dangerously violent criminals and dangerously violent soldiers, a short methodological and conceptual note is necessary. Throughout this piece, I will be using evidence from both American and Russian military actors to demonstrate that the process of soldier violentization is one that takes place in a number of different cultural contexts. This cross-cultural perspective is helpful in understanding the internal dynamics of violence, since it serves to partially isolate it as a variable. Though conceptually separating the production of violence from the historical circumstances in which it occurs can be a useful heuristic device, we should not go so far as to imagine that violence ever exists in a social or cultural vacuum. Violence is always produced within broader systems of meaning and behavior that vary through time and space.

Specifically, I am not making the argument here that military training methods are somehow timeless. Quite the contrary, the reason for the similarity of experience of Russian and American soldiers throughout the twentieth century is historical. In the wake of Napoleon's success, the international community of military planners implemented a fairly standard "technology" for creating soldiers. This technology was exported widely and quickly over the course of the nineteenth century through the careful study of foreign military systems, the translation of key texts of military theory in many different languages, and an entire set of practices that constituted the modern General Staff. This "staff revolution" happened throughout Europe and the Americas, and as a result, there have been significant regularities in the ways that military training, for instance, has been conducted (Gat, 1992). Understanding the ways that the violentization of soldiers and of criminals are similar and different therefore has significant potential for dealing with the related but distinct processes of state-sponsored and state-proscribed violence in a variety of different places on the globe.

PARALLELS OF VIOLENTIZATION

As Athens has argued, the first key stage of violentization is the brutalization of the individual. Over the course of the brutalizing process, subjects become desensitized to violence and change their view toward the production of violence. Without this personal transformation, most people prove reluctant to perform violence, a fact that military trainers around the world have long known. Russia's most influential voice on military training in the late nineteenth century, General M. I. Dragomirov, consistently warned officers to remember in this vein that soldiers were human beings and that they should "never imagine that a serviceman has superhuman qualities." The fear of death and the "instinct for self-preservation" were both natural and powerful (Dragomirov, 1956, p. 610). Only a strong (and equally natural) moral will could overcome this instinct. It was precisely this lack of training of the will that constituted the "fundamental sickness" of the modern era. The task of military trainers was therefore to undermine the "intellectual" instinct of self-preservation of its soldiers by conducting intensive training and inducing soldiers to exert their moral will to power through violence (Dragomirov, 1908[1880], p. 635).

As a result of this belief that modern societies produce weak-willed and selfish men, military officers consciously structured their training programs to "break down" the new recruit before "building him back up" in the proper military way. As it turns out, this process of breaking and building correlates directly to the phases of brutalization. First, individuals experience violent subjugation, through personally becoming the victim of a recognized authority figure who shows them that hierarchy and power are maintained through violent acts. Second, they witness a similar act of violent subjugation upon another member of their "primary group." Finally, their "brutalization" is completed via "violent coaching," during which novices are taught that violence is a *personal responsibility* which they cannot evade." That responsibility is underlined by the portrayal of violent actions against enemies as "glorious acts" and the violent actors as "heroes, or at least anti-heroes." These portrayals are almost always achieved by the telling and re-telling of personal narratives of the violent acts of relatives or close friends (Athens, 1989, pp. 47–48, emphasis in original).

The same processes of violent subjugation, personal horrification, and violent coaching were (and remain) mainstays of army training. From the very first days in military school in *fin-de-siècle* Russia, for instance, officer trainees were left with no doubt about the authority structure within the army or the methods by which it was maintained. Second-year students subjugated the first year students (who were called 'beasts') with near continuous hazing, "for which bullying is not an adequate translation." Many of the trainees dropped out under the pressure within the space of a month. In the eyes of the trainers themselves, the outcome was positive and not unlike the goal of violent subjugators described by Athens: "[I]ts beneficial result for the army was the development of respect for any superior – even for one only a year above you. Consequently, although hazing was illegal, the officers of the school, all of whom had experienced it in their own days, closed their eyes to it" (Littauer, 1993, pp. 13, 26).

These men went straight from their military schools to positions as junior officers, where, not surprisingly, they replicated their own training experience when training new conscripts. That training of enlisted men was even more unrepentantly violent than the training of officer candidates was. Soldiers not only were beaten by officers or NCOs on a regular basis for violations of regulations but also suffered violent acts at the hands of their fellow soldiers, who were forced to participate in the subjugation when men were ordered to "run the gauntlet" of stick-wielding comrades (Ignatyev, 1944, p. 146; Wildman, 1980, p. 34).

Violent coaching was also omnipresent. The narrative of the glorious and violent exploits of the regimental "family" in previous conflicts were a constitutive part of basic training, and lest soldiers forget over time, their barracks were filled with pictorial reminders of what constituted glory. Barracks walls were covered with paintings of heroic scenes of Russian martial exploits (Butovskii, 1893, p. 68; "List of evacuated materials" 1914, pp. 438–440). The themes of personal responsibility for committing violence and the reasons for doing so that were stressed by Athens were also emphasized by military trainers. This theme of individual responsibility was strongly emphasized during training sessions through numerous invocations of the notion of duty. World War I reservists were reminded of "why they were drafted" and the "responsibilities of a soldier," and those lessons were reinforced in following weeks by discussions about the evils and shame of self-mutilation, desertion, and the "duties of the honorable soldier after being captured" ("Weekly program," n.d., pp. 1–13).

The process of training new recruits in the United States Army during the Vietnam War was even more systematically brutalizing. The Russian army, on the eve of World War I, had no centralized training bases; soldiers simply joined their units and conducted all basic and advanced training while living alongside previously trained soldiers. The American practice of dedicating certain camps for the purpose of basic training resulted in a more uniform experience for its conscripts. The same profanity-laced tirades, the same marching songs, the same exercises are related by nearly every memoirist of the war.

Violent subjugation began immediately upon arrival in boot camp and did not relent until graduation. On the bus from the airport to camp, Phil Ball watched the three marine escorts on his bus stride the aisle abusing the scared young men. "I didn't think anyone was supposed to hit us in training," he recalled wryly, "but someone must have forgot to tell these escort chasers. One of them had a guy in a choke-hold, and another was punching him in the stomach. Richie and I caught the attention of these corporals somehow. They ran back to us and got right in Richie's face. 'You eye-fuckin' me boy? You think I'm pretty? Do you want to fuck me faggot?" Ball admitted that he was sure this was an anomaly and that once they got to the base "someone would take charge and start treating us like Marines: Wrong!" (Ball, 1998, p. 6) Every new recruit was intentionally humiliated and physically subjugated in a milieu in which violence was the only daily constant and bedrock of the community. Even the war receded from view. "Reference to the War served as a rhetorical device used occasionally by our drill instructors as a means of gaining our attention. In terms of impact, it was greatly overmatched by the immediate proximity of the low-crawl pit." (Russell, 1993, p. 28) Those who fought back against the conditions of the camp often did so through violence, which led, predictably, into a ratcheting up of abuse and, perhaps less predictably, into a co-optation of the most violent resisters. Especially troublesome men were sometimes made squad leaders to transform them from violators of the military code to its enforcers (Goldman & Fuller, 1983, p. 12).

At the same time that the daily processes of violent subjugation and personal horrification were taking place, violent coaching occurred. Men were taught the practical aspects of performing violence, of course, but just as importantly, they learned the violent outlook on the world held by their trainers. Even the most morally hardy and most inclined to nonviolence eventually caved under the pressure. Tim O'Brien was one of these men. He made it all the way through basic training before deciding in advanced infantry training that he could not reconcile himself to murder. He marched into the chaplain's office, declared his pacifist stance, and was told: "You know, this country is a good country. It's built on armies, just like the Romans and the Greeks and every other country . . . They do what the country says. That's where faith comes in, you see? If you accept it, as I do, that America is one helluva great country, well, then, you follow what she tells you. She says fight, then you go out and do your damnedest. You try to win." When O'Brien persisted, the chaplain exclaimed in exasperation "O'Brien . . . you're betraying your country when you say these things. I've met people who don't like Vietnam, sure, but you're icy about it. Where the hell do you fit the guts and bravery into your intellectual scheme? Where does God and the unknown fit in? Listen, I've *been* in Vietnam. I can tell you, this is a fine, heroic moment for American soldiers" (O'Brien, 1973, pp. 55–57). The chaplain's intellectual arguments were unpersuasive for O'Brien. Even so, at the moment he was about to desert, he was overcome by nausea and a sense of isolation and changed his mind, preferring to serve in Vietnam rather than flaunt social expectations. For him, as for so many other young men, this visceral sense of "duty," inculcated as a part of his civic and masculine self from childhood, was reinforced and recalibrated through military training. Even the most cynical of soldiers admitted that the army's technique in this regard was effective. "It played to our sense of schoolboy honor" (Russell, 1993, p. 29).

Brutalization is just the first stage in the violentization process, and in itself it is normally insufficient to make a subject dangerously violent. The next stage, according to Athens, is the belligerency stage, when the individual contemplates his situation and his relationship to violence, asking how he can avoid further victimization.[1] Many of these subjects decide that violence is a legitimate and effective course of action in certain circumstances. Though prepared to resort to lethal violence, the subject at this stage has decided to limit his actions to those in which it is both "absolutely necessary for the well-being of his body and mind" and those in which "he has at least some chance of success" (Athens, 1989, p. 60).

The belligerency phase of the soldier's personal transformation is not well-documented in the historical literature on Russia. A powerful model of the mental life of the Russian peasantry (from which the majority of enlisted men were drawn) has held that rural Russians in the early twentieth century had "primitive minds" and were unable to think abstractly (Pipes, 1992, pp. 157–158). In this view, Russian soldiers could hardly have been expected to ruminate extensively about the role of violence in their lives. This assumption about peasant mental weakness is contradicted by all the available evidence, however. Nothing is more clear from the few records of conscript thoughts still extant than that soldiers gave the experience of brutalization and the role of violence a great deal of thought. Iakov Dragunovskii remembered his military experience this way:

> I was taught discipline, taught to 'march,' to be not an independent rational man but a humble servant in the hands of the authorities, at whose command I must defend 'the Faith, the Tsar, and the Fatherland from all enemies foreign and domestic.' Those enemies greatly frightened me. What if I was ordered not just in words but in fact to kill? What could I do then, when I was horrified at the very thought? . . . The severity of service increased my aversion to it. Discipline. Fear for one's life. Bitterness.

Even Dragunovskii, though, who was later to adopt Tolstoyan nonviolence as a basic moral tenet, took a long time to resolve the nettlesome problem of violence, realizing over the course of World War I that he was "becoming brutalized. When I shot at the Germans from a trench, I did not feel any pity for them . . .. Our compassion for human beings disappeared . . .. I still thought this situation was necessary and willed by God. We had enemies and we had to kill them" (Edgerton, 1993, pp. 184–194).

Dragunovskii was probably quite typical of most soldiers. He followed orders and accepted the necessity for killing, but nevertheless carefully considered the question of his role in the war and the reasons for war. Several authors who spent time in the armed forces agitating for peace noted both the extreme interest of the topic (large crowds would gather around to debate) and the varied opinions that the soldiers had (Pireiko, 1926, p. 17; M. N. 1905: *passim*). In the end, after the shouting was done, most of the soldiers decided that when the time came they would have to commit violence and do it well. The dialogue regarding violence that soldiers conducted with themselves impacted not only the production of violence but the production of their selfhood as well. As several influential social theorists in the twentieth century have argued, individuals construct their "selves" precisely through this sort of soliloquy, in which the internalized voices of large communities, smaller primary groups, and influential individuals shape the actions and attitudes of every human being as he or she proceeds through life (Athens, 1994).

In contrast to the literature on Russian soldiers, the raft of memoirs from American soldiers makes clear that this process of belligerency was present and pronounced in the United States Army. The more intellectual phrased this question in philosophical form, as Tim O'Brien did during his fire watch duty in boot camp. "The rain is falling, and you feel comfortable. You listen, smiling and smoking. Will you go to war? You think of Socrates . . . Socrates, it has been told, was a brave soldier. You wonder if he had been a reluctant hero. Had he been brave out of a spirit of righteousness or necessity? Or resignation?" (O'Brien, 1973, p. 44). This was a difficult question to answer. O'Brien, for one, answered the question of how he should relate to violence quite clearly as basic training came to an end. He was ready to kill, starting with his drill sergeant. "We could get the man with one shot from an M-14, no problem. He'd taught us well. Erik [O'Brien's friend] laughed and shook his fist at the window. 'Too easy to shoot him' " (O'Brien, 1973, p. 47). Another recruit was more calm. He had never believed in killing and had even refused to fight back against bullies in his school days, taking punches without returning them. But he "also realized that enemy soldiers were not about to take the time to discuss my views with me. We would be communicating through the sight of a rifle, and I aimed to make my weapon talk straight and true" (Russell, 1993, p. 37).

The first two processes of brutalization and belligerency are important. They transform individuals from ones who had mostly sought to avoid violent confrontations to ones who accepted violence in their lives. But, as Athens rightly notes, they do not "create" violent men in and of themselves. They produce a "mitigated violent resolution" in which individuals become determined to "attack other people physically who unduly provoke him with the serious intention of gravely harming or even killing them." The subject now "awaits only the proper circumstances to test his newly developed resolve" (Athens, 1989, pp. 62–63). Ironically, this moment never comes for most soldiers. Soldiers usually serve in peacetime, and even when war breaks out most men in uniform do not engage directly in combat. This is a significant fact, since it is the combat experience that puts men in situations in which they can enter the final two stages of the creation of dangerously violent men. The importance of these latter stages is highlighted not only by Athens, but also by studies of the violent behavior of army veterans. When Ghislaine Boulanger surveyed 276 Vietnam veterans, 273 other veterans, and 452 nonveterans on their violent behavior, she found that there was no statistical difference between them in the incidence of physical fights, in the severity of injury inflicted during those fights that occurred, and in the rates of abusing spouses (Boulanger, 1986, p. 83).

When Boulanger controlled for combat experience, however, statistically significant differences emerged. 26.8% of combat veterans had gotten in a physical fight over the past five years, compared with 19.5% of noncombat veterans and 18.5% of nonveterans. Similar statistical differences appeared in responses as to whether they had inflicted serious harm (Boulanger, 1986, p. 85). A close study of the combat experience quickly reveals why this is the case. The third stage of violentization identified by Athens was that of the violent performance, when the individual who has made a mitigated violent resolution is put to the test. Obviously, men thrown into combat for the first time face this test. Indeed, many even look forward to combat as a way to demonstrate to themselves and their comrades that they are courageous, honorable, and fully masculine. They want to test their mitigated violent resolution and to find out whether they have "what it takes" (Goldman & Fuller, 1983, p. 157).

Some soldiers do not make these violent performances. They lie low, creep away, fire over the heads of the enemy, or become casualties before ever going on the offensive themselves. Many combat soldiers, however, do commit violence. The battle, though nearly always disorienting, terror-inducing, and soul-shaking, does eventually end, and the surviving soldiers reflect on their behavior. Many (perhaps most) are unsure whether they in fact inflicted casualties on the enemy, but they have ample evidence to judge their own performances. The most irrefutable evidence is that they are still alive, and this fact leads most to conclude that their violent coaches, though reviled at the time, were on target with their message. Violence in the form and manner in which it was taught by drill instructors *can* be effective. It can keep you alive. As one veteran put it, boot camp was "grueling and abusive, but it showed me that I was capable of far more than I ever believed possible. By pushing us beyond our limits, those mean drill instructors instilled a sense of self-confidence that would later save my life in Vietnam" (Ball, 1998, p. 9).

Even this initial performance and self-assessment is insufficient to make an individual dangerously violent. The final stage is virulency, in which the subject receives psychological rewards from his nearby community. Before the violent performance has a significant impact, this significance must be impressed upon the subject by other people. Athens writes that "[t]he opinions formed about his violent action by members of the subject's primary groups, especially friends, almost always ultimately have a far greater weight in the subject's shaping of his own opinion about his actions than those drawn by secondary group members, such as official authorities" (Athens, 1989, pp. 72–73). The opinions of primary and secondary groups are not always in contradiction, however. For military men, the assessment of violent action taken by primary and secondary groups is far more likely to coincide than in the case of criminals. The entire structure of military service is suffused with small-group and large-group benefits for men who are adept at violence. At the secondary group level, medals are awarded, promotions are granted, citations are sent home to families. At the equally important primary group level, bravery under fire leads to greater respect, trust, and sense of closeness. All of these are significant rewards that further erode whatever brakes upon violent activity that may have existed before the first battles. Soldiers are now prone to make "unmitigated violent resolutions," deciding to engage in violent acts where only minimal threats (or none at all) exist. Anger becomes the sufficient precondition. At this point soldiers begin to slip beyond the framework of military discipline and increasingly become dangerous not only to the enemy but also to civilians and indeed to themselves.

Let us return to our case studies one more time to see this process at work. In Russia during World War I, it took only a few weeks for soldiers to go through the compressed violentization process. Already brutalized and belligerent by the time they made it to the front lines, they quickly went through the process of violent performance and moved on to virulency. Within a month of the start of hostilities, the soldiers of the 24th Army Corps were already being chastised by their commander for their recent activities in occupied Galicia, where they had destroyed postal stations, cut telephone wires, sacked the estates of landowners and burned towns ("Order of 24th Army Corps," 1914, p. 113). The problem of violent looting was not limited to foreign regions, though, as Russian subjects complained as well that Russian soldiers were "treating them badly" as they passed through (Voitolovskii, 1926, p. 34).

As the war dragged on, acts of violence increasingly began to take place outside of the sanctioned areas of violent behavior. Armed robberies of civilians (especially Jews) in the front-line zones became commonplace, as did attacks upon whole villages. Civilian massacres were reported on both sides of the pre-war border. Individual acts of terror also mushroomed, as men robbed women clerks at gunpoint, attacked unarmed individuals, and committed sexual assaults. Soldiers themselves, not to mention civilians, admitted that they had become "wild beasts" (Shklovsky, 1984, p. 101; Littauer, 1993, pp. 149, 153; Rychkov, 1915, p. 12; "Report to Stavka," 1916, p. 35).

But we should note here that though the realm of violence had greatly expanded, it was not wholly indiscriminate. Much (though by no means all) of this explosion was linked to the wave of anti-Semitism and xenophobia that washed across Russia during World War I (Lohr, 2001). There are many examples of vicious behavior towards Jews in front-line areas. Fedor Stepun witnessed a Cossack riding in a carriage whipping not the horse, but a Jewish driver, who in turn was expected to beat the horse. In addition, he was present when an officer related an incident in which a soldier encountered a Cossack and complained that he had no boots and nowhere to go to get some. At first the Cossack suggested that the soldier search the trenches for boots to take off a corpse, but then they came across a Jew on the road. The Cossack then came up "with the magnanimous idea to give the soldier 'yid' boots." When the Jew protested, the Cossack came up with a yet more "humorous idea." He told the soldier to drop his pants and ordered the Jew to "kiss his ass and thank him for letting you live," an order that was obeyed. "It was horrible," Stepun wrote home, "that all of this could happen . . .. But it was more horrible that the narrator, telling the story over cognac, got such a tremendous response from his listeners" (Stepun, n.d., pp. 107–108).

The fact that the violence against civilians was directed mainly against social outcasts and enemy populations suggests two things. On the one hand, the countervailing official and social forces that normally kept violence within prescribed limits were weakened by the outbreak of war. On the other hand, they were still in evidence in sufficient strength to keep soldier-civilian relations from completely disintegrating. The difference between weakened limits and no limits at all became clear after the revolutions of 1917. These revolutions removed the social restrictions and much of the system of military discipline that had been imperfectly restraining soldiers in the first three years of the war. Over the course of the years of Revolution and Civil War (1917–1921), brutalized soldiers ran rampant. One soldier wrote privately that "[i]t's hard to live when all around all you see is disorder and only disorder. For so long everyone was ruled by the stick and the majority of Russians are people with no idea of the Motherland, honor or duty . . ." Another wrote. "Something horrible is reigning: train stations are blown up, supply stations are burned down . . . soldiers in the rear are hopping trains to Kiev and then stealing along the way, forming teams of runaways, which are then caught and sent back to their unit." Local authorities were helpless, unable "to take measures to halt this anarchy." In big cities, deserters, usually well-armed, took control of burgeoning gangs and routed police and militia alike, terrorizing even the capital (in which there were perhaps 50,000–60,000 deserters in July 1917) during the summer of 1917 for days on end. The result, as Tsuyoshi Hasegawa has noted, was that "the means to settle political differences were rapidly shifting from persuasion and compromise to physical violence" ("Spiski," 1917, p. 6; "Anonymous letter," 1917, p. 43ob.; "Telegram from estate steward," 1917, p. 66; Hasegawa, 1992, pp. 249–251).

Stories of American soldiers in a state of virulency in Vietnam are commonplace. The best known incident was the massacre of the civilian population at My Lai, but smaller scale incidents were almost daily occurrences. One brief recollection retold to Harry Maurer included a whole string of murderous acts: the napalming of a village housing mostly women and children, the shooting of an elderly man defecating near a highway, the slitting of prisoners throats. As Warren Wooten, the soldier in question, admitted "I was thinking less and less about my duty and more and more about, goddamn it, I've gotta survive this thing. Plus by that time I had committed enough mayhem over there that it was getting pretty disgusting" (Maurer, 1989, p. 155). Wooten was not alone. Most memoirists relate tales of haunting brutality, of torture, of corpse mutilation, and of dropping children to their deaths from helicopters. All also note the prevalence of the practice of "fragging," when unpopular soldiers or officers would be killed by their own troops in the heat of battle.

These incidents, we should note, were not atavistic acts of wilding, but instead reflected the transformation of the code of action that some soldiers followed. Only certain circumstances dictated fragging or child murder. In the latter case any suspicion of collaboration on the part of the child or their community was sufficient cause, especially if units had taken casualties from snipers or other guerrilla action. Violence never became totally meaningless, nor did it cease having a structure. Instead, the conditions of war *changed* the rules by altering the message given to soldiers by the "phantom communities" within their heads.

THE LIMITS OF THE PARALLEL

The many commonalities between the making of soldiers and the making of violent criminals are so clear that it is tempting to make rather sweeping claims about the similarities between combat veterans and dangerously violent criminals. This is certainly the approach taken by several recent authors (Rhodes, 1999; Shay, 1994). It seems to me, however, that there are too many questions that remain to be answered before such a straightforward conclusion can be reached. In this section, I would like to point out two important differences between criminals and soldiers, both of which are partial answers to the most obvious question we must ask when comparing these two groups: if the process of violentization is essentially the same, why are combat veterans significantly less likely to commit violent crimes after leaving the service than violent criminals are after leaving prison?[2]

As I noted before, combat veterans are significantly more likely to perform violence at home than others, but their rate of "recidivism," if you will, is still far lower than that of violent criminals. In Boulanger's study, 11.5% reported having been arrested for a violent crime in the past five years, and 26.8% reported having gotten in a fight in the past five years (Boulanger, 1986, p. 84). These numbers are certainly higher than the numbers for non-veterans (5.6% and 18.5% respectively), but they compare quite favorably with those of men released from prison after committing violent crimes. Recidivism rates for violent criminals vary from state to state and from year to year, but rearrest rates generally range between 33% and 50%. In Florida, the five year rate in 2001 was 37.0%; in Texas, the three year rates of reincarceration ranged from 41–48% depending on the year (Florida Department of Corrections, 2001, p. 21; State of Texas Criminal Justice Policy Council, 2001, p. 1). The difference in behavior is even more striking when we consider that most men with the experience of performing extreme violence on the streets are either never released from prison or are released much later in life. In addition, criminal recidivism rates do not reflect the scale and prevalence of violence in the prisons where many violent men go immediately following their violent acts on the streets. There is a certain amount of comparing apples and oranges here, of course, since the statistics I use were not compiled with an eye toward direct comparison, but the essential point that veterans are significantly less likely to commit extreme violence than ex-convicts seems clear enough. So what accounts for the difference?

The first difference between the violentization of criminals and that of soldiers is that there is a greater unanimity of "communities" regarding the activities of the latter. Violent criminals frequently experience a conflict between the messages of their primary community, which may approve of violent behavior, and the society as a whole, which does not condone it. The disapproval and sanctions of the society as a whole toward criminal behavior obviously does not prevent the creation of dangerously violent criminals, but it does make the process different than it is for soldiers in modern national armies, who are committing violence explicitly on behalf of the larger community, not in defiance of it. Soldiers are taught that there is a strict line between violent martial acts and violent criminal acts. As our parallel above showed, this line is more artificial than real, but even the artifice of the distinction plays an important part in "deviolentizing" demobilized soldiers. There is much room for further research on this topic, especially on the ways that individuals transform their attitudes when they return home from war. We know enough as a result of psychological studies of Vietnam veterans to know that this transformation is often painful and incomplete, but the parallel with violent criminals also shows that this is usually a *successful* transition in at least one respect; most men never commit extreme violence again (Lifton, 1985).

Historians have begun to point to one way that broad social approval helps men deal with this trauma by studying the role of memory and memorialization in postwar periods. Scholars have argued (correctly in my view) that the ways in which past wars are remembered are in sharp contrast to the lived experience of combat veterans (Mosse, 1990). This transformation of memory has several baleful effects, but it may also be the case that they significantly reduce internal violence in the wake of war. The creation of war myths may serve to reintegrate combat veterans into society by intentionally downplaying the violent acts they performed in wartime. This process of reintegration would of course have to take place at the individual level as well as the social level: veterans would have to rearrange their phantom communities and reinvent themselves with new soliloquies for this process to significantly reduce violent incidents in the civilian realm. If this hypothesis is correct, it would go a long way toward explaining why combat soldiers who hate war in their diaries end up coming to terms with it in their memoirs and then hawkishly promoting it in their political activities in the VFW.

The second difference has to do with the technique of violence itself. The acts of violence that are committed by soldiers and by criminals are normally very different. Criminals do not napalm city blocks or slaughter hordes of onrushing men with machine guns. They do not launch high explosive shells over the horizon at unseen enemies. It is also rare for them to select a target hundreds of yards away with a rifle and then to shoot a man they have never met and never seen. Soldiers have a wider palette of violent acts. The sorts of intimate, face-to-face violence normally conducted by criminals are indeed practiced by soldiers, especially those in a state of virulency. The bloody work of the bayonet in the trench, the fist and knife fighting of a surprise attack, and the incidences of rape and infanticide when soldiers run amok in civilian populations are all too easy to find in the historical record. But in the twentieth century, at least, this sort of personalized violence has not been the norm. Most of the murder has occurred at a distance with advanced technological means, a transformation of organized violence that some scholars have labeled "industrial killing" (Bartov, 1996).

This difference in the technique of violence is important. Criminologists have long known that individuals practice violence in highly specific ways. A man who murders with a knife is more likely to use the same weapon again rather than a gun; a rapist rarely pulls a gun on a bank teller. Violence is situational, for reasons that Athens makes clear. Individuals *prepare* for their violent acts by conducting conversations with themselves about their potential for violence and by making violent resolutions. They imagine future scenarios in which violence might be used and they frequently carry their personal violent tools with them in case those scenarios play out. While in uniform, soldiers do the same thing. But then they go home, take off their epaulettes, give the machine gun back to the supply sergeant, and leave the napalm-bearing plane in the hangar. They may continue to maintain violent resolutions and harbor violent fantasies, but they no longer are faced with the same type of violent scenarios they had experienced in war and they no longer have their specialized violent tools that were always a part of their violent imaginings. This does not mean, of course, that they are incapable of developing new violent scenarios and incorporating new violent tools, but this requires an additional step that many never make.

CONCLUSION

The comparison of the production of violent soldiers and the production of violent criminals has the potential for important insights into the bloody history of the modern age on battlefields and city streets alike. It is highly significant that the processes by which young men are transformed into violent criminals so closely parallels the way that they are trained as soldiers. In each case, "violent coaches" undertake a process to "break down" young men by making their "will" to commit violent acts stronger than what Dragomirov called their "intellectual desire for self-preservation." This coaching is normally done within the confines of a hyper-masculine moral code that stresses the importance of courage, of dynamic activeness, of "honor," and of duty. The methods of these coaches are unrepentantly violent. The new moral structure that violentized individuals adopt is constructed and confirmed by acts of brutality. Demonstrating authority, dominance, and effectiveness through violent acts systematically undermines the variety of notions of social relations and of social control that "recruits" had internalized in the "civilian" world. When put to the test in violent confrontations on the street or in the trenches, many men learn that the new code of behavior and of social interaction propagated by their violent coaches is both reliable and effective. They become new social beings with new outlooks on the world that are patently dangerous for those around them and for themselves.

But this parallel between criminals and soldiers is not a perfect one. The fundamental internal dynamic of violence remains fairly constant, but the context within which those violent acts take place is quite different. This difference in context produces a sharp difference in outcomes. This difference in outcome is most evident when we begin to consider the important process of "deviolentization." Combat veterans, at the end of their tour, are man for man some of the most dangerous individuals in any society. Accustomed to danger and death and proficient at destruction, one might expect that they would quickly become the scourge of any community unfortunate enough to host them. But, remarkably, the vast majority of these individuals cease their murderous ways and attempt to reintegrate into their home communities on a peaceful basis. They are far more successful at doing so than young men who wore prison uniforms rather than army uniforms.

Discovering how these veterans are able to resocialize will help us understand not only how societies effectively bring wars to an end, but also how violent criminals might successfully change their attitudes toward violence and the people around them. It is unfortunate that the parallel between soldiers and criminals should break down right at the point of pacification. Still, the most basic lesson of the comparison between soldiers and criminals is that individuals become violent mainly as the result of powerful processes of microsocialization and that their violent acts tend to take place within highly specific contexts. The experience of veterans also shows that this process can go both ways: even virulently violent men can become "deviolentized." It is probably not too outlandish to suggest that wise public policies that focus on changing the phantom communities of violent criminals and on depriving them of the contexts and tools that are present in their habitual violent imaginings might result in a similar "pacification" of at least some of the most dangerous men in our midst.

NOTES

1. In his latest work, Athens has relabeled this stage "defiance." Belligerency seems to me to be a better term for this process for soldiers, so I will continue to use it here (Athens, 2001, p. 737).

2. Another question that might benefit from using the lens of "violentization" is the question of why some troops go on rampages against civilian populations and some maintain firm discipline. As the close parallel between Russia and America suggests, the answer to this question is unlikely to lie in such amorphous areas as "national character" or the influence of dictatorial regimes.

REFERENCES

Abbink, J. (2000). Preface: Violation and Violence as Cultural Phenomena. In: G. Aijmer & J. Abbink (Eds), *Meanings of Violence: A Cross-Cultural Perspective* (pp. xi–xvii). Oxford and New York: Berg.

Anonymous letter to V. A. Maliuch (1917). Russian State Military-History Archive f. 1300, op. 1, d. 99, l. 43ob.

Archer, D., & Gartner, R. (1984). *Violence and Crime in Cross-national Perspective*. New Haven and London: Yale University Press.

Athens, L. H. (1989). *The Creation of Dangerous Violent Criminals*. New York: Routledge.

Athens, L. H. (1994). The Self as a Soliloquy. *The Sociological Quarterly, 35*(3), 521–532.

Athens, L. H. (2001). Violence, Theories of. In: P. Ferguson Clement & J. S. Reiner (Eds), *Boyhood in America: An Encyclopedia* (Vol. 2, pp. 733–742, L-Z). Santa Barbara, Denver, and Oxford: ABC-CLIO.

Ball, P. (1998). *Ghosts and Shadows: A Marine in Vietnam: 1968–1969.* Jefferson, NC: McFarland and Co.

Bartov, O. (1996). *Murder in Our Midst: The Holocaust, Industrial Killing, and Representation.* Oxford and New York: Oxford University Press.

Boulanger, G. (1986). Violence and Vietnam Veterans. In: G. Boulanger & C. Kadushin (Eds), *The Vietnam Veteran Redefined: Fact and Fiction* (pp. 79–90). Hillsdale, NJ: Lawrence Erlbaum Associates Publishers.

Butovskii, N. (1893). *O sposobakh obucheniia i vospitaniia sovermennago soldata (prakticheskiia zametki komandira rota)* (3rd ed.). St. Petersburg: Berezovskii.

Dragomirov, M. I. (1956). *Izbrannye trudy: voprosy vospitaniia i obucheniia voisk,* L. G. Beskrovnyi (Ed.). Moscow: Voenizdat.

Dragomirov, M. I. (1908[1880]). Perepiska M. I. Dragomirova s A. Drygal'skim. *Russkaia starina, 34,* 633–637.

Edgerton, W. (Trans., Ed.) (1993). *Memoirs of Peasant Tolstoyans in Soviet Russia.* Bloomington and Indianapolis: Indiana University Press.

Florida Department of Corrections (2001). Recidivism Report: Inmates Released from Florida Prisons.

Gat, A. (1992). *The Development of Military Thought: The Nineteenth Century.* Oxford: Clarendon Press.

Goldman, P., & Fuller, T. (1983). *Charlie Company: What Vietnam Did To Us.* New York: Ballantine Books.

Hasegawa, T. (1992). Crime, Police, and Mob Justice in Petrograd during the Russian Revolutions of 1917. In: C. E. Timberlake (Ed.), *Religious and Secular Forces in Late Tsarist Russia* (pp. 241–271). Seattle: University of Washington Press.

Ignatyev, A. A. (1944). *A Subaltern in Old Russia.* I. Montagu (Trans.). London, New York, and Melbourne: Hutchinson and Co.

Keane, J. (1996). *Reflections on Violence.* London and New York: Verso.

Litton, R. J. (1985[1973]). *Home from the War: Vietnam Veterans, Neither Victims Nor Executioners.* New York: Basic Books.

List of evacuated materials from Plotsk (July 1914). State Archive of the Russian Federation. Fond 1745, opis 1, delo 58, lists 438–440.

Littauer, V. S. (1993[1965]). *Russian Hussar: A Story of the Imperial Cavalry: 1911–1920* (Reprint ed.). Shippensburg PA: White Mane Publishing.

Lohr, E. (2001). The Russian Army and the Jews: Mass Deportations, Hostages, and Violence during World War I. *Russian Review, 60*(3), 404–419.

Maurer, H. (1989). *Strange Ground: Americans in Vietnam: 1945–1975, An Oral History.* New York: Henry Holt.

Mosse, G. L. (1990). *Fallen Soldiers: Reshaping the Memory of the World Wars.* New York and Oxford: Oxford University Press.

M. N. (initials only). (1905). *Na voinu!: zapiski krest'ianina prizyvnogo 1904 goda.* Christchurch, Hants, England: Svobodnoe slovo.

O'Brien, T. (1973). *If I Die in a Combat Zone: Box Me Up and Ship Me Home.* N.p.: Delacorte Press.

Order of 24th Army Corps (1914). Russian State Military-History Archive f. 2067, op. 1, d. 2904, l. 113.

Pipes, R. (1992). *Russia Under the Old Regime* (2nd ed.). New York: Macmillan.

Pireiko, A. (1926). *V tylu i na fronte imperialisticheskoi voiny: vospominaniia riadovogo* Leningrad: Rabochee izdatel'stvo "Priboi."

Report to Stavka from head of mobile field bakery No. 11 (1916). Russian State Military-History Archive f. 2003, op. 2, d. 810, l. 12.

Rhodes, R. (1999). *Why They Kill: The Discoveries of a Maverick Criminologist*. New York: Alfred A. Knopf.

Russell, N. L. (1993). *Suicide Charlie: A Vietnam War Story*. Westport, CT: Praeger.

Rychkov, G. (1915). Telegram to Stavka. Russian State Military-History Archive f. 2003, op. 2, d. 810, l. 12.

Sanborn, J. (forthcoming). *Drafting the Russian Nation: Military Conscription, Total War, and Modern Identity: 1905–1925*. Dekalb, IL: Northern Illinois University Press.

Shay, J. (1994). *Achilles in Vietnam: Combat Trauma and the Undoing of Character*. New York: Atheneum.

Shklovsky, V. (1984). *A Sentimental Journey: Memoirs: 1917–1922* (Rev. ed.). R. Shelton (Trans.). Ithaca and London: Cornell University Press.

Spiski korrespondentsii zaregistrovannoi v Novorossiiskoi voennoi tsenzuroi (1917). Russian State Military-History Archive f. 1300, op. 1, d. 99, l. 6.

State of Texas Criminal Justice Policy Council (2001). Recidivism Rate by Offender Type. (Accessed October 23, 2001: http://www.cjpc.state.tx.us/StatTabs/RecidivismRates/stattabsrecidvisimrates.html).

Stepun, F. (n.d.). *Iz pisem praporshchika artillerista*. Prague: Plamia.

Telegram from estate steward to Podol'sk provincial commissar (1917). Russian State Military-History Archive f. 2067, op. 1, d. 572, l. 66.

Voitolovskii, L. (1926). *Po sledam voiny* (2nd ed.). Leningrad: Izd. pisatelei.

Weekly program for the eight-week training course for enlisted men in reserve infantry units (n.d.). Russian State Military-History Archive f. 2000, op. 2, d. 2379, ll. 1–13.

Wildman, A. K. (1980). *The End of the Russian Imperial Army*. Princeton: Princeton University Press.

THE VIOLENT SOCIALIZATION SCALE: DEVELOPMENT AND INITIAL VALIDATION

Ginger Rhodes,[1] George J. Allen,
Joseph Nowinski and Antonius H. N. Cillessen

ABSTRACT

Athens' (1992) conceptual model of violent socialization explicates early developmental processes that lead individuals to employ violence as a preferred method of handling disputes, getting one's way and circumventing anticipated trouble. Athens' four-stage model has six major socialization components. The model was developed from a sociological perspective involving participant observation of incarcerated felons. The present study describes the development of an instrument, the Violent Socialization Scale (VSS), to assess components of Athens' conceptual model. Test items were generated in accord with underlying theoretical propositions and then were subjected to classical test construction procedures. Two additional scales measuring aggression and traumatic stress, both with well-established validity, were used to validate the components of the VSS. Respondents were 69 incarcerated adult males and 99 male college students, the latter serving as a comparison group. Exploratory factor analyses yielded six discrete subscales that matched the hypothesized components of violence

**Violent Acts and Violentization: Assessing, Applying, and Developing Lonnie Athens'
Theories, Volume 4, pages 125–145.**

development: Violent Subjugation, Personal Horrification, Violent Coaching, Belligerency, Violent Performances, and Virulency. All six VSS subscales showed high internal consistency reliabilities. The incarcerated group scored significantly higher on all subscales than did the comparison group. All six subscales exhibited convergent validity with existing measures of self-reported aggression and trauma. Finally, mediational analyses indicated that consistent with the theory, violent coaching mediated the relationship between violent subjugation and aggression.

INTRODUCTION

Major historical views of violence assume that aggression is expressed with minimal conscious volition. These views encompass theories that aggressive people act out of frustration (e.g. Dollard, Doob, Miller, Mowrer, Sears, Ford, Hovland & Sollenberter, 1939), that they model belligerent behaviors observed during childhood (e.g. Bandura & Walters, 1959), or that they exhibit particular constitutional (Witkin, 1977) or personality characteristics (e.g. A. Heilbrun, L. Heilbrun & K. Heilbrun, 1978). A more recent view (Athens, 1992) attributes violence to conscious, volitional, goal-directed activity. Athens offers a persuasive four-stage developmental model that describes how individuals undergo violent socialization, or "violentization." The model contains six components, each of which defines a distinct social experience. Athens emphasizes that these socialization events are significant events, more influential than the many easily-forgotten moments experienced in daily life. Although people may have such experiences at any age, the most common period of occurrence is late childhood to mid-adolescence. As the underlying theory is explicated in other chapters in this journal, we present only a brief overview of the six components.

The first stage of "violentization" is labeled "Brutalization" by Athens. Brutalization encompasses three components: Violent Subjugation, Personal Horrification and Violent Coaching. Each of these components has a common element, that of harsh treatment by a primary group member. Athens maintains that Brutalization can develop within any primary group, even in adulthood.

Violent Subjugation is the experience of being forced to acquiesce to the control of an authority figure from one's primary group. The authority figure forces the novice to obey commands and to show proper respect, through either coercive or retaliatory violence or the threat of such violence.

The coercive approach has more short-term impact. Coercion typically begins with the authority figure making a demand which the novice either openly defies or shows reluctance to follow. This resistance, in turn, prompts the authority figure to beat or threaten to beat the novice. Once a beating begins, the novice becomes fearful that he[2] cannot tolerate the pain and begins to feel terror. His increasing panic finally leads the novice to signal his willingness to comply with the authority figure's demand. The authority figure then stops the beating.

The retaliatory approach often begins with the authority figure accusing the novice of past willfulness. The primary difference between the coercive and retaliatory approaches is that the novice's first signal to submit does not end the beating. The authority figure continues the violence until the novice ends all resistance and often until the novice is physically prostrate and emotionally dazed, only then accepting the novice's complete submission. This method has more lasting impact. The novice remembers the interminable violence long afterward.

Regardless of the particular approach, the feelings that result for the novice are much the same. The novice first feels humiliated because he is unable to stop the violence. Humiliation turns to rage for being subjected to such mistreatment. The burning rage the novice feels eventually evolves to a desire for revenge. The novice wants the authority figure to feel the same humiliation.

Personal Horrification occurs when someone close to the novice is violently subjugated. The novice can experience Personal Horrification through seeing or hearing violence being directed toward a peer, and may feel as if he were experiencing that violence himself. The novice considers intervening to help the victim but concludes that the risk is too great. Once again, the novice feels helpless before a violent authority figure. That humiliation again turns to rage, but now he directs his feelings toward himself in the form of shame that he cannot protect himself or the victim. For this reason, Personal Horrification is especially traumatic.

The third component is Violent Coaching, the credible instruction that violent action is the personal responsibility of the novice. The one necessary qualification for a violent coach is that he must be credible, someone the novice perceives to be or to have been an authentically violent person. The coach does not necessarily teach the novice how to fight or defend himself. Instead, the coach teaches the novice that, when provoked, taking violent action is a personal obligation.

The coach can use various methods, including vainglorification (e.g. boasting about his own past exploits, portraying himself as taking violent action against victims who "deserve it"), ridicule (e.g. contrasting his confidence to the novice's fear), haranguing (e.g. talking so often about violent actions that eventually the novice incorporates the need as his own to attack others), or direct coercion (e.g. if the novice does not attack a provocateur, the coach threatens that *he* will attack the novice). Coercion, in particular, sends a clear message to the novice that he must use violence.

In Athens' second developmental stage, labeled "Belligerency," the novice finds himself in a troubling emotional state. He has been repeatedly assaulted or threatened and has watched others whom he values being similarly mistreated. These noxious experiences arouse in the novice a sense of shame and rage at his inability to stop the brutalization. The violent coach's ability to protect himself emphasizes the novice's inadequacies. The novice thus begins to brood and reflect on the meaning of his current existence and to ruminate on his future. He comes to see clearly the point the coach was making: that the way to stop being brutalized is to take violent action. As a result, the novice decides thereafter to use all necessary force when seriously confronted; he makes a "mitigated violent resolution" (Athens, 1992, p. 62).

Violent Performances, the third stage, begins after the novice arrives at this mitigated violent resolution, when he proceeds to experiment with violence as a defensive measure. Depending on the success of the novice's violent performances, he may advance to further violent acts or reconsider his decision.

Successful violent encounters can lead to a more sinister outcome, the fourth and final stage, which Athens calls "Virulency." If the novice's community acknowledges the success of his violent acts by showing fear and respect, and, in turn, the novice begins to value that new reputation, he may conclude that if violence works so well when defense is required, it should work even better when he is not being challenged. The novice may then expand his resolution to use violence even in situations where he is not provoked (an "unmitigated violent resolution"). Over time, violence thus becomes a core part of his personal identity. Athens argues that the choice to harm or kill others with little provocation occurs if, and only if, an individual has been successfully socialized through all six components of Violentization.

PURPOSE OF THE PRESENT STUDY

Athens conducted his research using the participant-observer method common to sociology, and did not extend his model to include any systematic nomothetic method of measurement. The goals of this study were to develop a reliable and valid measure of violent socialization and to evaluate its various types of validity. To assess construct validity, we hypothesized that factor analyses of the Violent Socialization Scale (VSS) would yield six internally consistent factors that would represent the six components described by Athens. We next hypothesized that incarcerated adult males would score higher on all six subscales than a comparison group of male university students. Finally, we hypothesized that factors from the scale would correlate highly with existing and validated measures of aggression and traumatic distress.

METHOD

Participants

Validation data were drawn from two populations; 99 male college students, ranging in age from 18 to 30 (mean age = 19.4 years) and 69 prisoners (ranging in age from 19 to 55, mean age = 31.4 years) who were incarcerated in a medium-security corrections facility. The prisoners were recruited from a list of men seeking placement in anger-management treatment groups offered from the mental health unit. Informed consent was obtained from all interested participants. All participants were male, most were Caucasian, and all spoke English. Students completed the questionnaires in groups of approximately 20; inmates completed the measures in groups of five to seven in a group meeting room located in the prison's mental health unit.

Assessment Instruments

In addition to the VSS, Buss and Perry's (1992) Aggression Questionnaire (AQ) was also given. To assess posttraumatic stress, Horowitz, Wilner and Alvarez's (1979) Impact of Events Scale (IES) was administered. All participants also completed a demographic form that assessed age, years of education, number of arrests and number of convictions. Participants were also asked to indicate the geographic region in which they lived as children and the most prominent family constellation in which they were raised during their childhood.

Aggression Questionnaire (AQ). The AQ is a 29-item self-report questionnaire which measures four aspects of aggression: physical aggression (PA; nine items), verbal aggression (VA; five items), anger (A; seven items), and hostility (H; 8 items). Participants responded to each item on a five-point scale, with possible endorsements ranging from *extremely uncharacteristic of me* (1) to *extremely characteristic of me* (5). The internal consistency of the AQ is strong with an overall alpha coefficient of 0.89; subscale alphas were 0.85 for PA, 0.72 for VA, 0.83 for A, and 0.77 for H. The measure also has shown good test-retest reliability (Buss & Perry, 1992).

Impact of Events Scale (IES). The IES is a 15-item self-report questionnaire that assesses posttraumatic stress for a specific life event, which is defined by participants as salient during the past seven days. The scale measures two aspects of responses to stressful events: intrusive experiences (e.g. traumatic imagery, dysphoric feelings and bad dreams) and avoidance of trauma-related feelings and situations. Participants responded to each item on a four-point Likert scale: *not at all* (0); *rarely* (1); *sometimes* (3); and *often* (5). The measure has demonstrated highly acceptable internal consistency with alpha coefficients ranging from 0.79 to 0.92. The average alpha for the intrusive subscale (7 items) is 0.86 and the avoidance subscale (8 items) is 0.90 (Horowitz, Wilner & Alvarez, 1979).

Construction of the Violent Socialization Scale

The initial version of the VSS consisted of 91 items that were drawn for theory relevance according to Athens' (1992) model. In many cases, the items reflected the actual phrases used by the incarcerated felons to describe their experiences as reported in *The Creation of Dangerous Violent Criminals* (Athens, 1992). A first draft of the measure was evaluated by seven graduate students and two faculty knowledgeable about the theory. Participants were asked to respond to each item on a six-point Likert-type scale. The possible endorsements ranged from *never* or *not at all* (1) to *frequently* or *almost always* (6).

If participants did not have the personal experiences that comprised particular constructs of Violent Subjugation and Personal Horrification, they were given the option of skipping the items that assessed those constructs. (When entering the data, no answer was considered a *never* choice.) Participants who reported experiencing some element of violence completed those items pertaining to that particular component. In addition, those participants were asked to indicate the relationship of the person involved in the perpetration of violence (i.e. father, mother, stepfather, stepmother, brother, sister, or other).

RESULTS

The reliability of the VSS was assessed by Cronbach alpha analysis; the content validity of the scale was assessed by analyzing the factor structure of test items. Following these analyses, the VSS was shortened to 59 items. Convergent and discriminant validity were then determined by evaluating correlations between the final version of the VSS and other previously validated instruments of aggression and trauma. When appropriate, tests were performed on the student and prisoner groups separately. Group means and standard deviations were examined for both the individual and combined samples.

Preliminary Factor Analyses

To reveal the underlying structure of the VSS, multiple factor analyses were performed. Exploratory factor analysis was used to evaluate whether the VSS items clustered into logical and empirically coherent subsets (Tabachnick & Fidell, 2001). These subsets should theoretically reveal the constructs of the model. The factor structure underlying the VSS was evaluated through analyses that forced solutions of two factors, four factors, and six factors. The selection of these specific forced solutions was theory-driven: two factors representing nonviolent and violent stages, four factors representing the model's four stages, and six factors representing the model's six constructs.

Following varimax rotations of the various solutions, loadings were evaluated for the presence of "marker" items. Marker items were defined as those items loading above 0.30, being the most highly loaded on that one particular factor, and loading low on other factors. The six-factor solution proved the best fit, yielding 59 marker items loading above 0.30. This solution accounted for 60.3% of the total variance.

Table 1 presents the item loadings of the 59 items and associated factors that comprise the VSS; marker items are presented in bold. Six factors emerged, corresponding (in order of their magnitude) to Athens' conceptions of Violent Subjugation (19 items), Personal Horrification (11 items), Violent Coaching (nine items), Virulency (nine items), Belligerency (six items), and Violent Performances (five items). In general, these items loaded substantially on the factors they were theoretically expected to and did not load on other factors.

Reliability Analyses

The internal consistency of the VSS items within individual factors was evaluated by Cronbach alpha computations. These coefficients are presented in Table 2, separately for the two samples and also for the aggregated data. The coefficients are acceptable, ranging from 0.69 to 0.97. The magnitude of these coefficients justifies the inclusion of all 59 items on their respective subscales.

Comparison of Scores Reported by Students and Prisoners

Group differences theoretically should show prisoners scoring higher than the college men on all VSS factors and also on corresponding criterion scales. Table 3 presents means and standard deviations for all six VSS subscales as well as for the criterion measure subscales. Three multivariate analyses of variance were calculated to evaluate differences between the two subsamples. Significant multivariate F-values were followed by univariate Bonferroni t-tests, corrected for degrees of freedom and subscale overlap. The first multivariate analysis, which contained all six VSS subscales, was significant, $F(6,161) = 19.82$, $p < 0.001$. Bonferroni t-values, which are also presented in Table 3, indicate that the prisoners scored significantly higher ($p < 0.001$) than students on all

Table 1. VSS Items and Loadings for A Forced Six-Factor Varimax
Rotated Solution.

ITEM	FACTOR	VS	PH	VC	VR	BL	VP

When I was growing up a significant person in my
life would . . .

		VS	PH	VC	VR	BL	VP
(1)	threaten to harm me physically.	**0.67**	0.22	0.25	0.06	0.00	0.11
(2)	beat me or whip me.	**0.71**	0.24	0.34	0.05	0.16	0.21
(3)	punish me for being disrespectful.	**0.45**	0.13	0.16	0.24	-0.11	0.17
(4)	"go crazy" (lose control) when beating or whipping me.	**0.62**	0.16	0.31	-0.03	0.13	0.16
(5)	do or say things to scare me.	**0.59**	0.22	0.30	0.09	-0.02	0.10
(6)	force me to do what he or she wanted.	**0.59**	0.23	0.18	0.19	-0.12	-0.04

When I was growing up . . .

(7)	I would get a beating or whipping without knowing why.	**0.60**	0.17	-0.01	0.08	0.28	0.05
(8)	I was told I did not show proper respect to the right people.	**0.31**	0.19	0.24	0.10	0.04	-0.07
(9)	I was told I did things that deserved beatings or whippings.	**0.75**	0.31	0.27	0.05	0.14	0.08

When I was getting a beating or whipping . . .

(10)	I had to show respect before the beating would stop.	**0.65**	0.22	0.06	0.00	-0.07	-0.04
(11)	I had to say I was sorry before the beating would stop.	**0.56**	0.16	0.11	0.00	-0.15	0.00
(12)	Even if I said I was sorry, the beating still did not stop.	**0.56**	0.09	0.26	0.10	0.22	0.13
(13)	I had to scream or cry for the beating to stop.	**0.67**	0.16	0.23	0.07	0.10	-0.07

After the beating or whipping stopped . . .

(14)	I was angry.	**0.71**	0.35	0.26	0.00	0.04	0.17
(15)	I was ashamed.	**0.68**	0.15	-0.04	-0.02	0.22	0.15
(16)	I was confused.	**0.71**	0.29	0.13	0.03	0.27	0.03
(17)	I was afraid.	**0.73**	0.20	0.13	0.08	0.28	0.08
(18)	I was enraged.	**0.63**	0.44	0.37	0.02	-0.01	0.06
(19)	I wanted to get back at the person who beat me	**0.65**	0.37	0.41	0.06	0.03	0.08
(20)	When I was growing up I witnessed someone important to me getting beaten up or whipped.	0.34	**0.78**	0.24	-0.03	0.13	0.09

When that person was getting a beating or whipping . . .

(21)	I was angry.	0.30	**0.88**	0.17	0.05	0.09	0.15
(22)	I was ashamed of myself for not doing something.	0.26	**0.83**	0.24	0.02	0.17	0.06
(23)	I was afraid to do anything to help.	0.28	**0.79**	0.14	-0.03	0.18	0.06
(24)	I was enraged.	0.29	**0.84**	0.25	0.04	0.16	0.08

Table 1. Continued.

ITEM	FACTOR	VS	PH	VC	VR	BL	VP
When that person was getting a beating or whipping . . .							
(25)	It felt like I was getting the beating, too.	0.35	**0.77**	0.25	−0.05	0.17	−0.01
(26)	I thought about trying to stop the beating.	0.22	**0.87**	0.14	0.00	0.10	0.14
(27)	I tried to stop the beating.	0.19	**0.66**	−0.06	0.05	0.00	0.05
(28)	I felt like it was my fault that he or she was being beaten.	0.37	**0.53**	0.14	0.15	0.02	0.00
(29)	I felt helpless to stop the beating.	0.23	**0.81**	0.23	0.06	0.08	0.05
(30)	I wanted to get back at the person who did the beating.	0.32	**0.79**	0.29	0.03	0.10	0.12
When I was growing up a significant person in my life . . .							
(31)	threatened to hurt people who showed him or her disrespect.	0.29	0.36	**0.58**	0.20	0.06	0.06
(32)	told me the best thing to do was physically attack someone who threatened me.	0.32	0.31	**0.70**	0.04	0.07	0.14
(33)	told me that people would get you if you didn't get them first.	0.34	0.34	**0.71**	0.01	0.01	01.12
(34)	told stories about taking people out (beating, hurting or killing them).	0.34	0.19	**0.67**	0.17	0.01	0.02
(35)	said I could never be as tough as he or she was.	0.24	0.03	**0.52**	0.06	0.10	0.16
(36)	said I should do whatever it took to win my fights.	0.30	0.25	**0.72**	0.11	0.02	0.28
(37)	said it was important to be the winner.	0.19	0.03	**0.60**	0.03	0.05	0.09
(38)	praised me if I won my fight.	0.19	0.30	**0.68**	0.21	−0.06	0.17
(39)	made me feel proud for not being afraid to fight.	0.17	0.31	**0.67**	0.22	−0.04	0.22
Now when I think about other people pushing me around . . .							
(40)	I feel ashamed.	0.11	0.16	0.08	0.16	**0.61**	−0.06
(41)	I feel confused.	0.07	0.19	0.10	0.04	**0.73**	−0.07
(42)	I feel afraid.	0.13	0.08	0.10	−0.07	**0.74**	−0.05
(43)	I feel like I deserved it.	0.25	−0.03	−0.07	0.17	**0.35**	−0.09
Now when I think about not standing up for the people close to me . . .							
(44)	I feel confused.	0.00	0.17	0.10	−0.02	**0.67**	0.20
(45)	I feel afraid.	0.00	0.04	−0.13	0.01	**0.71**	0.14
How do the following statements describe the way you feel now . . .							
(46)	It is my responsibility to protect myself and people I care about.	0.23	0.13	0.27	0.09	0.15	**0.44**

Table 1. Continued.

ITEM	FACTOR	VS	PH	VC	VR	BL	VP
	How do the following statements describe the way you feel now . . .						
(47)	When people try to push me around, I stop them.	0.03	0.14	0.19	0.07	−0.02	**0.78**
(48)	When people try to push around people I care about, I stop them.	0.11	0.01	0.15	0.10	−0.03	**0.83**
(49)	I will protect myself even if I get hurt.	0.90	0.01	0.11	0.03	0.08	**0.74**
(50)	I am proud of my ability to take care of myself.	0.06	0.18	0.11	0.15	−0.03	**0.62**
	People who know me (as I am now) would . . .						
(51)	give me what I want because they are afraid of me.	0.11	0.02	−0.20	**0.77**	−0.11	0.20
(52)	do what I tell them without asking questions.	0.09	−0.05	−0.16	**0.68**	−0.14	0.30
(53)	say I am dangerous.	0.04	0.24	0.22	**0.75**	0.04	0.14
(54)	show that they're afraid of me.	0.09	0.18	−0.12	**0.78**	−0.05	0.15
	How do the following statements apply to you today?						
(55)	I am dangerous.	0.05	−0.10	0.21	**0.63**	0.10	0.01
(56)	I like to pick fights.	−0.02	−0.22	0.26	**0.61**	0.03	−0.07
(57)	I fight when people don't do what I tell them.	0.09	−0.06	0.18	**0.69**	0.08	−0.02
(58)	I attack someone just because I want to.	−0.06	−0.10	0.15	**0.69**	0.14	−0.05
(59)	I am full of hatred.	0.21	0.13	0.28	**0.53**	0.26	−0.02

Factor marker loadings are in bold.
All marker loadings > 0.30.

Factor 1 = Violent Subjugation (VS)
Factor 2 = Personal Horrification (PH)
Factor 3 = Violent Coaching (VC)
Factor 4 = Virulency (VR)
Factor 5 = Belligerency (BL)
Factor 6 = Violent Performances (VP)

six subscales, with the largest differences occurring on Violent Subjugation, Personal Horrification, and Violent Coaching.

The second multivariate analysis, which contained the physical aggression, verbal aggression, anger, and hostility Buss-Perry subscales, was significant, $F(4,153) = 23.01$, $p < 0.001$. All four univariate t-tests were significant, indicating that the prisoners reported engaging in significantly more ($p < 0.001$) physical and verbal aggression and experiencing more intense anger and hostility. The final

Table 2. Internal Consistency Reliabilities (Cronbach's Alphas) of VSS Subscales for Prisoner, Student, and Combined Samples ($N = 168$).

FACTOR	PRISONERS	STUDENTS	COMBINED
Violent Subjugation 19 items	0.94	0.91	0.95
Personal Horrification 11 items	0.95	0.95	0.97
Violent Coaching 9 items	0.92	0.85	0.92
Belligerency 6 items	0.79	0.73	0.78
Violent Performances 5 items	0.69	0.83	0.79
Virulency 9 items	0.85	0.87	0.86

Table 3. Means and Standard Deviations of the VSS and Criterion Measures for Prisoner and Student Samples ($N = 168$).

Measure	PRISONERS Mean	SD	STUDENTS Mean	SD	Bonferroni t-value
Violent Subjugation	51.87	22.50	29.47	11.01	8.54***
Personal Horrification	35.57	18.59	13.87	9.43	9.93***
Violent Coaching	28.21	13.62	16.16	7.42	17.38***
Belligerency	14.48	6.81	11.40	4.59	3.50***
Violent Performances	26.16	3.98	23.95	4.74	3.17**
Virulency	18.18	8.20	14.38	6.61	3.31**
Aggression Questionnaire					
Physical	29.75	7.65	21.03	7.00	7.32***
Verbal	17.22	3.98	14.91	4.56	3.23**
Anger	23.45	5.72	16.72	4.94	7.81***
Hostility	26.49	6.65	18.27	6.15	7.89***
Total	96.91	19.81	70.93	18.40	
Impact of Events					
Intrusive	19.74	7.17	7.45	8.77	9.05***
Avoidance	21.82	7.27	9.57	9.31	8.59***

Note: *$p < 0.05$. **$p < 0.01$. ***$p < 0.001$.

analysis, which contained the IES subscales, also was significant, $F(2,154) =$ 48.41, $p < 0.001$, with derivative univariate analyses indicating that the prisoners experienced significantly greater ($p < 0.001$) intrusive imagery and traumatic avoidance compared to the students.

Relationships Among VSS Subscales

Bivariate correlations assessed associations among the VSS subscales. These interscale correlations are presented for the combined sample in Table 4. Violent Subjugation, Personal Horrification and Violent Coaching were most highly intercorrelated, more so than with the remaining VSS subscales. This result is consistent with the model; together, these three components comprise the Brutalization stage of Violent Socialization.

Identical interscale correlations were also computed separately for the prisoner and student subsamples and the significance of differences between corresponding coefficients was evaluated by z-tests. These comparisons revealed several interesting relationships. First, prisoners showed a similar intercorrelation among Violent Subjugation, Personal Horrification and Violent Coaching to the student sample. The intercorrelation for the prisoners was slightly, but not significantly larger than the student sample. Similarly, Violent Coaching was significantly associated with Violent Performances for both prisoners ($r = 0.44$, $p < 0.001$) and students ($r = 0.34$, $p < 0.001$), with the difference between these coefficients being nonsignificant.

The coefficient describing the relationship between Violent Subjugation and Belligerency for prisoners ($r = 0.30$, $p < 0.05$), however, was significantly larger than the correlation found for students ($r = 0.03$, $p > 0.05$), $z = 2.12$, $p < 0.05$. This identical pattern was found for the relationship between Personal Horrification and Belligerency and also between Violent Coaching and Belligerency, both of which were significantly higher for prisoners.

Convergent and Predictive Validity of VSS Subscales with Criterion Measures

Validity coefficients assessing the magnitude of relationships among the VSS subscales and criterion measures for the entire sample are presented in Table 5. All but one of the 42 coefficients were significant, with 36 at $p < 0.001$. Coefficients for the individual prisoner and student samples are not shown, but showed outcomes similar to those reported in Table 5. For prisoners, Violent Coaching was most strongly correlated with both physical aggressiveness and hostility; Virulency correlated most strongly with physical aggressiveness as

Table 4.   Correlations among VSS Subscales for the Entire Sample
(*N* = 168).

SUBSCALE	PH	VC	BL	VP	VR
Violent Subjugation (VS)	0.68***	0.65***	0.30***	0.31***	0.30***
Personal Horrification (PH)		0.60***	0.35***	0.30***	0.17*
Violent Coaching (VC)			0.27***	0.43***	0.34***
Belligerency (B)				0.09	0.16*
Violent Performances (VP)					0.26***

Note: VS = Violent Subjugation; PH = Personal Horrification; VC = Violent Coaching; BL = Belligerency; VP = Violent Performances; VR = Virulency. *p < 0.05. **p < 0.01. ***p < 0.001.

Table 5.   Convergent Validity Coefficients Between VSS Subscales and
External Criteria for the Entire Sample (*N* = 168).

SCALE	AQ PHY	AQ VER	AQ AGR	AQ HOS	AQ TOT	IES INTR	IES AVD
Violent Subjugation	0.52***	0.30***	0.44***	0.48***	0.53***	0.52***	0.48***
Personal Horrification	0.49***	0.28***	0.46***	0.53***	0.53***	0.49***	0.53***
Violent Coaching	0.68***	0.45***	0.53***	0.59***	0.68***	0.48***	0.40***
Belligerency	0.25**	0.15	0.37***	0.45***	0.37***	0.32***	0.26***
Violent Performances	0.40***	0.32***	0.22**	0.22**	0.35***	0.28***	0.17*
Virulency	0.53***	0.33***	0.43***	0.29***	0.48***	0.34***	0.18*

Note: AQPHY = Aggression Questionnaire (AQ), Physical; AQVER = AQ, Verbal, AQAGR = AQ, Anger; AQHOS = AQ, Hostility; AQTOT = AQ, Total; IESINTR = Impact of Events (IES), Intrusive; IESAVD = IES, Avoidance. * *p* < 0.05. ** *p* < 0.01. ***p < 0.001.

well. For students, Violent Coaching was most strongly correlated with physical aggressiveness as well as the other criteria associated with violence.

A more sophisticated multivariate analytic predictive strategy involved regressing each of the VSS subscales onto each criterion variable, in hierarchical fashion. Table 6 summarizes only the significant outcomes of these analyses for the entire sample. Violent Coaching was a significant predictor for all four Buss-Perry aggression subscales. Violent Coaching, however, was not a reliable predictor for either of the trauma subscales.

Violent Subjugation was the strongest predictor of the Intrusive Imagery associated with traumatic stress, accounting for 27% of the variance. Personal Horrification accounted for an additional 3% of the variance; another 6% of the variance was accounted for by Virulency. In the final model, 36% of the

Table 6. Hierarchical Regression Analyses Predicting External Validity Criteria From VSS Subscales For The Combined Sample ($N = 168$).

Dependent variable	R^2	ΔR^2	Predicted by	β	t-value
Physical Aggression	0.27	0.26	Violent Coaching	0.48	5.98***
	0.59	0.57	Virulency	0.35	6.02***
Verbal Aggression	0.20	0.19	Violent Coaching	0.36	3.42***
	0.26	0.23	Virulency	0.19	2.47*
Anger	0.30	0.29	Violent Coaching	0.28	2.95**
	0.34	0.32	Belligerency	0.16	2.37*
	0.41	0.38	Virulency	0.29	4.22***
Hostility	0.30	0.29	Personal Horrification	0.19	2.03*
	0.39	0.37	Violent Coaching	0.39	4.25***
	0.44	0.43	Belligerency	0.25	3.78***
IES-Intrusive	0.27	0.26	Violent Subjugation	0.21	2.03*
	0.30	0.29	Personal Horrification	0.20	2.01*
	0.36	0.33	Virulency	0.20	2.75**
IES-Avoidance	0.30	0.29	Personal Horrification	0.39	3.68***

Note: IES = Impact of Events Scale. $*p < 0.05$. $**p < 0.01$. $***p < 0.001$.

variance of Intrusive Imagery was accounted for by the three predictors. Personal Horrification only predicted 30% of the variance of Traumatic Avoidance.

Mediation of Outcomes by Violent Coaching

In combination, these analyses suggest that violent domination generates traumatic symptomatology. Such domination, by itself, however, does not necessarily translate into aggressiveness or Violent Performances. Our previous analyses implied that Violent Coaching is a critical factor in creating violent resolutions to conflict in later life.

We employed a series of mediational regression analyses to assess the extent to which Violent Coaching mediated the relationship between violent domination and multiple indices of aggressive or traumatic outcomes. Baron and Kenny (1986) suggest testing for mediating variables through using ordinary least-squares multiple regression. Mediation is established through demonstrating that: (1) the predictor variable is correlated with the outcome variable; (2) the predictor variable is correlated with the presumed mediating variable; (3)

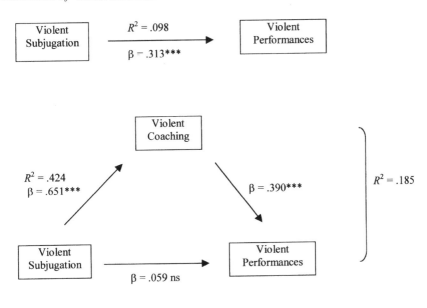

Note: *p < .05. **p < .01. ***p < .001.

Fig. 1.   Mediational analysis showing full mediation of relationship between violent
subjugation and violent performances by violent coaching.

the mediator variable accounts for more variance than the predictor variable;
and (4) the effects of the predictor variable do not remain significant after
controlling for the effects of the mediating variable.

Figure 1 presents the results of this analysis method with Violent
Performances as the outcome variable and Violent Subjugation as the predictor
variable. This figure can also be used to help interpret Table 7, which
summarizes the mediating effects of Violent Coaching on existing relationships
between Violent Subjugation and multiple outcome indices of violence and
trauma. Simple regression of Violent Subjugation onto Violent Performances
indicated the existence of a significant relationship ($\beta = 0.313, p < 0.001$) which
accounted for 10% of the variance. When Violent Coaching was entered into
the regression, however, the paths between Violent Subjugation and Violent
Coaching and also between Violent Coaching and Violent Performances became
significant. The formerly reliable path between Violent Subjugation and Violent
Performances became nonsignificant and the overall variance accounted for in
the model almost doubled to 19%.

Table 7. Mediating Effects of Violent Coaching on Relationships Between Violent Subjugation and Multiple Outcomes of Aggression and Trauma.

Predictor variable	Outcome variable	R^2/β	Mediating variable	β
Violent Subjugation	Violent Performances	0.098/0.313***		
	Violent Coaching	0.424/0.651***		
	Violent Performances	0.185/0.059 ns	Violent Coaching	0.399***
Violent Subjugation	Aggression Physical	0.27/0.517***		
	Violent Coaching	0.424/0.651***		
	Aggression Physical	0.473/0.092 ns	Violent Coaching	0.621***
Violent Subjugation	Aggression Verbal	0.089/0.298***		
	Violent Coaching	0.424/0.651***		
	Aggression Verbal	0.202/0.017 ns	Violent Coaching	0.461***
Violent Subjugation	Aggression Anger	0.196/0.443***		
	Violent Coaching	0.424/0.651***		
	Aggression Anger	0.289/0.158 ns	Violent Coaching	0.417***
Violent Subjugation	Aggression Hostility	0.235/0.484***		
	Violent Coaching	0.424/0.651***		
	Aggression Hostility	0.363/0.150 ns	Violent Coaching	0.490***
Violent Subjugation	Trauma Avoidance	0.228/0.478***		
	Violent Coaching	0.424/0.651***		
	Trauma Avoidance	0.237/0.390***	Violent Coaching	0.127 ns
Violent Subjugation	Trauma Intrusive	0.266/0.516***		
	Violent Coaching	0.424/0.651***		
	Trauma Intrusive	0.294/0.357***	Violent Coaching	0.231*

Note: *$p < 0.05$. **$p < 0.01$. ***$p < 0.001$.

This identical pattern was found using Violent Subjugation and all four Buss-Perry indices of aggression (see Table 7). In every case, the addition of Violent Coaching rendered nonsignificant the direct path between the domination and aggressive outcome, led to significant pathways through Violent Coaching. Thus, Violent Coaching mediated fully relationships between subjugation and aggressive or violent outcomes.

Violent Coaching, however, did not mediate prior significant relationships between Violent Subjugation and indices of traumatic avoidance or intrusive imagery. Figure 2 presents the path model between Violent Subjugation and Traumatic Avoidance. In this model, Violent Subjugation was predictive of Violent Coaching but Violent Coaching did not predict reliably Traumatic Avoidance. The addition of Violent Coaching also had negligible influence on raising the amount of variance accounted for by the overall model. An identical outcome was found when using Intrusive Imagery as the outcome variable

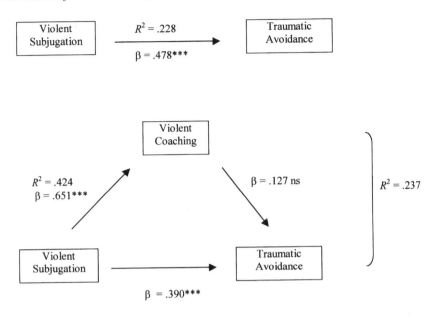

Note: $*p < .05.$ $**p < .01.$ $***p < .001.$

Fig. 2. Mediational analysis showing that violent coaching does not mediate the relationship between violent subjugation and traumatic avoidance.

(Table 7). In combination, these results suggest that the experience of violence by itself will trigger traumatic outcomes. The presence of Violent Coaching, however, seems to be instrumental in moving victims of violence toward themselves becoming perpetrators of violence.

DISCUSSION

The outcomes of this investigation indicated that Athens' (1992) model of violent socialization can be measured quantitatively in a reliable manner. In addition, standardized processes of test construction and validation yielded concurrent support of the underlying theory. Initial content validity was established through the emergence of six internally consistent factors that corresponded with the six major constructs of Athens' theory. The subscales measuring these constructs manifested acceptable internal consistency in the combined sample as well as in individual samples of college men and male prisoners.

Athens' "violentization" model delineates a more detailed understanding of the presumed socialization processes than some of its closest predecessors, although it does share similarities to Mosher and Tomkins' (1988) "macho personality scripts." Mosher theorized that the development of hypermasculine or "macho" personality style is influenced heavily by parental use of contempt and humiliation. Mosher also articulated the role of violent coaching, although not in the same graphic detail as did Athens. Mosher described characteristics of the macho personality as involving three elements, "danger is exciting," "violence as manly," and "callused sexual attitudes toward women," and developed a psychometrically valid instrument to assess this constellation. Athens' model fleshes out these childhood exposure components from the later stages of attempting violent actions and the subsequent internalization of those chosen behaviors.

VSS interscale correlations found Violent Subjugation, Personal Horrification and Violent Coaching to be highly interrelated. According to Athens' model, these three components are the necessary experiences of the first developmental phase of violent socialization, namely Brutalization. This strong relationship was found for the combined and individual populations, although the correlations were slightly larger for the prisoner sample than the student sample.

Mediational analyses also supported Athens' (1992) contention that Violent Coaching is a central socialization component in teaching people to be characteristically vicious. Violent Coaching was found to fully mediate relationships between Violent Subjugation and other forms of aggressive acting out and hostility. These findings, in particular, suggest that Violent Coaching could be the missing component for researchers puzzled about the inconsistent outcomes of childhood maltreatment (i.e. Gorman-Smith, Tolan, Loeber & Henry, 1998; Lewis, Shanock, Pincus & Glaser, 1979; Weeks & Widom, 1998; Widom, 1998). Athens' model makes it clear that children forced to endure Violent Subjugation and Personal Horrification do not necessarily turn to violent behavior. The addition of Violent Coaching, however, appears to set the stage for the potential development of later physical aggressiveness.

From a pragmatic perspective, our findings suggest that treatment interventions may focus most usefully on either preventing coercive child rearing practices or providing prosocial alternatives to violent coaching. Preventing the brutalization of children continues to be a daunting task, but cross-generational cycles of violence may also be reduced by providing non-violent models to young people who have been treated violently. Non-violent coaching is a central component in many emerging school-based programs, including conflict resolution and peer mediation interventions (Loeber & Farrington, 1998; Orpinas, Kelder, Frankowski, Murray, Zhang & McAlister, 2000). Loeber and

Farrington's study of violent juvenile offenders indicated that early intervention is crucial. These investigators also found that the most effective interventions include a number of approaches, such as: school-wide monitoring and reinforcement of prosocial behavior as well as use of prosocial models from the wider community. Additional outcome studies that supported martial arts training (Smith, Twemlow & Hoover, 1999) and interactive art and drama participation (Long & Soble, 1999) all require the active involvement of pro-social non-violent models.

Our results indicated that prisoners reported higher levels of PTSD than did students. For both samples and the combined group, Violent Subjugation and Personal Horrification correlated strongly and in a positive direction with both intrusive and avoidant traumatic distress. Violent Coaching, however, did not mediate fully these relationships. Very little research on traumatic stress has focused on how anger, aggression, and hostility are specifically associated with trauma responses. Beckham and Moore (2000) suggested that anger may be a central feature of PTSD responses. They argued that anger is a key survival response in traumatic situations. Collins and Bailey (1990) investigated presumed causal links between PTSD symptoms and violent occurrences. They found support for the hypothesis that PTSD symptoms precede violent action. These findings, in combination with our results, suggest that violence may be a function of either a fearful/defensive reaction or a calculated attempt to coerce or control others. Although it is premature to create a typology of violence, these two dynamics would have very different implications for how to best intervene to reduce violence.

Limitations of the Current Investigation and Directions for Future Research

The study has two important limitations. First, the sample sizes was relatively small, especially the prisoner sample. It would be of interest to assess two larger samples involving general-population incarcerated men and serially violent incarcerated men, that is, prisoners who manifest longstanding patterns of violent crime.

A second but related limitation is that the incarcerated men were chosen from a pool of men who had contacted the mental health unit to enroll in an anger management program. This selection criterion may have biased the sample against having a larger percentage of men who met Athens' criterion for being virulent. This limitation, however, is balanced by the fact that men with the most extensive criminal records (Simon, 1999) typically offer the least reliable self-reports.

In Table 1, we presented the VSS items in their entirety so that the VSS can be used by other investigators who study the development and perpetuation of violence.[3] More work needs to be done on scale validation, for example, determining the congruence between self-report and evaluations by informants who know the respondents well. Even though the VSS was conceptualized as a trait measure, it might prove useful as an indicator of change following preventive interventions. Athens' original research included interviews with women; future research on the VSS should include a sample of women. It also could be of value to assess a sample of people who no longer utilize violence as a means of dispute resolution. Understanding the transformative changes (Miller & C'de Baca, 2001) that such individuals undergo would provide more information about creating a society that is freer of fear and violence.

NOTES

1. This research was part of a master's thesis by the first author, under the tutelage of the remaining three authors.
2. We have deliberately chosen to use male pronouns in describing the dynamics of Athens' model because it was developed from interviews conducted with men.
3. Copies of the VSS may be obtained from either Ginger Rhodes or George Allen at no charge and may be used for research or clinical purposes. We ask that researchers make available to us any findings that pertain to scale validity and/or utility.

REFERENCES

Athens, L. H. (1992). *The Creation of Dangerous Violent Criminals*. Urbana, IL: University of Illinois Press.

Bandura, A., & Walters, R. H. (1959). *Adolescent Aggression*. New York: Ronald.

Baron, R. M., & Kenny, D. A. (1986). The moderator-mediator variable distinction in social psychological research. *Journal of Personality and Social Psychology, 51*, 1173–1182.

Beckham, J. C., & Moore, S. D. (2000). Interpersonal hostility and violence in Vietnam combat veterans with chronic posttraumatic stress disorder. *Aggression and Violent Behavior, 5*, 451–466.

Buss, A. H., & Perry, M. (1992). The aggression questionnaire. *Journal of Personality and Social Psychology, 6*, 452–459.

Collins, J. J., & Bailey, S. L. (1990). Traumatic stress disorder and violent behavior. *Journal of Traumatic Stress, 3*, 203–220.

Dollard, J., Doob, L. W., Miller, N. E., Mowrer, O. H., Sears, R. R., Ford, C. S., Hovland, C. I., & Sollenberger, R. T. (1939). *Frustration and Aggression*. New Haven: Yale University Press.

Gorman-Smith, D., Tolan, P. H., Loeber, R., & Henry, D. B. (1998). Relation of family problems to patterns of delinquent involvement among urban youth. *Journal of Abnormal Child Psychology, 26*, 319–333.

Heilbrun, A. B., Heilbrun, L. C., & Heilbrun, K. L. (1978). Impulsive and premeditated homicide: An analysis of subsequent parole risk of the murderer. *Journal of Criminal Law & Criminology, 69*, 108–114.

Horowitz, M. D., Wilner, N., & Alvarez, W. (1979). Impact of events scale: A measure of subjective stress. *Psychosomatic Medicine, 41,* 209–218.

Lewis, D. O., Shanock, S. S., Pincus, J. H., & Glaser, G. H. (1979). Violent juvenile delinquents. *Journal of the American Academy of Child Psychiatry, 2,* 307–319.

Loeber, R., & Farrington, D. P. (1998). Never too early, never too late: Risk factors and successful interventions for serious and violent juvenile offenders. *Studies on Crime and Crime Prevention, 7,* 7–30.

Long, J. K., & Soble, L. (1999). Report: An art-based violence prevention project for sixth grade students. *Arts in Psychotherapy, 26,* 329–344.

Miller, W. R., & C'de Baca, J. (2001). *Quantum change: When Epiphanies and Sudden Insights Transform Ordinary Lives.* New York: The Guilford Press.

Mosher, D. L., & Tomkins, S. S. (1988). Scripting the macho man: Hypermasculine socialization and enculturation. *The Journal of Sex Research, 25,* 60–84.

Orpinas, P., Kelder, S., Frankowski, R., Murray, N., Zhang, Q., & McAlister, A. (2000). Outcome evaluation of a multi-component violence-prevention program for middle schools: The students for peace project. *Health Education Research, 15,* 45–58.

Simon, L. M. J. (1999). Are the worst offenders the least reliable? *Studies on Crime and Crime Prevention, 8,* 210–224.

Smith, J., Twemlow, S. W., & Hoover, D. W. (1999). Bullies, victims and bystanders: A method of in-school intervention and possible parental contributions. *Child Psychiatry & Human Development, 30,* 29–37.

Tabachnick, B. G., & Fidell, L. S. (2001). *Using Multivariate Statistics* (4th ed.). New York, NY: HarperCollins.

Weeks, R., & Widom, C. S. (1998). Self-reports of early childhood victimization among incarcerated adult male felons. *Journal of Interpersonal Violence, 13,* 346–361.

Widom, C. S. (1998). Child victims. *Applied & Preventative Psychology, 7,* 225–234.

Witkin, H. A. (1977). Criminality, aggression and intelligence among XYY and XXY men. In: S. A. Mednick & K. O. Christiansen (Eds), *Biosocial Bases of Criminal Behavior* (pp. 165–188). New York: Gardner Press, Inc.

FROM VIOLENT JUVENILE OFFENDERS TO DANGEROUS VIOLENT CRIMINALS: A TEST OF ATHENS' THEORY

G. Roger Jarjoura and Ruth Triplett

ABSTRACT

Though research has established a number of factors that predict youths at-risk for violent offending, the ability of these factors to distinguish serious dangerous offenders who will continue to offend is limited. Athens' (1989, 1997) theory of violentization attempts to explain dangerous violent offending and provides a means for identifying the most violent offenders. Using 18-year-old youths from a high-security juvenile facility, we explore the ability of Athens' theory to this end. Results of the analysis provide support for the theory, but also raise some questions that do not appear to be answered by the theory.

INTRODUCTION

One need not look very far to find evidence that juveniles are capable of serious forms of violent behavior. The media is only too willing to supply us with continuous messages that support this conclusion. The highly publicized school shootings in the 1990s emphasized to the public the violence that youths can

Violent Acts and Violentization: Assessing, Applying, and Developing Lonnie Athens' Theories, Volume 4, pages 147–173.
© 2003 Published by Elsevier Science Ltd.
ISBN: 0-7623-0905-9

commit. Research, though, helps put the issue of juvenile violence into its proper perspective. As Howell (1997) notes, fewer than one-half of 1% of all U.S. juveniles (between the ages of 10 and 17) are arrested for a violent offense in a given calendar year. Despite this, in 1999, juveniles did account for 16% of all arrests for the Violent Index Crimes (Snyder, 2000). Yet, as Howell (1997) observes, many of these arrests were for relatively minor acts (i.e. the degree of injury was negligible). In fact, Elliott and Tolan (1999) find that only 5–8% of the juvenile offenders engaging in violence actually perpetrate serious forms of predatory violence on others. Further, despite claims of an epidemic of youth violence in the early 1990s, Cook and Laub (1998) show that the proportion of violent arrests involving a juvenile was at the same level it was in 1965.

Despite the research, juvenile justice policies are largely driven by the perception of an epidemic of juvenile violence (Elliott & Tolan, 1999). In the rush to respond to public demands that something be done about violence among juveniles, these policies tend to focus on control, rather than prevention, and make little effort to distinguish between types of violent offenders. There is evidence that we can prevent involvement in violent offending among juveniles (Elliott & Tolan, 1999). The difficulty in prevention, though, is in predicting which juveniles will be violent offenders and, in particular, which will fall into the 5–8% who commit serious violent offenses. Predictors of juvenile violent offending (see for example, Brewer et al., 1995) are not effective at distinguishing between juveniles who commit violent offenses and the more dangerous violent criminals.

The central question of the current study is: how can we effectively identify those juvenile offenders that will commit the most serious violent offenses? One theory designed to answer this question is Athens' (1989) theory of violentization. In this paper, we briefly describe Athens' theory of the creation of dangerous violent criminals and provide an exploratory analysis of the theory using a sample a high-risk juvenile offenders serving time at a state-run juvenile correctional facility. The paper concludes with a discussion of the findings and implications for juvenile justice policy.

RISK FACTORS FOR JUVENILE VIOLENCE

There is now a large literature on the predictors of violent juvenile offending. In their review of the research on risk factors for violent offending, Brewer et al. (1995; see also Hawkins et al., 1995; Howell, 1997; Howell & Hawkins, 1998) consider four classes of predictors – community, family, school and individual factors. Research has shown there are a wide variety of community-level factors that increase the likelihood of juvenile violence. Economic deprivation in the community, as characterized by substandard living conditions and extreme levels of poverty and unemployment, is one risk factor. Violence is also more likely in disorganized neighborhoods and in those neighborhoods where there are high rates of residential mobility. Increased access to firearms and exposure to media portrayals of violence at the community-level are also associated with higher levels of violent delinquency (see, also, Allen et al., 1999; Fagan & Wilkinson, 1998).

Research has also identified factors at both the family and school levels that are predictive of violent juvenile offending. Brewer et al. (1995) point to several family-related risk factors. These include poor discipline and supervision by parents, family conflict, and parental attitudes that support the use of violence (see also Gorman-Smith & Avery, 1999). Two factors are most notable among the school-related factors: antisocial behavior that is persistent in the early school years and poor school performance.

Finally, Brewer et al. (1995) identify several individual-level risk factors. For instance, early onset of delinquent activity and association with delinquent peers are both related to participation in violent delinquency. Elliott (1994) emphasizes the important role of the peer group in the onset of serious violent offending. In particular, he points to peer normlessless and peer sanctions, which affect the exposure of the youth to delinquent peers, as being critical to the involvement of the youth in serious forms of violence. Use of alcohol to the point of intoxication is another risk factor for juvenile violence (Brewer et al., 1995). Violence is also more likely for youths that suffer some form of brain damage or that experienced complications during the prenatal stage. Personality characteristics, such as delinquent attitudes, rebelliousness, a propensity towards sensation seeking, and low impulse control, are all risk factors for involvement in violent forms of delinquency. Finally, Farrington (1998) also points to attention deficit as a predictor of violence in juveniles.

Despite the amount of empirical support regarding the validity of these predictors, there are two important facts they do not help us reconcile. First, given that only 5–8% of juveniles engaging in violent crime actually commit serious forms of violence (Elliott & Tolan, 1999), some researchers argue that not all violent offenders are equally violent. Athens (1989) is a strong proponent of this argument. He argues that there exists a class of "dangerous violent criminals" that are distinct from other violent offenders. According to Athens, what distinguishes the dangerous violent offender is the commission of violent crimes with minimal or no provocation. Second, research has also found there is both continuity and change in aggressive behavior over the life course (Huesmann & Moise, 1999). Children rated low in terms of aggression are most likely to continue to exhibit low levels of aggression as adults. A similar pattern is found for those children rated as medium in levels of displayed aggression. The continuity of aggressive tendencies is less evident, though, for those children exhibiting high levels of aggressive behavior. In fact, as Huesmann and Moise (1999) point out, most highly aggressive children do not grow into highly aggressive adults.

What factors can help identify dangerous violent criminals that will likely continue in their violent offending? Several scholars (Athens, 1989; Huesmann & Moise, 1999; Moore & Tonry, 1998) suggest that to understand how one becomes a dangerous violent criminal, we must look beyond the factors traditionally considered and, instead, examine social experiences.[1] Athens (1989, 1997) provides a potentially useful strategy.

ATHENS' THEORY OF VIOLENTIZATION

In his book *The Creation of Dangerous Violent Criminals*, Athens (1989) lays out a theory of violentization that takes us beyond traditional predictors of violent offending to the social experiences of the youth. Athens uses a strong symbolic interactionist background to formulate a theory that centers on individuals' social experiences. Rather than seeing a person as merely a biological, psychological or sociological being, Athens seeks to develop a theory that "integrates, rather than segregates, the factors playing upon them from inside and outside the skins of their bodies" (1989, p. 80).

The theory describes four stages of violentization, all of which must occur before a person becomes a dangerous violent criminal. The first stage in this theory is Brutalization. This stage is actually a composite of three distinct elements: violent subjugation, personal horrification, and violent coaching. These three elements represent different aspects of "cruel treatment at the hands of others that produces a lasting and dramatic impact on the subsequent course of their lives" (p. 27). To understand why brutalization has the impact that it does, Athens differentiates between primary and secondary groups. He defines primary groups as "a group characterized by regular, face-to-face interaction and intimate familiarity between its members, such as a family, gang, or clique, whereas a secondary group can be characterized by the absence of the quality of intimacy" (p. 28). Violent subjugation and personal horrification result from experiences in the primary group. Violent coaching can come from secondary as well as primary groups.

In violent subjugation, the first element of Brutalization, an authority figure (either bona fide, such as parent to child, or would-be, such as step-parent to stepchild or husband to wife) from the subject's primary group uses violence to force the subject to submit to their demands. There are two avenues for the use of violent subjugation: coercion and retaliation. With coercion, "authority figures employ violence or the threat of violence to force the subject to comply with some command (including to show respect) which the subject displays some reluctance to obey or refuses to obey outright" (p. 29). With retaliation, "authority figures use violence to punish subjects for past disobedience to them or for a present display of disrespect towards them" (p. 31). Coercive subjugation has the goal of achieving immediate, short-term compliance and is usually carried out until the subject offers to comply. On the other hand, retaliatory subjugation has the goal of future and long-term compliance and so, is carried out until the authority figure has had enough.

The next element of Brutalization, personal horrification, occurs when the subject hears or sees the violent subjugation of another person within the subject's primary group (e.g. a mother, a sibling). While this is a particularly painful experience for subjects, it is made more so by the tendency for them to blame themselves for not being able to protect the victim. The subject is likely to conclude "that it was his impotence rather than the subjugator's wickedness which was principally responsible for the episode of violent subjugation which he only a few minutes ago stood by and witnessed" (p. 41).

The final element of Brutalization is violent coaching (Athens, 1989). In violent coaching, the subject receives messages about how to behave in situations of conflict. The coach is typically a member of the subject's primary group but may also come from the secondary group. The message delivered during violent coaching, according to Athens, is, typically, that the subject should never back down or walk away from a conflict. In contrast, the subject is encouraged to use violence and to use enough violence to make sure he or she will win the conflict. The subject is not taught skills – how to attack or how to fight – they are simply encouraged to be prepared to do what it takes to triumph.

Typically Brutalization has been completed by the early years of adolescence. By the end of this stage, the subject is in a state of confusion and turmoil, and is ready for the next stage of violentization – Belligerency. During this stage, Athens (1989) argues that the subject is reflecting on human nature. The subject is wondering how people can be so cruel as to treat him or her in the way he or she was treated. The subject realizes that reality is very different from the way in which personal relationships are characterized in books, movies and television. The subject is motivated to figure out a way to prevent being brutalized in the future. The solution that is identified tends to involve using violence to ward off the potential for future brutalization experiences. At the conclusion of the Belligerency stage, Athens predicts the subject will resolve to use whatever force is necessary to protect him or herself.

Having resolved to resort to violence to solve problems, the subject is prepared for the third stage in the process, that of Violent Performances (Athens, 1989). With the right conditions in place, the subject acts in a violent way. According to Athens (1989), an important part of violent performances is the outcome, since there can be a conditioning effect on the subject. He predicts that winning the conflict makes it more likely the person will resort to violence again in the future. If, on the other hand, the subject experiences defeat, especially if it occurs on a repeated basis, Athens predicts he or she may move out of the trajectory of becoming a serious violent criminal.

A successful violent performance is followed by a social reaction. This sets the stage for the fourth phase in this process – Virulency (Athens, 1989). Here, persons close to the subject will react to the violent performance of the subject. It will become clear to the subject that the perception that others have of him or her is now different. In fact, some people may now express a feeling of unease due to the violent potential of the subject. Realizing that others are now wary of him or her, the subject is likely to feel a sense of importance. The subject may now resolve to resort to violence against others in future situations. As Athens notes, "the subject is ready to attack people physically with the serious intention of gravely harming or killing them with minimal or less than minimal provocation on their part" (p. 79). The subject has become a dangerous violent criminal.

If this theory is correct, then we should be able to draw from it to distinguish between violent youthful offenders and those who Athens classifies as dangerous violent offenders. A fair test of the ability of the theory to do this should come from using a sample of 18-year-old youths serving time at a state juvenile correctional facility of the highest-security level. By age 18, a youth would have passed through most, if not all, of the stages of Athens' theory if he or she is going to (Athens, 1989). A high-security facility is where the most violent juvenile offenders would be sent. Even given the relative rarity of the dangerous violent offender, we should be able to capture some of them in a representative sample from such a facility.

THE CURRENT STUDY

Beginning in the fall of 1999, the first author conducted a series of life-history interviews with male juvenile offenders. The youths interviewed consisted of all of the 18-year-old males in custody at the highest security-level facility in a Midwestern state during the month of November 1999. This gives us a good cross-section of the variety of offenders in the state system, but does not consider those youths waived to adult court (perhaps the most serious juveniles of all).

Twenty-five youths participated in the life-history interviews.[2] For each interview, the researcher and the youth met on a series of occasions until the life history was complete. Completed interviews lasted between three hours (the shortest interview) and twelve hours (the longest interview).

The interviews themselves focused on the entire life span of the youth, from birth through age 18. The life of the youth was split into periods: from birth to pre-kindergarten, from kindergarten through the end of elementary school, middle school, and high school. During each phase, the youths were invited to talk about their family, school, neighborhood, and peer experiences. Special attention was paid to events that held significant meaning for the youths and to the quality and nature of relationships with family, peers, and teachers. In addition, significant attention was paid to the involvement of the youth in juvenile delinquency and the juvenile justice system. Questions were also posed regarding experiences with gangs, guns, drugs, and sexual activity. Finally, the youths were invited to share their aspirations for the future.

At the completion of the study, transcripts of the interviews were prepared. These transcripts serve as the raw data for the analysis reported here. At the time we began this analysis, 18 transcripts were ready for consideration. As such, the sample size for this analysis is 18. For each transcript, each author conducted an independent assessment, coding for evidence of the four stages of Athens' theory. The two independent ratings were compared, allowing for an assessment of the inter-rater reliability of the coding scheme.

The life-history interviews were part of a project whose purpose was primarily focused on assessing the rationality of juvenile justice policies. During the interviews, though, it became evident that the vast majority of the sample had experienced some form of severe victimization as a young child, and for the most part, had never been afforded an opportunity to work through the personal issues that arose from those experiences. Rhodes (1999) introduced us to the work of Lonnie Athens. His theory seemed particularly relevant for understanding the role that violence had played in the lives of these subjects. After studying Athens' theory of violentization, we felt that we could provide a fairly reasonable test of the theory with the data from the life-history project.

We went through the life histories looking for evidence of each of the stages of brutalization, belligerency, violent performances, and virulency. From the narratives, we looked for reports of incidents meeting the criteria for each of these stages, as described by Athens (1989). For each of the subjects in this analysis, then, we should be able to predict whether they fall into the category "dangerous violent criminal". If the subject has been through all four stages of Athens' theory, then we would predict that this person would be a serious violent criminal. If, on the other hand, the subject has not experienced all four of the stages, then we would predict this person would not be a serious violent criminal.

For the stage of Brutalization we scanned the narratives for examples of incidents of violent subjugation, personal horrification, and violent coaching each categorization following Athens' description. Violent subjugation involves physical violence performed against the subject by an authority figure from his primary group. From the description in the narrative, we are able to determine if the incident is an example of coercive or retaliatory subjugation. In most cases, the subject gave an explanation for how the violent incident began. For instance, Subject 7 reported the following incident:

> I was sitting there talking to my friend [on the phone] and [my stepfather] had started talking shit to me and I was like, I was like, "O.K., yeah alright." You know, just kind of talking shit to him and everything and I was like, "W___ I'm going to let you go." So I got off the phone, and he was like, he looks up at me and he was like, "Man you know what me and people that I work with call people like you?" I looked at him, I was like "Yeah." I said, "Do you know what people like me and my buddies call people like you?" And he was like, "What?" And I said, "Assholes!" And man, he just went off on. He ran up to me and stuff and he started yelling at me and stuff. And I was like, I was "Yeah, alright, whatever man, get out of here," you know. He followed me all the way up the stairs and he grabbed ahold of me and started throwing me and shit and everything. And then I made it up the stairs you know and I was like, "Man, get the hell away from me, man." I was like, "Please!" Now I was like, "Man if you really care about me just leave me the fuck alone." And he was like, "No you're not gonna talk to me like that in front of my kids," and everything. Ran at me and throwing me around and hitting me with stuff and he took – I had a drum seat, like a seat that went to drums you know. And you know how it has those pads on the ends? Well the pads were off of it and it was just metal that came down he took that and was hitting me with that and scratched me all up and everything. And then I threw him off of me and stuff, man. And he took me and threw me across the room and so I took off. I run out of my room and I go downstairs. And my little brothers and sisters, I remember, was staring at the top of the stairs and they was down at the bottom of the stairs crying and telling him to get off of me. They was like, "Leave him alone daddy, leave him alone!" and everything and he just wouldn't stop, he wouldn't listen to them. So I made it through to the garage because the garage was connected to the house and I was gonna go out the garage, open the garage door and cut out. And I started going out there and I had on some necklaces and stuff and he ran out there after me and he turned me around and he grabbed me by my shirt and he tried throwing me by my shirt and he ripped my shirt all the way down to like right here. And he broke my chains and everything and he just dropped them and I looked at him and I was like "O.K." I was like, "Thanks, so now you are going to buy me some new chains, right." I picked them up and he was like, "I don't give a fuck about them chains," and all this and yelling and I can't say exactly what he said cause I can't really remember. And so, then he was like, "Get your ass in the house," and he threw me inside and everything. And I was like . . . So I took the chains and I just threw them on the table and I was going to walk upstairs and he kept yelling at me all the way up the stairs, throwing me some more. And I got up in my room and stuff, man he picked me up and slammed me on the ground and everything. And I was like,

"Please man," I was like, "man if you really love me like you say you do, man just leave me the hell alone, please!" I was begging him, I was like "Man, just leave me alone." I was like, "Man I will sit here all day and night, I don't care, just leave me alone." And he had gotten up and everything and said his last words and he started walking out and my door was still open. I went over and I grabbed my phone. I got on it and I was kind of crying and shit and I called my friend's house and he was sitting right there so I didn't want to say nothing so I was sitting there and I was like kind of talking to him and he was just standing there and he was like, my friend was, he was like, "Well, hey man, I'm going to get up off of here." And I was like, "No man, don't hang up, just hold on." And he was like, "Why?" And I said, "No, just don't," you know, and he was sitting there. And he was like, "Why?" And I was like, "Because, man, he's beating on me." And he was like, "What?" And the next thing I know, BAM! I got smacked in the head with something. I think it was like a little G. I. Joe or something like that. And I was like, "See man!" And he started yelling, "How the fuck you going to say I'm beating you?" and all this. And he came over and ripped the phone out of the wall and everything, and threw it across the room and broke it and everything. He starts yelling at me and throws me around a little bit more and stuff, man. And probably about ten minutes later, my buddy's mom came over. She just walks up the steps, you know, and I see her and she's like, she's like, "C___ just calm down. Just let me take him out here and talk." And he's like, "No he ain't going nowhere, Goddamn it!" and all this. She's like, "I'm not taking him nowhere. We are just going to go out front and talk. And she's like, "Come on N_____," and came in there and got me. And I went downstairs and we went out front and everything. And she was like, "What happened?" and all this, and I told her the whole story. And so we went out and sat in her car, you know, and she gave me a cigarette. And I was like, she was like, well she was like, "The cops are on their way. I already called them." And I was like, "Yeah!" That was like the only thing that made me feel good at the time. I was like, "Good." We was sitting there talking and she was like, "Man, he's gone out of control." And I was like, "Shit I know," you know. My shirt was all ripped up and everything and I was like, "Man, he done broke my chains and everything." She's like, "O.K." And I was showing her all the scratches and everything and then the cops came and I told them what happened and everything. And they was like, "O.K., well he says he didn't do all that," and they was like, "Do you want him to go to jail?" And I was like, "Hell yeah!" I didn't say "hell yeah," but they was like, "Do you think you could take care of your little brothers and sisters until your mom comes home?" And I was like, "yeah, I can do that." They was all like, "Well, just stay in the house and stay calm, he's not going to be there." So they took him to jail.

Next, we scanned the narratives for examples of personal horrification. Here, we were looking for examples of violence performed against a member of the subject's primary group, such as a parent or sibling, in which the subject blamed himself for not protecting the victim. In most cases, the subject described the context of the incident and his reaction to the violent incident. There is generally enough information to classify the incident as personal horrification or not. Here is an example, as described by subject 19:

One of the clear pictures I get is seeing my mother being held up against the wall. He's got his legs held up against her stomach and the wall when she was pregnant. I walked in the door and seen it. That was a scary picture. From then on, I vowed not to let her get abused. I would get myself abused. If I ever seen anybody hit my mother I would throw a fit or if I seen him being mean to my mother I would start in yelling and I would take the pain for her.

We then scanned the narratives for examples of violent coaching. Here we were looking for references by the subject to messages he received from members of his primary group or secondary group about the necessity of using violence against others. It was important that there be some indication of the subject's reaction to these messages. This would allow us to consider whether this was received as coaching. It should be noted that since the life-history interviews were not structured to provide a test of Athens' theory, this is one aspect of the theory that we found difficult to capture in the narratives. Subject 5 gives one of the best examples.

I met this kid that got me into a lot of trouble . . . I ain't never get into a fight all the way until I was in fifth grade. Then people started pickin' on me and stuff. I was real little when I was younger, and they'd be like, he came up to me one day and said "Why do you let people mess with you like that?" He started fillin' my head full of dumb stuff and I just got fed up with it and started fightin' back. He was sayin', "Man, you should beat them dudes up," "Don't let 'em pick on you like that or else they'll keep pickin' on ya." And like, "you're a cool dude," and stuff like that, and "you shouldn't, you know what I'm saying, let 'em bully you." And I was like, I thought about it for awhile, and I was like, Yeah, I probably shouldn't . . . Then finally I just snapped and started chokin' this one kid.

After checking for all three elements of brutalization, we then examined whether a subject also experienced belligerency. We scanned the narratives to find evidence of the way that the youth was conceiving the role that violence was likely to play in his life. Many of the subjects have described their "rules" for using violence. From these, we can determine if the subject has actually experienced belligerency. Here, where subject 2 reflects on his relationship with his mother, is an example of belligerancy:

It was just kind of, I didn't really like her. I kind of hated her cause she was subjecting me to this and I was thinking why did you bring me into this world and have me feel these kind of feelings . . . frustration, anger, worthlessness, I felt like I was alone except for my little brother. I just found myself always going out of the house. Trying to be out of the house as much as possible. Even up to when I got locked up I was always trying to stay away from home. I hated going home.

In terms of violent resolution, consider, once again, subject 2:

I use to beat [my brother] up all the time. Make him tough so he wouldn't have to go through anything like I did . . . Make him like me. Thought if I beat him up now it would save him a lot of pressure later because then he would know how to fight. I use to make him fight me back. So he'll get stronger. That way if a situation occurs and instead of him running like a ho, he can stand up for himself. Don't let people take anything from him and stuff like that . . . He's the type of person that I am now. That I was. He don't take no shit from nobody.

After scanning for evidence of belligerency, we then examined the narratives for evidence of violent performances. Any reported acts of violence were explored in as much detail as the youths were comfortable discussing. In the case of violent performances, we also looked for evidence of social reactions and personal interpretations of the meaning that violence is likely to take in this person's life. Consider this excerpt from subject 5:

> Then finally I just snapped and started chokin' this one kid. I didn't really want to hit him, I didn't hit him, I just choked him and I looked at him. I looked at him in the eye, and I could tell he was scared and I let him go. As long as I got my point across. He came over and started pushin' me and stuff. I just grabbed him by the throat, and threw him on the ground and I just started chokin' him. I drew my hand back, like I was gonna hit him, and he just looked at me and he had this scared look in his eyes. Everyone was yelling "Hit him, hit him!" But, I just didn't hit him. I don't know why, I just couldn't do it for some reason. In a way I did actually [like that he was scared of me]. It gave me that feel of superiority that I like. Wow, if he's gonna be afraid of me, then maybe I should do that to the rest of the people and then maybe they won't talk to me either. I thought about it for a long time. I think that's what threw me off track, in a way. 'Cause I've been in a lot of rumbles.

In terms of the use of unmitigated violent resolution, consider the following excerpt from subject 2:

> We were just in the status room and he called me a gay bitch or something like that. I was just hot about being locked up in general. Being in Boys School, I was on level one watching T. V. in the Status Room and he was talking shit to me so I got up and went over there and pushed his head and he got up. I was like "call me a bitch again dude, call me a bitch," so I pushed him. He wouldn't fight me so I just started sticking him and I just kept hitting him. People would make fun of him and stuff because of that cause he used to talk all that shit and he wouldn't fight nobody. So people make fun of him. I'd be trying to sit in the day room and watch T.V. and he'd get in an argument with somebody else and they be "Don't let me go call H____," and that would make me feel bad. Because now his reputation is shattered.

Subject 20:

> I quit working at Arby's cause this dude there was being racist. Like, I was dipping the fries out of the fry machine and, uh, dude, he burnt me somehow. I got real mad at him. From the grease, he burnt me. I got mad – he was like the manager. So, like, one day I'm out [on the strip] and I'm drunk, you know. Me and my buddy, we drank two fifths of E & J. Uh, so I seen him and I was like, "that dude burnt me." We sitting like, on the corner of Kent and Wabash. So we chillin' and I'm sitting on my car, right? I turn my head and I get hit on the side of the face with an egg and it's the dude that worked at Arby's with me. So I'm played it cool and in the back of my mind, I'm like, "he better not catch a red light." He caught a red light. So I creeped around his car and just hit him through his window. There was glass sticking all out of his face and stuff.

As we scanned the transcripts for evidence of the stages of violentization, we also coded each subject in terms of other predictors of risk for violent offending. These were economic deprivation in the community, high rates of residential mobility, access to firearms, poor discipline and supervision by parents, family conflict, parental attitudes that support the use of violence, antisocial behavior in the early school years, poor school performance, early onset of delinquent activity, association with delinquent peers, use of alcohol to the point of intoxication, delinquent attitudes, rebelliousness, a propensity towards sensation seeking, and low impulse control. Given the nature of the life histories, we were not able to code for brain damage, complications during prenatal development, or attention deficit.

FINDINGS

The first question we examine is, how well do the traditional predictors of violent offending at the community, family, school and individual level work? In Table 1, we rated each of the subjects on the basis of these predictors. From the literature, we expect that anyone with three or more of these factors is at risk for violence. We were able to identify at least three risk factors for each of the subjects in the study. What is even more striking, however, is that most of the subjects could be classified as having evidence of a majority of the risk factors. Thus, using the traditional predictors we find that each of the subjects is at risk for involvement in violence. In fact, all 18 of the subjects we examined in this analysis have engaged in some form of violent offending. Fifteen of the subjects were actually serving time at the juvenile correctional facility for a violent offense.

On the basis of this analysis, we find that we could have predicted violent offending in this sample with an impressive degree of accuracy. Yet, these youths had committed acts that ranged in the level of seriousness. Further, we know from the risk assessment literature that violent offending is not necessarily a predictor of further involvement in violence (Andrews & Bonta, 1998). Violent offending is not a good predictor of further involvement in offending of any kind (Andrews & Bonta, 1998). So given that we are concerned about the risk of these youths for continued involvement in serious violent offending, we need to look beyond these traditional risk factors. As such, we assess the subjects as to their fit with Athens' theory.

In Table 2, we provide a summary of the categorization of each of the youths along the four stages of violentization described in Athens' theory. In the first stage, Brutalization, we considered whether the subjects had experienced the three elements as described by Athens: violent subjugation, personal

Table 1. Classification of Subjects Based on Predictors of Violence.

Subject	Community-Level				Family-Level				School-Level	
	I. High rates of poverty, unemployment	II. High rates of mobility	III. Access to firearms	IV. Media portrayals of violence	I. Poor supervision	II. Poor discipline	III. Family conflict	IV. Parental support of violence	I. Antisocial behavior in early school years	II. Poor school performance
1									✓	
2		✓	✓		✓	✓	✓	✓	✓	✓
5			✓	✓	✓	✓	✓	✓		
6			✓	✓	✓	✓	✓	✓	✓	✓
7			✓	✓			✓	✓	✓	✓
8			✓	✓	✓	✓	✓			✓
9					✓	✓	✓			
10	✓	✓	✓		✓	✓	✓		✓	✓
11		✓			✓	✓	✓		✓	✓
12	✓	✓			✓	✓	✓		✓	
13		✓	✓	✓	✓	✓	✓	✓	✓	✓
14	✓		✓		✓	✓	✓			
15					✓	✓	✓			
17		✓	✓		✓		✓		✓	
18	✓	✓			✓	✓	✓	✓	✓	
19	✓	✓			✓	✓	✓	✓	✓	✓
20	✓	✓	✓		✓	✓	✓	✓		✓
24			✓		✓		✓			

Table 1. Continued.

						Individual-Level			
Subject	I. Early onset of delinquent activities	II. Association with delinquent peers	III. Use of alcohol to point of intoxication	IV. Brain damage	V. Complications during prenatal care	VI. Delinquent attitudes	VII. Rebelliousness	VIII. Propensity towards sensation seeking	IX. Low impulse control
1	✓	✓	✓			✓		✓	✓
2	✓	✓	✓			✓		✓	✓
5	✓	✓	✓			✓	✓	✓	✓
6	✓	✓				✓	✓	✓	✓
7		✓	✓			✓	✓	✓	✓
8						✓	✓	✓	✓
9									✓
10	✓	✓	✓			✓	✓	✓	✓
11	✓	✓	✓				✓	✓	✓
12	✓	✓	✓			✓	✓	✓	✓
13	✓	✓	✓				✓	✓	✓
14		✓					✓	✓	✓
15		✓	✓			✓	✓	✓	
17		✓					✓		
18	✓	✓	✓			✓	✓	✓	✓
19	✓	✓	✓			✓	✓	✓	✓
20	✓	✓	✓			✓	✓	✓	✓
24		✓					✓	✓	

horrification, and violent coaching. We found that eight youths experienced violent subjugation. It is interesting to note that in this sample, we were more likely to find examples of retaliatory subjugation than coercive subjugation, although for some of the subjects, there was clearly a combination of the two:

Subject 20:

> I ain't never been beat that bad in my life. I mean, I got hit, like, my dad would take a belt and hit me real hard against my back with it and then when he went to whip my butt he switched the belt around and hit me with the buckle and stuff. I got *beat* bad. Then I got beat so bad to where, like, he hit me once, POW, it split my skin open. After that, he made me take a bath in salt water. He said that would seal the cuts quicker. I cried and cried. He came in there and punched me in my mouth cause I was crying so much. He told me I had to stay in there until he told me that I could get out. All it did was just burn. I tried to stay still but you got to move sometimes and boy it burned.

Subject 19:

> I do remember L____. That's the one, that was probably the most devastating point in my life. That's what switched my whole self around. I mean I was being abused. I watched my mother being beat three nights after we moved in with him. Threw her over couches and beating her constantly. It was horrifying. I mean, he constantly beat her. He'd torment me and beat me and make me eat shit. He tied me up with an extension cord and put me in an oven and that was stupid man. All I did was I was playing around with him, playing around with little M____. I told him, man, I was like, "tell him no, tell him no", just playing around with him, and M____ went and told on me, and I got put in an oven. He turned it on. I wasn't in there very long, though. He let me out. It was kinda like being in a cremator, you know, not knowing if you were going to die or not, not knowing how bad you were going to be burnt. I thought I was gone.

In remaining faithful to the conceptualization of subjugation by Athens, we found several examples of subjects that had been abused, but did not meet the qualifications for violent subjugation. According to Athens, subjugation would take place at the hands of a "bonafide or would-be authority figure" from the subject's primary group. In addition, the purpose of the violence should either be a form of coercion or retaliation. As such, some of the youths that had been abused, particularly those reporting sexual abuse, should not be considered as having experienced violent subjugation. Consider, for example, Subject 1. He reported being sexually abused by an adult "friend" over a period of several months:

> I was molested when I was 11, by this dude named R____. That happened for like six months to a year. I was young and he was, like, grooming me I guess, me and my cousin. And he had this Jaguar and lots of money and he'd buy me stuff and let me drive this Jaguar. Eleven years old and I was driving this Jaguar. He would let me basically do anything. He'd give me money and buy me drugs and alcohol. Stuff like that. I wasn't really much of a drug user back then, but . . . Actually I was riding my bike through Friendly

Table 2.　Classification of Subjects Based on Athens' Theory of Violentization.

Stages of Violentization	Brutalization			Belligerency		Violent Performances	Virulency	
Subject	I. Violent Subjugation (coercion/retaliation)	II. Personal Horrification	III. Violent Coaching	I. Reflects on cruelty and how to stop violence	II. Chooses violence	I. Use of violence	I. Social Reaction increases sense of importance	II. Resolve to use violence in future
1	*	*	*	✓	✓	✓	✓	✓
2†	✓	✓	✓	✓	✓	✓	✓	✓
5	✓	✓	✓	✓	✓	✓	✓	✓
6	*	✓	✓	✓	✓	✓	✓	✓
7	✓	✓	✓	✓	✓	✓	✓	✓
8	*	*	*	✓	✓	✓	✓	✓
9†	*							
10	*	*	*	✓	✓	✓	✓	✓
11†	✓	✓						
12†	✓	✓						
13	*		*					
14		*	*	✓	✓	✓	✓	✓
15†	*		*					
17	✓	*	*	✓	✓	✓	✓	✓
18†	✓	✓	✓	✓	✓	✓	✓	✓
19	✓	✓	✓	✓	✓	✓	✓	✓
20	✓	✓	*	✓	✓	✓	✓	✓
24	*	*	*					

† sex offense included in list of offenses.

Village, this trailer park that's right next door to ours, and he rolled up in the Jaguar and my cousin J____ was like, "Hey what are you doing?" And I was like, "Nothing." So he asked if I wanted to go for a ride and I was like, "Where you going?" "Just for a ride and chill." So I put my bike up at my house and they picked me up at my house and we started going for a ride. Next thing I know we pull up in his driveway and he gets out and goes inside and I noticed J____ pulling up his pants, I was like, "What's that all about?" He was like, "He was playing with me while we were driving." And I was like, "You let that go on?" He was like, "Yeah, he gives me money and stuff." At first I thought it was sick, and then he was like, well, "Well he'll give you money, too." And he was telling me all sorts of stuff that he'd do for me. So I was like, sure I'll try it, cause I'll try anything. I liked what I was getting out of it. I was getting money and clothes. All the clothes I never asked my dad for, I was getting. So I was like, this will work. [I had to let him] just, suck me off and play with me. That was it. Sometimes he wanted me to have sex with him, he let me stick my thing in him, but I didn't do it that often, only like once or twice. I didn't really like it.

As this "friend" would not qualify as an authority figure, and since he was not resorting to coercive violence, we would not classify this as an example of violent subjugation. Similarly, Subject 11 relates being molested by a 16-year-old cousin who was babysitting him when he was six or seven. The subject reports being traumatized by the incident and attributes some of his inability to control his anger to having been sexually abused. Yet, even if the cousin could be seen as an authority figure, the details of the abuse do not fit Athens' conception of coercive or retaliatory subjugation.

The second element of brutalization is personal horrification. Of the eight youths reporting violent subjugation, seven also experienced personal horrification. Here we found many examples of violence in the home that was directed at someone in the subject's primary group, generally either the mother or another sibling. The subjects reported many incidents in which they either witnessed or could hear the abuse as it occurred. Subject 5 relates:

My mom ex-husband, he was an asshole. Ya know what I'm sayin'? He ain't never really, I mean he used to start a fight and beat on my mom and us kids all the time. He really, he used to scream at us all the time and all that. I wanted to kill the dude. I used to want to kill him every day, but I was too little. I couldn't do anything. Plus I probably woulda got beat up myself. I would just watch it.

Some of the subjects reported efforts on their part to attract the abuse onto themselves as a way to protect their loved ones. As Athens notes, the combination of the personal horrification and the violent subjugation appeared to increase the impact of the brutalization experiences.

Of the seven youths experiencing both subjugation and horrification, five experienced violent coaching. As the life-history interviews were not *designed* to test Athens' theory, we found as we read through the transcripts that it was not always clear whether violent coaching had taken place. Since Athens is clear on what the message of the violent coaching tends to be, however, we are able to infer some of this from the comments of the subjects. As Athens notes, the message that is delivered in violent coaching tends to emphasize that it is a personal responsibility for the subject to take violent action against a person that behaves in a provocative manner (although the level of provocation does not always warrant a violent response). The subjects were asked to discuss how they learned to be violent and their impressions on how violence might be useful. From the responses of the subjects, we get some insight into how these attitudes were shaped and reinforced. Consider subject 6. In talking about how he would raise a son, he describes how he was coached:

> When I have a son, I'm not gonna teach my son, I mean I'm gonna teach him to walk away, but at the same time, I'm gonna teach him like my daddy taught me. Cause if you think about, I don't think my daddy taught me bad. Cause he always told me "if a person big enough to pass a lick, they big enough to get one," you know what I'm saying, but, it's exceptions to some of the people. You know what I mean, you don't hit older grown-ups and, you know what I mean, the police, and stuff like that. But, if it's, you know what I'm saying, somebody, your age group, your peer group, you know what I'm saying, they hit you back, you know what I'm saying, I mean if they hit you, you hit 'em back. I'm not gonna have my son just letting somebody hit him and he "Ah, My daddy told me to walk away". Naw, cause I'm gonna be mad then, you know what I mean, naw, you defend yourself. You know what I'm saying . . . I mean if you can walk away, go on and walk away. You know what I mean. But if you have to defend yourself, you gotta do what you gotta do. You know what I mean. And if you sit there, if he get beat up, so be it, you know what I mean. As long as I know he was out there and he defended hisself. He didn't just let this man run all over him. Cause if he do it then the next person will think they can do it, then. . . . Naw, my son ain't gonna be like that.

Stage 2 of Athens' theory is Belligerency. It is during this stage that the subject goes through a period of personal reflection on the meaning of the brutalization experiences that have been endured. In trying to understand why this has happened to him or her, and with a strong motivation for avoiding such experiences in the future, the subject now resolves to use violence against others when provoked though the provocation would seem minimal to many. For the subjects that experienced all three stages of brutalization, all five of them reported a pattern of violent behavior throughout middle school and the subsequent years. They reported being prepared to fight other youths, even without what others would consider great provocation. It is clear from the narratives that these youths were motivated to change the perception that others had about them. They wanted to make sure that they were not viewed as potential victims. Subject 7 reflects here on the usefulness of violence:

If it's called for. But I mean, if it's not, you know, something that's pretty minor, it's not real, you know, like, a real big loss, it's not really [called for]. I mean, in a way, yeah because I mean, sometimes, that's what you've gotta do to earn your respect, you know. To keep from other people doing it. You know, cause once one person do it, they all think they can. "Well, he robbed him and he didn't do shit, well shit, I'm going to." You just let somebody do the shit, it's gonna keep happening, you know. That's the way that you get a name for yourself, I guess.

We found from the transcripts, however, that it was not only the boys that we classified as having experienced brutalization who reflected on the role of violence. We found that seven other subjects had also considered the potential for violence to serve their needs in a manner that seemed to fit Athens' description of belligerency. These subjects all had one thing in common. They all could be characterized as having a mitigated violent phantom community. Athens describes a mitigated violent phantom community as resulting from "past significant social experiences" (1997, p. 139) that encourage the subject to take "violent action when someone either threatens to dominate them physically or seeks intentionally to irk them by opposing their domination or attempting to dominate them" (1998, p. 679). This is at least suggestive of the fact that these subjects indeed experienced brutalization at an earlier point.[3]

Yet, if brutalization was not suffered at the hands of their family members, then from where? Other factors that seem to be important are the violent contexts in which these youths were living. Besides the violence they experienced directly or which they committed, there were many reports of violence in the environment – many reported friends that died at an early age. There were also sisters who were stabbed and raped, and grandmothers and parents who were victims of a wide range of violence. Gangs, as well as drugs, were common in the neighborhoods these youths described growing up in. It was not uncommon for them to describe their school as a place of violence. Further, behavioral norms among their peers, cultural values, defensive behaviors that allow for an expression of pent-up frustration and rage, all seemed important in the explanations these youths gave for their violence.

In Table 2, we indicate the subjects with mitigated violent phantom communities with an "*" in the columns for brutalization. There are seven subjects that can be so classified. We distinguish them from the other subjects that we identified above to signify that we believe they were brutalized, but only find evidence by proxy (i.e. phantom communities). From this point on, we consider these subjects in each of the subsequent stages of violentization.

Reflections of the usefulness of violence, of course, paved the way for violent performances and the further resolve to resort to violence in social interactions (stages 3 and 4 of Athens' theory). In our sample we find that all five youths who experienced the full range of brutalization and who also experienced belligerency can also be classified as having engaged in violent performances. We also believe they successfully completed the stage of virulency. We also found this to be true of the other seven youths who we believe experienced brutalization, at least in part through their mitigated violent phantom communities, and who went on to experience belligerency. They all went on to engage in violent performances and fit the characteristics of the stage of virulency.

Athens points to a special form of violent performance. He refers to this as the "violent personal revolt." Here the subject directs the violence toward a person that has been a subjugator. Consider the following examples:

Subject 20:

> I would go to work and come back and my mom would have a black eye and she told me she fell and stuff like that. I can't do nothing cause I haven't seen it. Then one day my dad got drunk and thought he could beat up my mom and me and it wasn't happening. I told him like two days after I got out: "Don't let me catch you cause I'm not that little kid no more. I'll do something to you." I guess he thought I was playing with him. I beat him up . . .

Subject 5:

> I hated it. I hated every minute of it. I used to hate all her boyfriends with a passion. I used to want to kill her ex-husband. I used to hate him so much. I still do, ya know what I'm sayin'? If I ever saw him, I probably wouldn't do nothin' now but about two years ago, I probably woulda tried to kill him where he was standin' at. I don't know. I'm over it now. It made me feel betrayed sometimes, that my mom would let him, ya know what I'm sayin', do that to me.

It is clear from the findings thus far that Athens' theory of violentization is applicable to some of the youths in the sample. Does it distinguish, though, between those youths who are serious violent predators and those who are not? We use two criteria to assess the differences between those in the sample who met the criteria of Athens' theory and those who did not. First, we consider the seriousness of the acts themselves. Second, and perhaps more importantly, we consider the level of provocation that led up to violent acts. Athens predicts that dangerous violent criminals commit their acts with little or no provocation.

In terms of the seriousness of the violent acts, all of the subjects had been involved in violence, ranging in the level of seriousness. In Table 3, we present the offenses for which the subjects had been most recently incarcerated as well as the subjects' own reports of their most violent acts. Many had committed some extremely serious offenses. As a group, the 18 subjects hit, stabbed and shot people, robbed people at gunpoint, and tortured animals. They kidnapped,

Table 3. Incarceration Offense and Most Violent Act of Each Subject.

Subject	Incarceration Presenting Offense	Most Violent Act (Self-Reported)
1	Possession of Controlled Substance (D Felony)	Drive-by Shooting
2	Child Molest – Deviate Sexual Conduct (B Felony)	Drive-by Shooting
5	Conspiracy (D Felony)	Kidnapping w/ Torture
6	Criminal Recklessness w/ weapon (D Felony)	Aggravated Battery with Motor Vehicle
7	Possession/ own machine gun (C Felony)	Intimidation with Deadly Weapon
8	Escape (C Felony)	Battery
9	Child Molest – Fondling (C Felony)	Child Molest – Fondling
10	Criminal Confinement (D Felony)	Stabbing
11	Child Molest – Fondling (C Felony)	Fights
12	Child Molest – Fondling (C Felony)	Child Molest – Fondling
13	Battery w/ Serious Bodily Injury (C Felony)	Aggravated Battery
14	Aggravated Battery (B Felony)	Aggravated Battery
15	Child Molest – Fondling (C Felony)	Child Molest – Fondling
17	Intimidation of Law Enforcement (D Felony)	Armed Robbery
18	Child Molest – Fondling (C Felony)	Child Molest – Fondling
19	Battery w/ Bodily Injury (D Felony)	Aggravated Battery
20	Carrying Handgun (A Misdemeanor)	Aggravated Battery w/ Firearm
24	Conspiracy (B Felony)	Criminal Recklessness w/ Deadly Weapon

Note: In this state, misdemeanors increase in severity from C to A and felonies increase in severity from D to A.

raped, had shoot-outs with the police, and molested younger children. With one exception, though, we were able to distinguish by seriousness those who fell under Athens' theory and those who did not. Each of the 12 subjects that we classified as having experienced all four stages of violentization reported at least one act that Athens would classify as "substantially" violent. Of the six subjects that did not experience the full range of the four stages of violentization, only one (subject 13) reported a substantially violent act.

According to Athens, it is not the seriousness of the offenses that is most distinguishing, but the level of provocation, with dangerous violent criminals needing little or none. Level of provocation also varied with a pattern supporting Athens' distinction. Subject 14 was charged with aggravated battery after stabbing a man three times. Here he describes the incident:

> My sister paged us, like, "Come pick me up." I was like "Alright." So me, F____, and E____ go. We head up Hammond, go get some liquor. I'm just gone. I'm just out. Tell E____, "You drive." I'm in the middle, F____'s right here. Cause my truck, it only holds three people. The rest of the people have to sit in the back. So I'm sitting there. We go

there, and S____ comes out and she's mad. "I think he's over at P____'s with that bitch, blah blah blah." "Let's go to P____'s." You know what I'm saying. We're all friends – me, P____, F____. J____ was one of my best friends. He's dating my sister, I guess he's cheating on her. That's not my business. Me and F____ get in the back, we're drinking, keeping it low. You know what I'm saying, you know, we're still in daylight. We go to P____'s house. It was about a one or two-minute drive. I pull up and that girl was there, I pulled up next to her car, I'm not thinking nothing and S____'s yelling to P____, "He ain't here." "Why is his car here?" "Well he ain't here." P____ comes down and starts talking shit to her. "Aaah, he ain't here, get out of here, blah, blah, blah . . . you're going to get these people mad, blah, blah, blah." Cause a police officer used to live over there, too – we didn't know him. I'm just sitting there with E____ and F____, my driver door's open, I'm sitting there, drinking, smoking some weed, then J____ comes down and they get to arguing, then I hear, Bam, bam, bam, and I turn around and my sister's on the ground. She's crying. I was like, "What the fuck!" and I grabbed my knife and I wanted to walk towards him, but I was like "No, I can't." So I slashed the girl's tires and I started scratching her paint, and did her other tire. J____'s like "It ain't none of your business." He saw me. "It ain't none of your business." Running to me, he swung at me. I was like, "Dude!" I stabbed him like three times. He backed up, I was kind of shocked, but I wasn't and it just turned nighttime like that. All before that I was on top, now at that moment I'm like, "Damn." I put the knife down and put it inside the truck, shut the truck. He was clutching his stomach, took his shirt off, laid on the ground and there was some stuff coming out of his stomach and I'm looking at him and my sister was crying, "Oh, are you all right?" "Look, man, he just hit you." And P____ was like, "Just leave."

Subject 7 reports even less provocation:

Did you sometimes resort to violence when it wasn't called for?
Yeah. Like a kid said something to my little sister. I ran up to him and choked him and then threw him off his bike and everything. That all wasn't really called for. (Laughs) That wasn't too called for, but . . . I mean, in my eyes I thought it was, because, man, that's my family, man. He called her like a "ho" or "whore" or something and then I seen him riding his bike and I jumped out of my car and ran up to him and grabbed him by his neck and threw him off, you know, said my words to him and threw him on the ground and let him know not to do the shit no more. I mean that's my family man. I don't let nobody mess with them, you know. I mean if they're family, you know, whether you're full-blooded family or you're just my family you know. I mean, shit, I'ma look out for you like that, cause in my eyes, we're the same. I gotta take care of mines, man. That's the way I was always taught.

Subject 6 describes here the fights he had at school:

If you bump into me, right, then I'll fight you. Even if it was an accident, I'd be like, "Your fault, man." And you would say something. You could be like, "Alright man," and then I'm like "what?" and the people, they'd be like, "I know you ain't going to let him talk to you like that." I guess it was just the reputation I had built for myself. Cause I hated it when somebody bumped into me I'd be like, "My fault, man." They like, "I know it's your fault." "But what do you mean?" "You know what I mean." I hate that. I'm trying to tell you, "Dude, I'm sorry," but people crowd around you like, "aw you going to let him talk to you like that?" I don't know. I guess I at the time, I guess I was trying to prove myself to people but, I see it wasn't worth it. Like when somebody, "Are you going to let them talk to you like that?" Then I would probably say, "Man I'll beat this fool's butt," or something like that. And then by me saying that, I've done got him mad cause he like, "Well whatever, you won't do nothing to me." "What's up then?" "What you gonna do?" We'd get into a fight.

Not all acts of violence reported, however, were lacking in reasonable provocation. Each of the subjects who fell under Athens' theory also committed acts of violence in situations of provocation.

A good test of this theory would also consider evidence of predictive validity. We would expect that those who went through all the stages of violentization would be more likely to continue offending than those who did not. All of the subjects were released from the juvenile correctional facility at some point during the period of December 1999 to October 2000. At the time of the writing of this paper (December 2001), we examined whether any of the youths had returned to prison on a new offense. Two of the 18 subjects are currently serving time in prison. Both are serving time for a violent offense. Subject 1 is serving 5–10 years for robbery and aggravated battery. Subject 2 is serving 2–4 years for child molesting. Subject 2 fit the classification of a dangerous violent criminal based on our analysis. Subject 1 was classified as fitting Athens' theory once we considered the role of the mitigated violent phantom community. Thus, 17% of the group that we would classify as dangerous violent criminals has reoffended in a violent manner, compared with 0% of those predicted to not be dangerous violent criminals. The sample is small, but the results are suggestive in their support for Athens' theory.

DISCUSSION

Though research has established a number of factors that are useful in predicting those at risk for violent offending, their ability to identify the 5–8% who commit the more serious forms of predatory violence is limited. Athens' theory of violentization offers a way to make distinctions among violent juvenile offenders by examining the social experiences of offenders. Is this a potentially useful classification tool for identifying the youths that should be targeted for intervention?

Though we must be mindful of the fact that this is an exploratory study and one based on data not designed specifically to test this theory, we did find support for Athens' theory and, thus, its potential usefulness for classification. All of the subjects in this sample have engaged in some form of violent offending. All of the subjects would have been identified as "at-risk" based on the traditional community, school, family and individual factors identified in the literature. Only a portion (67%) went through all the stages identified in Athens' theory of violentization, thus meeting the criteria for a dangerous violent criminal. This finding itself suggests a meaningful way to identify those delinquents that are at-risk for becoming dangerous violent offenders.

Further, it is clear from this analysis that there are meaningful distinctions to be made about child abuse experiences. Based on Athens' theory, not all forms of abuse are examples of brutalization. In particular, we found that while two-thirds of the youths in this sample experienced some form of physical or sexual abuse as a child, many of them did not experience the concomitant horrification and coaching that is required in the theory of violentization. This was, interestingly, most common among youths who had been sexually abused. In fact, in our sample, most of the youths who were sexually abused were not the victims of an authority figure, either bona fide or would-be – a necessary condition for subjugation – and their victimization experiences were not aimed at coercion or retaliation.

Another key point from this analysis is that adolescent sex offenders, though placed in this maximum security setting and thought of as violent offenders, tended not to fit Athens' criteria for dangerous violent criminals. Five of the six subjects that did not experience all four stages of violentization were serving time for a sex offense. Each of these youths was charged with molesting (i.e. fondling) a child under the age of 14. The nature of the specific act does not fit the violent nature of the behaviors that Athens is seeking to explain in his theory. While public attitudes view sex offenses as very serious (and certainly the victims of sex offenses are often as traumatized as victims of other violent offenses) it would appear that this type of offending cannot be explained by Athens' theory. In addition to the degree of violence and the level of injury that results, another element of mismatch has to do with the reaction of others to the sex offense. Virulency is said to emerge from social reactions that imply fear, awe, and even respect on the part of others close to the subject. Yet, these are not typically social reactions to forms of sexual offending. Instead, the sex offender is more likely to experience disgust and disapproval from the reaction of others. This is unlikely to reinforce the behavior.

The findings also illustrate an important aspect of the theory that we believe is difficult to study. Researchers have now begun to recognize the important role that abuse has in increasing risk for future offending. Widom and her colleagues (Widom & Ames, 1994; Weeks & Widom, 1998; Kaufman & Widom, 1999) provide us with some of the strongest evidence on this point. One of the contributions that Athens makes to our understanding of this connection lies in the fact that his theory helps us understand why some who are abused go on to commit serious violent crimes and others do not. Part of his theory's ability to do this is through the explicit definition of brutalization. Its emphasis on the primary group for violent subjugation and horrification, and on the coercive and retaliatory nature of the abuse, helps distinguish it from measures of abuse that focus simply on the existence of an act of abuse. Yet, in terms of testing this theory, one must directly address two specific challenges in collecting data. First, can we get offenders to discuss brutalizing experiences from their past? If we can, then a second issue is how to get the subjects to describe experiences of violent subjugation in ways that allow us to appreciate the qualities that differentiate it from other forms of abuse. In the life history interviews conducted here, the first author was able to establish a strong rapport with the subjects and was able to get them to discuss earlier experiences in great detail. Unfortunately, at the time of the interviews, there was no plan to test the theory of violentization, and so we did not ask the specific questions that would allow us to examine all stages of violentization. Future tests of this theory need to more specifically anticipate these challenges.

Does Athens' theory help us identify the most serious violent criminals? The analysis presented here, while admittedly exploratory, suggests that Athens' conception of violentization may indeed allow for useful distinctions between juvenile offenders. It would appear that the classification system in place in this state successfully identifies the most serious violent offenders for placement at this facility. This particular facility houses all the adolescent sex offenders in the state, as well as other high-risk offenders. In our sample, there was only one non-sex offender that did not fit the criteria for a dangerous violent criminal. For the most part, we found that when the youths experienced all four stages of violentization, they also had engaged in serious violent acts of aggression toward others. We believe our findings point to the importance of the theory and the perspective that it takes. Like the work of Katz (1988) and others who encourage us to understand the social experiences and mind frame of offenders, this theory has the potential for great power.

There are two additional questions that we believe are not adequately addressed by this theory. First, what should the response of the criminal justice system be for those offenders that have experienced all four stages of violentization? Athens (1989) suggests that there are some offenders that are not amenable to rehabilitation. In his discussion of the policy implications of his theory, Athens identifies points of intervention prior to the completion of the virulency stage. In our analysis, we noted that two of the offenders in this sample went back to prison on new violent offenses soon after their release. Yet, the remaining ten offenders had not recidivated after at least one year in the community. Of course, we do not have enough information to claim that this is evidence of rehabilitation, maturation, or even a lack of detection of ongoing offending. This is an area that deserves further examination in future analyses.

A second, related question has to do with the level of remorse of the offenders in this sample. In Athens' theory, there does not seem to be a place for remorse if the subject has progressed through all four stages of violentization. In this sample, some of the youths meeting the criteria for all four stages of Athens' theory were much less likely to express remorse for their offending behaviors. Others, while capable of serious forms of violence, expressed regret over the harm that had been caused. They also reported feeling ashamed about the things they had done. This may be a critical distinction between dangerous violent criminals that are beyond rehabilitation and others engaging in serious forms of violence and amenable to treatment. At the very least, it is an issue worthy of further examination.

NOTES

1. There are several examples of the examination of social experiences in explaining juvenile violence (see, for example, Anderson, 1999; Canada, 1995). The focus of this paper, however, is on the most serious, dangerous, predatory violent offenders.
2. There were 28 youths aged 18 or older at the facility at the start of the project. Three of these youths chose not to participate.
3. In response to an earlier version of this chapter, Athens argued that juveniles would not believe in violent norms or values without having experienced brutalization.

REFERENCES

Allen, L., Jones, S. M., Seidman, E., & Aber J. L. (1999). Organization of exposure to violence among urban adolescents: Clinical, prevention, and research implications. In: D. J. Flannery & C. R. Huff (Eds), *Youth Violence: Prevention, Intervention, and Social Policy* (pp. 119–141). Washington, D.C.: American Psychiatric Press.

Anderson, E. (1999). *Code of the Street: Decency, Violence, and the Moral Life of the Inner City.* New York: W. W. Norton.

Andrews, D. A., & Bonta, J. (1998). *The Psychology of Criminal Conduct.* Cincinnati, OH: Anderson Publishing.

Athens, L. H. (1989). *The Creation of Dangerous Violent Criminals.* London: Routledge.

Athens, L. H. (1997). *Violent Criminal Acts and Actors Revisited.* Chicago: University of Chicago Press.

Athens, L. H. (1998). Dominance, ghettos, and violent crime. *Sociological Quarterly, 39*, 673–691.

Brewer, D. D., Hawkins, J. D., Catalano, R. F., & Neckerman, H. J. (1995). Preventing serious, violent, and chronic juvenile offending: A review of evaluations of selected strategies in childhood, adolescence, and the community. In: J. C. Howell, B. Krisberg, J. D. Hawkins & J. J. Wilson (Eds), *A Sourcebook: Serious, Violent, and Chronic Juvenile Offenders* (pp. 61–141). Thousand Oaks, CA: Sage Publications.

Canada, G. (1995). *Fist Stick Knife Gun: A Personal History of Violence in America.* Boston: Beacon Press.

Cook, P. J., & Laub J. H. (1998). The unprecedented epidemic in youth violence. In: M. Tonry & M. H. Moore (Eds), *Youth Violence (Crime and Justice*, Vol. 24, pp. 27–64). Chicago: University of Chicago Press.

Elliott, D. S. (1994). Serious violent offenders: Onset, developmental course, and termination – The American Society of Criminology 1993 Presidential Address. *Criminology, 32*, 1–21.

Elliott, D. S., & Tolan, P. H. (1999). Youth violence prevention, intervention, and social policy: An overview. In: D. J. Flannery & C. R. Huff (Eds), *Youth Violence: Prevention, Intervention, and Social Policy* (pp. 3–46). Washington, D.C.: American Psychiatric Press.

Fagan, J., & Wilkinson, D. L. (1998). Guns, youth violence, and social identity in inner cities. In: M. Tonry & M. H. Moore (Eds), *Youth Violence (Crime and Justice*, Vol. 24, pp 105–188). Chicago: University of Chicago Press.

Farrington, D. P. (1998). Predictors, causes, and correlates of male youth violence. In: M. Tonry & M. H. Moore (Eds), *Youth Violence (Crime and Justice*, Vol. 24, pp. 421–475). Chicago: University of Chicago Press.

Gorman-Smith, D., & Avery, L. (1999). Family factors and youth violence. In: D. J. Flannery & C. R. Huff (Eds), *Youth Violence: Prevention, Intervention, and Social Policy* (pp. 231–251). Washington, D.C.: American Psychiatric Press.

Hawkins, J. D., Catalano, R. F., & Brewer, D. D. (1995). Preventing serious, violent, and chronic juvenile offending: Effective strategies from conception to age 6. In: J. C. Howell, B. Krisberg, J. D. Hawkins, & J. J. Wilson (Eds), *A Sourcebook: Serious, Violent, and Chronic Juvenile Offenders* (pp. 47–60). Thousand Oaks, CA: Sage Publications.

Howell, J. C. (1997). *Juvenile Justice and Youth Violence.* Thousand Oaks, CA: Sage Publications.

Howell, J. C., & Hawkins, J. D. (1998). Prevention of youth violence. In: M. Tonry & M. H. Moore (Eds), *Youth Violence (Crime and Justice*, Vol. 24, pp. 263–315). Chicago: University of Chicago Press.

Huesmann, L. R., & Moise, J. F. (1999). Stability and continuity of aggression from early childhood to young adulthood. In: D. J. Flannery & C. R. Huff (Eds), *Youth Violence: Prevention, Intervention, and Social Policy* (pp. 73–95). Washington, D.C.: American Psychiatric Press.

Katz, J. (1988). *Seductions of Crime.* New York: Basic Books.

Kaufman, J., & Widom, C. S. (1999). Childhood victimization, running away, and delinquency. *Journal of Research in Crime and Delinquency, 36*, 347–370.

Moore, M. H., & Tonry, M. (1998). Youth violence in America. In: M. Tonry & M. H. Moore (Eds), *Youth Violence (Crime and Justice*, Vol. 24, pp. 1–26). Chicago: University of Chicago Press.

Rhodes, R. (1999). *Why they Kill: The Discoveries of a Maverick Criminologist.* New York: Alfred A. Knopf.

Snyder, H. N. (2000). *Juvenile Arrests, 1999.* Washington, D.C.: U.S. Department of Justice.

Weeks, R., & Widom C. S. (1998). Self-reports of early childhood victimization among adult male felons. *Journal of Interpersonal Violence, 13*, 346–361.

Widom, C. S., & Ames, A. (1994). Criminal consequences of childhood sexual victimization. *Child Abuse and Neglect, 18*, 303–318.

AFTERWORD: WHERE DOES VIOLENTIZATION GO FROM HERE?

Jeffery T. Ulmer

As Richard Rhodes (1999) has noted, Athens' work on violence (which I refer to as violentization theory for ease of discussion)[1] tends to provoke two polar responses, people either appreciate it or they ignore or dismiss it. In my experience in using his work in the classroom and in talking about his work with friends, relatives, and colleagues, those who appreciate the visceral sensibility of Athens' ideas tend to have some kind of personal experience with violence and violent actors (either through personal experience, ethnographic research, or both). This pattern is vividly illustrated by Randy Starr's narrative and interpretation of his biography in violentization terms. Matthew Dumont does an admirable job of embedding Athens' work and thought in his own life experience as a victim, witness, and abortive perpetrator of violence (as does R. Rhodes, 1999).

R. Rhodes (1999) calls Lonnie Athens a "maverick criminologist," and notes that some scholars of violence have dismissed and rejected Athens' work in part because of its "maverick," unconventional quality. Rhodes is justified in drawing this portrait, since Athens has certainly been treated as a maverick (when he has been treated with at all) by the field. But a closer examination of his work shows that it is actually rooted in well-established traditions in sociology and criminology, and his ideas are far from outlandish. The theoretical dimension of Athens' work is squarely based in the general sociological perspective of symbolic interactionism (Athens is, of course, a student of Herbert Blumer) and is compatible with the criminological theory of differential

Violent Acts and Violentization: Assessing, Applying, and Developing Lonnie Athens' Theories, Volume 4, pages 175–183.
© 2003 Published by Elsevier Science Ltd.
ISBN: 0-7623-0905-9

association. Basically, the theme animating Athens work and Rhodes' book is that substantial violent acts (like any other acts), are the product of definitions of situation and self favorable to violence. These definitions and selves are in turn generated through a contingent four-stage process of violent socialization (or violentization). And these selves, situational definitions, and socialization processes are in turn embedded within the dominance orders of and dispute norms of corporal communities that foster violence. This emphasis on the causal importance of definitions of situations, and the focus on minded, agency-possessing actors in two-way relationships with their social contexts lodges this theory squarely within symbolic interactionism (Maines, 2001). Symbolic interactionism, and its roots in pragmatist philosophy, are nearly as old as American sociology itself, and interactionism's place in sociology is stronger than ever (Maines, 2001).

The broader theory of self, social acts, and communities from which violentization derives is based in, but departs significantly from, more traditional symbolic interactionist theory (Mead, 1934; Blumer, 1969; Stryker, 1980). As Athens (personal communication) describes:

> Unlike Mead and Blumer, I make dominance rather than sociality the basic principle on which all communities are organized. Second, unlike them, I make the temporal locus of the social act a present that is tilted toward the past or future, rather than one always centered perfectly in the present. Finally, I see the self as based on a "phantom community" whose locus is the past, rather than a "generalized other" whose locus is the present. Thus, I emphasize how people have biographies that affect their present actions through shaping their phantom communities.

In criminology, Athens' theory of violentization (including its extension to the community level, see Athens 1998, and Athens, this volume) incorporates insights from differential association/social learning theory and labeling theory[2] into a broad, overarching interactionist theory of violence. However, it does not fit neatly into either differential association or labeling theories, since it is based on Athens' distinctive and much broader interactionist theory of the self, social acts, and communities (phantom and corporal) (see Athens, 1994, 1995).

Differential association/social learning theory has the distinction of being the most empirically supported and well established one in criminology (see Warr, 2002; Akers, 1998).

The structural, group level manifestation of differential association/social learning theory is *differential social organization*. Groups are organized differently in terms of valued skills, dominance orders, cultural definitions and norms, vocabularies of motives, and network relationships. Groups' organization can potentially be favorable for crime in general, and/or for specific kinds of crimes, or for specific kinds of crimes in specific circumstances. The norms, values, meanings, skills, and definitions found within these groups can be favorable to particular kinds of crime, or crime in general. With his conception of civil, malignant, and turbulent major and minor communities and their change (especially in the first contribution in this volume), Athens develops a unique theory of the social organization of violence.

The individual-level manifestation of differential association/social learning theory is the *differential association process*. This is the theory of differences in association with criminal messages and opportunities, and has been elaborated by several other researchers beyond Sutherland's original formulation (see reviews by Akers, 1998; Warr, 2002; Ulmer, 2000). Criminal behavior becomes more likely to the extent that individuals learn and internalize pro-criminal norms, values, meanings, skills, and definitions through socialization and social learning processes within the kinds of pro-criminal group contexts described above. Pro-criminal definitions will have varying degrees of influence on individuals depending on the source, emotional intensity, priority, frequency, and duration of the individual's contact with the definitions.

Violentization clearly posits a process by which individuals learn messages favorable to using violence to accomplish goals, such as winning dominance disputes (which implicitly includes goals like gaining compliance and exerting social control), gaining emotional satisfaction, or obtaining money. Violentization specifies mechanisms, stages, contingencies, and experiences involved in a socialization process that produces serious, persistent violent behavior.

According to Athens, violentization also improves upon differential association theory in two ways. First, he views Sutherland's (1947) original conception of individual actors as too passive and too culturally determined, and his conception of communities and cultures too static. He argues that his conception of the self as based in phantom communities is more agency-oriented and dynamic than Sutherland's. In fact, Athens argues that his conception of the self and phantom communities provides a missing link of personality and agency that Sutherland himself sought.

Methodologically, Athens' work relies on ethnographic observation and interviews, and his theory was developed by analyzing these data with the logic of analytic induction. Although such methods are not as widespread as deductive hypothesis testing with quantitative data and statistical models, ethnographic research has a long and respectable history in sociology and (to a lesser extent) criminology. The ethnographic tradition is literally as old as American empirical sociology itself (Maines, 2001), and the process of developing theory through inductive analysis of data (either ethnographic or quantitative) is described in Glaser and Strauss's (1967) methodological classic, *The Discovery of Grounded Theory*. Of course, once theoretical ideas are developed from data in this manner, they can then be tested as deductive hypotheses, and tested with a variety of types of data (e.g. statistical, historical/comparative, ethnographic, discourse analysis), in further empirical studies.

Where do we go from here? I think two developments are essential for future progress, refinement, and maturation of the theory of violentization and violent acts. First, all elements of the theory must be further tested by high quality research. We need more ethnographic, statistical, historical, and cross-national data and analysis to test and refine the theory's key propositions. Contributions to this volume have made a start in each of these directions.

In my view, among the most interesting issues to be addressed by future research are the following. First, research should flesh out the mutual relationships between the person/self, situational, community, and cultural levels of the theory. Empirical research should pursue violentization's "mesostructural" dimensions (Maines, 1982; Hall & McGinty, 1997), that is, the ways in which cultures, communities, situations, and selves mutually interrelate to produce or mitigate violentization.

Relatedly, a second direction of research I find fascinating is the potential for violentization theory to illuminate the role, or lack thereof, of culture and media in violence. That is, research should test Athen's proposition that, if community or even society-wide cultural norms, messages, discourse, media images, etc. cause serious violence, they do so *through* violentization. In other words, Athens' theory posits that violence-favorable definitions of situations are the proximate cause of serious violent acts, that violentization is the process by which these definitions of situations are learned, violentization is made more or less likely by the nature of communities' dominance dispute norms, and cultural rules for using violence. This causal chain needs further testing and fleshing out empirically.

Third, research should address the intriguing questions raised by Josh Sanborn (this volume) about the similarities and differences between violent criminals and combat soldiers in terms of violentization and careers in violent behavior. Sanborn draws many parallels between combat soldiers and violent criminals, but also points out key differences, and hypothesizes a "deviolentization" process that differentiates combat veterans from violent criminals. Athens, on the other hand, thinks Sanborn understates the degree of involvement of returning combat veterans in serious violence, and seems to be more pessimistic about the notion of returning combat veterans' "deviolentization" (personal communication). This is a fascinating, important, and highly socially relevant set of questions that can only be answered with systematic empirical comparison of violent criminals and combat veterans. Such research would specify similarities in violentization between the two groups, but also key differences, such as how the military structural and cultural context, bureaucratic authority structures, or modern war technology[3] might mediate or sidetrack the violentization process. Research should also explore and test the notion of deviolentization among both soldiers and criminals.

Richard Rhodes' contribution raises a similar set of issues regarding violentization and war crimes, also the subject of his new book. Indeed, it would seem impossible for human beings to commit genocide and other atrocities on others, at least through face-to-face action, without undergoing violentization. An obvious and timely arena to further explore this would be to examine the role of violentization and violent communities in wartime atrocities committed in Rwanda and the former Yugoslavia. More generally, R. Rhodes provides historical support for violentization, and further makes the point that violentization is a traumatic process of adaptation that it destructive to those that undergo it as well as their victims.

Fourth, I would like to see more empirical specification of the stages of violentization. For example, are the stages truly a sequence that must be gone through all the way, each dependent on the previous one? On the other hand, is it possible to short circuit the violentization process, jump from one stage to a higher one and skip some in between, as Jarjoura and Triplett's study in this volume implies? If the latter is possible, which stages are essential and which can be skipped? In other words, are all of the stages necessary causes of serious violent careers, or are some stages sufficient causes without the others?

Fifth, more progress needs to be made in quantitatively measuring and analyzing violentization. I am very gratified to see that Ginger Rhodes and her colleagues (this volume) have done a great service to the field by developing and validating the Violent Socialization Scale. I find the scale itself well-constructed and their confirmatory factor analyses and validity checks very convincing. Future research should replicate G. Rhodes et al.'s scale and validation analyses, and further assess the scale's predictive validity, with different samples.

Ethnographic research is indispensable for studying social processes, while quantitative data is useful for measuring the outcomes of processes and comparing them across large numbers of cases (for a review, see Ulmer, 2001). Of course, quantitative measurement and analysis of this kind does not permit the depth of information or the processual detail provided by the ethnographic interviews or life history narratives collected by Athens and by Jarjoura and Triplett, and exemplified by Randy Starr's story (this volume). But recognizing the value and necessity of ethnographic research should not blind us to the fact that quantification and statistical analysis is also indispensable is social science (for elaboration of this argument, see Ulmer, 2001). Such data and analysis allow investigation of larger samples and permit larger scale comparisons across groups, communities, or even cultures. Ideally, research should progress using quantitative measures and more in-depth ethnographic data collection in tandem.

Sixth, Richard Restak's satirical treatment of using neuroscience in the service of social control points to issues of growing seriousness and relevance. Restak thoughtfully critiques neuro-biological views of violence, which are becoming much more common and are quite palatable to policy makers and large segments of the public, at least in the U.S. (see Conrad, 1997). Restak uses violentization as the foundation for much of his criticisms. Furthermore, both Starr/Athens and Dumont in this volume argue that violentization can account for the violent acts of mentally ill people as well as the non-mentally ill. As neuro-biological views of violence, and crime in general, become more prominent, work like Athens' that is squarely sociological provides a valuable counter position to remind people that violence is inherently a social act, that all social acts are produced through interpretive processes of social definition, and that the acts and the interpretive processes themselves are embedded in, reflect, and potentially modify larger social contexts (see Maines, 2001). Any understanding of violence that does not recognize this is impoverished.

Finally, I believe the theory of violentization must now be brought into greater dialogue with other sociological research and theory on violence. In other words, I think it is time for the theory of violentization to lose its maverick status. For whatever reason, several sociological treatments of violence reach similar conclusions to Athens' work, but do not seriously engage in dialogue with it. Such a dialogue would uncover key common ground and differences between violentization and other theories of violent behavior. Other work on violence could incorporate insights from violentization theory, and violentization theory might profitably benefit from research findings from studies animated by other violence theories. I choose two examples, but there are surely other bodies of work on violence that could profit from dialogue with violentization and vice versa.

First, Richard Felson's (see Felson, 1992, 1993, 1996, 2002) instrumental theory of aggression and violence, like Athens', depicts these as goal-oriented behaviors arising out of interpretive decision-making. Felson's theory draws mostly from rational choice theory, but also symbolic interactionism, especially the works of Sheldon Stryker (1980) and Erving Goffman (1959). Felson argues that violence and aggression are usually instrumental, used to gain compliance, settle disputes, or otherwise exercise coercive power. The decision to use violence or aggression in this way arises from interpretive decision processes in which actors assess rewards and costs, the likelihood of success or retaliation, the reactions of audiences, and the situational context. It seems to me that much could be gained by delineating the common ground as well as the key points of divergence between Athens' and Felson's theories.

Second, violentization theory is obviously very relevant to domestic violence (a topic that Felson's work also discusses at length[4]). Two bodies of work that should be brought into dialogue are violentization theory and Michael Johnson's theory of domestic violence. Like Athens does with violence and violent offenders in general, Johnson and his colleagues make distinctions between types of domestic violence and types of domestic violence offenders (for a review of this body of work, see Johnson & Ferraro, 2000). Johnson distinguishes between: (1) "common couple violence" (that which does not involve a general pattern of one partner controlling the other, arises in the heat of specific disputes, and is more likely to be mutual); (2) "intimate terrorism" (violence is part of a larger pattern consisting of one partner trying to control or dominate the other, is less likely to be mutual, is more likely to escalate and result in serious injury); (3) "violent resistance: (violence as self defense or resistance to the violence of the other partner); and (4) "mutual violent control" (both partners are controlling and violent). Johnson and Ferraro (2000) also discuss distinct types of perpetrators of domestic violence found in studies of male battering: (1) "family only" (engages in sporadic or single episodes of battering, and only within his family); (2) "generally violent-antisocial" (consistently engages in a wide variety of violence, both in and out of the family); and (3) "dysphoric-borderline" (engages in violence only in a family context out of deep emotional dependence on their partner).

The applicability of violentization to the typologies above should be obvious. First, future research could examine the relationship between types of domestic violence, such as intimate terrorism, and violentization. That is, are perpetrators of intimate terrorism and mutually violent control more likely to have undergone violentization? Second, research could also investigate the parallels between what the research above calls "generally violent-antisocial" batterers and violentization. An implication of these parallels is that the most injurious and severe domestic violence may be intimately connected to violentization. Such an implication would, of course, come as no surprise to Athens.

In sum, future assessments should recognize Athens' contributions to symbolic interactionism in general and criminological theory in particular. Interactionists would do well to engage, incorporate, use, and evaluate Athens' distinctive theory of the self and its phantom communities. Criminologists should recognize violentization for what it is – a broad and distinctive interactionist theory of violence (and perhaps even other crime) that incorporates insights from differential association and labeling theories (see also Ulmer &

Spencer, 1999). Criminologists may disagree with it, debate it, or find support for it, but they should no longer ignore it.

In conclusion, I return to a key set of points made by Dumont in his contribution. Violence in one form or another vexes every human society and every historical epoch. As Dumont says, contemporary American society is obsessed with violence – we both fear it and romanticize it. Violence brings us into contact with the bare facts of how easily life can be disrupted or ended at the hands of others. Violence is inextricably intertwined with human suffering and anguish. Unlike some questions in the social sciences, understanding violence is not just an interesting intellectual puzzle or academic debate. At stake is our ability to understand, and hopefully to some degree prevent, a significant amount of misery among both the victims and perpetrators of serious violence. Athens may really be onto something – something big. Isn't it worth it to find out more?

NOTES

1. Athens now refers to his total theory as "violentization" (including its older conceptualization of violent acts and its new community dimensions), and uses the term "violentization process" to refer to the specific socialization process that produced serious violent careers.

2. The influence of labeling theory can be seen in, for example, Athens' conceptualization of the stage of virulency in the violentization process.

3. Think of the difference, for example, between the content of the socialization necessary to make individuals willing and able to shove a sword through an opponent's chest, vs. to bomb a city from 25,000 feet in the air.

4. It should be noted that Felson and Johnson disagree about several key issues in domestic violence (see Felson, 2002).

REFERENCES

Akers, R. (1998). *Social Learning and Social Structure: A General Theory of Crime and Deviance.* Boston: Northeastern University Press.

Athens, L. (1994). The Self as a Soliloquy. *The Sociological Quarterly, 35,* 521–532.

Athens, L. (1995). Dramatic Self Change. *The Sociological Quarterly, 36,* 571–586.

Athens, L. (1998). Dominance, Ghettos, and Violent Crime. *The Sociological Quarterly, 39,* 673–691.

Blumer, H. (1969). *Symbolic Interactionism.* Englewood Cliffs, NJ: Prentice-Hall.

Conrad, P. (1997). Public Eyes and Private Genes: Historical Frames, News Constructions, and Social Problems. *Social Problems, 44,* 139–154.

Felson, R. (1992). Kick 'Em When They're Down: Explanations of the Relationship Between Stress and Interpersonal Aggression and Violence. *The Sociological Quarterly, 33*(1), 1–16.

Felson, R. (1993). Predatory and Dispute-Related Violence: A Social Interactionist Approach. In: R. Clarke & M. Felson (Eds), *Advances in Criminological Theory* (Vol. 5, pp. 189–235). New Brunswick, NJ: Transaction.

Felson, R. (1996). Big People Hit Little People: Sex Differences in Physical Power and Interpersonal Violence. *Criminology, 34*(3), 433–454.

Felson, R. (2002). *Violence and Gender Reexamined.* Washington, D.C.: American Psychological Association.

Glaser, B., & Strauss, A. (1967). *The Discovery of Grounded Theory.* Chicago: Aldine.

Goffman, E. (1959). *The Presentation of Self in Everyday Life.* New York: Doubleday.

Hall, P., & McGinty, P. (1997). Policy as the Transformation of Intentions: Producing Program from Statute. *The Sociological Quarterly, 38*, 439–468.

Johnson, M. P., & Ferraro, K. (2000). Research on Domestic Violence in the 1990s: Making Distinctions. *Journal of Marriage and the Family, 62*, 948–963.

Maines, D. (1982). In Search of Mesostructure: Studies in the Negotiated Order. *Urban Life.*

Maines, D. (2001). *The Faultline of Consciousness: A View of Interactionism in Criminology.* New York: Aldine de Gruyter.

Mead, G. H. (1934). *Mind, Self, and Society.* Chicago: University of Chicago Press.

Rhodes, R. (1999). *Why They Kill: Discoveries of a Maverick Criminologist.* New York: Knopf.

Stryker, S. (1980). *Symbolic Interaction: A Social Structural Version.* Menlo Park, CA: Benjamin/Cummings.

Sutherland, E. (1947). *Principles of Criminology.* Philidelphia: Lippincott.

Ulmer, J., & Spencer, J. W. (1999). The Contributions of an Interactionist Approach to Research and Theory on Criminal Careers. *Theoretical Criminology, 3*(1), 95–124.

Ulmer, J. (2000). Commitment, Deviance, and Social Control. *The Sociological Quarterly, 41*, 315–336.

Ulmer, J. (2001). Mythic Facts and Herbert Blumer's Work on Race Relations. *The Sociological Quarterly, 42*, 289–296.

Warr, M. (2002). *Companions in Crime: The Social Aspects of Criminal Conduct.* New York: Cambridge University Press.

SUBJECT INDEX

macho personality scripts 142
major community(ies) 19–21, 37
malevolency 17, 63, 65
malignant minor community(ies) 26–31,
    34–37
marginally violent person 23, 25, 27,
    32–33, 74
media x, 47, 147, 149, 159, 178
mental illness xi, 48, 73, 81
minor community(ies) 19–23, 27, 29–34,
    36,–38, 177
mitigated violent resolution 11, 13, 17,
    114–115, 128
mutual violent control 181
My Lai 117

Nazi SS xi, 94

pacification 97, 122
personal disorganization 7, 10, 17, 24,
    27, 31
personal horrification 8, 10–11, 47, 55,
    57, 110, 112, 126–127, 130–131,
    134–138, 142–143, 150–151, 154–155,
    163
personality characteristics 126, 149
phantom community(ies) 49, 55, 63, 66,
    68–69, 73–74, 80, 118, 120, 122,
    165–166, 169, 176–177, 181
phantom others 45, 64, 73–74
posttraumatic stress 129
PTSD 143

quantitative data 177, 179

rational choice theory 180
retaliative subjugation 8

Schutzstaffel (SS) 93–106
self, the ix, 45, 176–177, 181
selves 24, 27, 96, 113, 176, 178
sex offender(s) 170–171
situational definition 176
social act ix, 176, 180
social control 48, 121, 177, 180
social interaction ix, 121, 165
social learning theory 176–177

social structure x
social trepidation 17–18, 65
soliloquy 113
subculture of violence 2
subordination 6
symbolic interactionism 175–176,
    180–181
symbolic interactionist ix, 150, 176

turbulent community(ies) xi, 30, 32
turbulent minor community(ies) 29–31,
    34–37

ultra-violent person 23, 30, 73

Vietnam 63, 108, 111–112, 114–115,
    117, 119
violent act(s) x–xi, 47, 49, 83, 110, 116,
    119–122, 128, 166–167, 171, 176,
    178, 180, 182
violent coaching 8, 10–11, 47, 55, 61,
    96, 98, 106, 110, 112, 126–127, 131,
    134–143, 150–151, 154, 156, 161,
    163–164
violent community(ies) 35, 37, 179
violent dominance engagement(s) 8,
    12–18, 23–39, 56, 60
violent notoriety 17, 18, 65, 98, 101
violent performance(s) 12, 38, 44, 47,
    58, 98, 108, 115–116, 126, 128,
    131, 134–140, 152–153, 157,
    165–166
violent resistance 181
violent socialization 93–94, 96, 98, 100,
    106, 125–126, 128, 130, 136,
    141–142, 176, 179
violent subjugation 8–11, 13, 17, 38, 47,
    55, 57, 70, 110–112, 126, 130–131,
    134–143, 150–151, 154, 158, 161,
    163, 171
violentization ix–xi, 1, 6–8, 10, 12,
    17–19, 24, 27, 30, 35–36, 39,
    47–48, 51, 54–55, 60, 73, 94,
    107–109, 112, 115–116, 118–119,
    122, 126, 128, 142, 147–148,
    150–151, 153, 158, 162, 165–167,
    169–172, 175–182